Bluecoated Terror

The publisher and the University of California Press Foundation gratefully acknowledge the generous support of the Ahmanson Foundation Endowment Fund in Humanities.

Bluecoated Terror

JIM CROW NEW ORLEANS AND
THE ROOTS OF MODERN POLICE BRUTALITY

Jeffrey S. Adler

UNIVERSITY OF CALIFORNIA PRESS

University of California Press
Oakland, California

© 2024 by Jeffrey Adler

Library of Congress Cataloging-in-Publication Data

Names: Adler, Jeffrey S., author.
Title: Bluecoated terror : Jim Crow New Orleans and the roots of modern
    police brutality / Jeffrey S. Adler.
Description: Oakland, California : University of California Press, [2024] |
    Includes bibliographical references and index.
Identifiers: LCCN 2023044874 (print) | LCCN 2023044875 (ebook) |
    ISBN 9780520385603 (hardback) | ISBN 9780520402348 (paperback) |
    ISBN 9780520385610 (ebook)
Subjects: LCSH: Police brutality—Louisiana—New Orleans—History—
    20th century. | Crime and race—Louisiana—New Orleans—History—
    20th century. | Discrimination in law enforcement—Louisiana—New
    Orleans—History—20th century.
Classification: LCC HV7936.P725 A435 2024 (print) | LCC HV7936.P725
    (ebook) | DDC 363.2/32—dc23/eng/20231212
LC record available at https://lccn.loc.gov/2023044874
LC ebook record available at https://lccn.loc.gov/2023044875

33 32 31 30 29 28 27 26 25 24
10 9 8 7 6 5 4 3 2 1

CONTENTS

ACKNOWLEDGMENTS

I incurred more debts writing this book than I can possibly repay. Friends, colleagues, and archivists were extraordinarily generous, and I am delighted to, at the very least, thank them. Maura Roessner, my editor at the University of California Press, played a particularly important role. She proposed the project and supported it in every way, providing encouragement, exceptional guidance, and constructive suggestions as the idea blossomed into a book. Working with her has been an absolute joy. Her colleagues at the University of California were first-rate as well, and I feel fortunate to have had help from such skilled professionals. Two extremely thoughtful readers for the press offered trenchant insights that improved my analysis in countless ways.

Like every historian, I could not have undertaken my research without the archivists and librarians who found sources and secured my access to them. I was lucky to have had the opportunity to work with Irene Wainwright. Though now retired, she served as the head archivist of the Louisiana Division/City Archives and Special Collections at the New Orleans Public Library when I began my research. Knowledgeable and creative, Irene helped me to locate the core source material for the project. The interlibrary loan staff at the University of Florida's Smathers Library also deserves special thanks.

In a challenging time for my academic discipline, the Center for the Humanities and the Public Sphere at the University of Florida awarded me a subvention grant. I deeply appreciate the Center's support. As institutions of higher education have cut back on research funding for the humanities, CHPS has stepped forward, helping me and many colleagues.

Student research assistants contributed to the project as well and have been professional and diligent beyond their years. I am grateful for the hard work of Robert Zuchowski, Shayna Schulman, Anthony Delgado, Natalia Debno Shevin, and Meagan Frenzer.

While I enjoyed every second I spent on this project, I also confronted a series of formidable recent challenges—including a serious health crisis, an accident that left me without the use of my right arm for three months, and, of course, a pandemic—and often relied on an amazing circle of friends, who provided moral and intellectual support at every turn. I hope that Tom Gallant, Mark Hirsch, Nina Caputo, Luise White, Steve Noll, David Johnson, Carolyn Conley, Matt Gallman, and Nancy Olsen, my sister, understand how much I value their friendship.

Four historians, all accomplished scholars, were especially generous. David Johnson, Carolyn Conley, and Matt Gallman read every chapter, helped me develop my ideas, and provided perceptive insights—and did so without hesitation as I bombarded them with questions and inundated them with drafts. The book is stronger for their wisdom and suggestions. They are terrific friends. Brandon Jett also provided much-appreciated help, sharing his vast knowledge of Jim Crow policing and data from his own important research.

As always, I need to thank my dogs, who have been constant companions and provided—mostly—welcome distractions. Charlie died as I was completing the manuscript, and I miss him. Millie has been an endearing, playful companion, and the newcomer, Sam, like Charlie and Millie, came from a local shelter, and he has introduced a bit of mischief and chaos to the household. They enrich my daily routine, adding—and imposing—balance and fun.

More than anyone, Barbara Mennel has contributed to the book and to my life. She listened to every inchoate thought about the history of American police brutality, pored over every chapter, and demonstrated unwavering patience as I seemed to hijack every conversation over every breakfast and dinner to float my ideas about race, law enforcement, and social justice in Jim Crow America. But her contributions extend far beyond this. She has sustained me during medical crises, helped me to deal with every challenge, shared and heightened every moment of joy, and has been a remarkably generous and wonderful life partner.

Introduction

TYRE NICHOLS, GEORGE FLOYD, Breonna Taylor, Laquan McDonald, Michael Brown, Eric Garner, and a horrifyingly long list of other African American citizens have died at the hands of policemen in the opening decades of the twenty-first century. These killings reflect a century-old police practice of using deadly force against African Americans. During the decades after World War I, New Orleans law enforcers, for example, fatally shot Louis Joseph, Percy Thompson, Charles Handy, Wilbert Moore, and dozens of other African American men. Police officers during both eras beat, tortured, and killed African Americans at dramatically higher rates than whites and more often employed coercion to extract confessions, shot unarmed suspects, and deployed preemptive deadly force during arrests. These practices bred—and continue to breed—gaping racial disparities in American criminal justice, inflicting searing social and political ruptures on the nation. Trends in police violence are not identical in the two periods, but they are chillingly similar, grounded in systemic racial discrimination. *Bluecoated Terror* explores the early twentieth-century roots of modern police brutality.[1]

It focuses on racialized criminal justice in the interwar South because this was a formative era for the institutionalization of such violence. Racialized police brutality was not new a century ago, though it increased significantly and assumed new forms during the decades after World War I. Before the Great War, white civilians, as slave patrollers, night riders, and lynchers, committed the lion's share of interracial murders, but cops rapidly supplanted them during the 1920s and 1930s.[2] Every form of police violence, from aggressive searches to murders, soared and became commonplace components of urban law enforcement, forging a racial disparity in brutality that has persisted and that roils twenty-first-century America. The rate of fatal police shootings of African Americans, for example, swelled to five times the white level during the interwar period and has narrowed but remains far higher. Thus, examining the early institutionalization of this race-based gap sheds light on modern police brutality and especially on the crucial blurring of race control and law-and-order policing. For early twentieth-century white Southerners, and many others across the nation, violent police methods for preserving white supremacy seemed justified and consistent with the rule of law. One hundred years ago, racial brutality became baked into the core operation of law enforcement and criminal justice. Echoes of this elision of racial dominance and law and order lingered long after Jim Crow waned and continue to haunt modern America.

Racial disparities in criminal justice grew rapidly in the interwar South and metastasized across the nation. These differentials became more pronounced and virulent with the modernization of the American police, the expanding authority of prosecutors, and the increasing use of prisons, rather than rough justice, to punish those perceived to be challenging racial custom and disrupting order.[3] Before the Great War, patrolmen typically inflicted punishment on suspected criminals and suspicious individuals, clubbing them with their billies.[4] When cops arrested suspects, grand juries rarely returned indictments and prosecutors seldom filed charges and secured few convictions. Even for the most heinous felonies, three-quarters of offenders escaped punishment of any sort. The crime surveys of the 1920s exposed the amateurish, feeble state of American criminal justice and unleashed a wave of legal reform and expansion.[5] Throughout the nation, but particularly in the South, the municipal police quickly gained greater responsibility for controlling crime but also for managing racial order. With this early twentieth-century shift, formal criminal justice institutions became mechanisms for preserving a white definition of "law and order," and race-based differentials in law enforcement widened. Cops, more than self-appointed white sentinels, assumed tasks of controlling criminals and African American citizens.

Early twentieth-century Southern police officers, still nearly all white, embraced a worldview consisting of a series of overlapping binaries. They divided society into crude blocks, categorizing citizens as good or bad, honest or deceitful, respectable or dangerous, orderly or disruptive, law abiding or criminal, and white or Black. Moreover, these binaries elided. According to early twentieth-century ethnographers, Southern cops believed that good people were honest, respectable, orderly, law abiding, and white, whereas bad people were deceitful, dangerous, disruptive, criminal, and usually African American.[6] Insisting that their mandate was to serve the needs of the first group, police officers saw African Americans as menacing, lying, violent predators, and they defended law and order and safeguarded social stability accordingly. Jim Crow reshaped the operation of the legal system when cops replaced vigilantes and prisons supplanted street justice as punishment. And policemen and prosecutors established and cemented their authority with voters, virtually all white in the heyday of disfranchisement, by preserving this racialized conception of social order and, hence, targeting African Americans.

Southern racial violence has deep historical roots, but a seismic shift occurred during the first half of the twentieth century, redefining American law enforcement and criminal justice. Police brutality emerged as the primary method of safeguarding racial dominance, rapidly supplanting rough justice. The latter did not disappear but contracted sharply. White Americans, particularly in the urban South, increasingly relied on law enforcers to buttress white supremacy. Police violence and mob violence shifted in opposite directions. During the first three decades of the twentieth century, the number of lynchings plunged by 81.7 percent, while police homicide surged.[7] In New Orleans, for example, cops began to commit the overwhelming majority of white-on-Black homicides. At the start of the new century, civilians committed nearly three-fourths of these murders. By the early 1930s, policemen killed two-thirds of African American residents murdered by white New Orleanians. In a three-decade span, the civilian white-on-Black homicide rate contracted by 70.9 percent.[8] Interracial violence assumed a different form, for the rate of police white-on-Black killings more than doubled. Nonlethal racial violence changed in comparable ways. Parallel shifts occurred in Memphis, Atlanta, Birmingham, Mobile, and throughout the urban South.[9] In the largest cities, with the most developed legal institutions, the transformation occurred fastest and most completely. In smaller towns and rural areas, the process was more protracted, and formal and informal mechanisms of race control overlapped. "Once the classic method was the rope. Now it is the policeman's bullet," a civil rights activist explained.[10] This "present lynching technique," according to a Birmingham observer, "has all but superceded [sic] the old method of lynching."[11] Police violence against African American residents became an "accepted practice," a New Orleans writer lamented.[12]

Reflecting the new role of the state, racial disparities in arrests, indictments, convictions, incarcerations, and executions soared as well. The toxic blend of aggressive policing and racialized law enforcement also encouraged the increasing use of force to extract confessions from African American suspects, even after the 1931 publication of the attorney general's Wickersham Commission report ignited a national scandal over the use of sadistic third-degree interrogation tactics.[13] These practices channeled skyrocketing numbers of African American suspects into criminal courts and then prisons, which, in turn, generated seemingly objective social-scientific evidence to support stereotypical associations of race and criminality.[14]

Racialized police brutality became an intentional, coherent law enforcement strategy in the urban South during the decades after the Great War, no longer operating as an informal, individual practice. To be sure, some patrolmen and detectives remained especially violent, but the wider use of brutality to manage race relations and maintain an overtly racialized notion of social stability and public safety became formalized and a "standard procedure."[15] Police brutality assumed a central role in the preservation of "law and order." Prosecutors, elected officials, and police leaders encouraged violent methods, while most white Southerners—and most white Americans—endorsed such an approach to crime fighting and protecting law-abiding (white) citizens. "Negroes are Negroes to police officers. All are regarded as potential criminals. Clubs, guns, and public opinion uphold the 'law' in cases of Brutality to Negroes," a Birmingham editor observed.[16] By the 1930s, violence against African Americans changed from an ad hoc, civilian practice to an established law enforcement strategy. Moreover, Southern mayors, police chiefs, and district attorneys not only tolerated beating and wantonly shooting African American men, they defended such violence as justified and consistent with the rule of law. Defining targeted police brutality as a necessary, lawful activity institutionalized racialized violence, embedding it in the core mission of the American criminal justice system.

This transformation was more calculated and purposeful than merely operating as a by-product of long-standing racial attitudes. To the contrary, policymakers, cops, and criminal justice officials explained and defended their racialized practices, especially reserving brutality for African American suspects. Simply put, African Americans were criminals, a linkage that blended well-entrenched white assumptions about race with the social-science research of the era.[17] The elision invoked early twentieth-century scientific racism to explain and justify the anxieties of Southerners who insisted that the early Great Migration flooded cities with vicious predators and thus endangered good, honest, decent, respectable, law-abiding white residents.[18] The police had to protect them and employ unflinching methods to preserve law and order.

In the eyes of white Southerners, one sociologist explained in 1940, "Negroes are just 'natural killers.'"[19] White editors echoed this view. New Orleans journalists, for example, maintained that African Americans committed the lion's share of violence in the city. "Most of the murders in New Orleans," the *New Orleans Item* reported in 1924, "are committed by negroes."[20] Many white residents often expressed this view in more unvarnished ways. A Louisiana lawyer, for instance, attributed violent crime to "murderous n-----s" and "baboons."[21]

When homicide rates surged during the 1920s, white city dwellers insisted that African Americans had laid siege to their communities, placing them in dire danger. The nation's murder rate swelled by 19.2 percent between 1920 and 1925. In Southern cities, it surged much more, rising by 52 percent in Memphis, 120 percent in Nashville, and 139.2 percent in New Orleans. The region had four-fifths of the nation's most murderous urban centers, and white residents claimed that African American newcomers were responsible for the violence. "The increase," the *New Orleans Times-Picayune* argued, "is all on the side of the negroes."[22] "Were it not for the colored murders," the city's police superintendent explained, "New Orleans and the entire South would have an excellent record."[23] Similarly, a Birmingham observer concluded that the stratospheric violence was "due to the large per cent of Negroes in these Southern cities."[24]

White Southerners—the electorate in the region—demanded that the police protect them from these predators and employ any means necessary to do so. Due-process protections and constitutional restrictions on the use of torture and coercion in law enforcement, they charged, undermined crime fighting, endangering law-abiding citizens. Legal constraints on police authority "coddled" murderers and rapists. In order to safeguard constitutional order, cops must be granted "license" to employ aggressive methods of preserving law and order, including third-degree interrogations and the preemptive use of deadly force.[25] By virtue of their criminality, criminals sacrificed their rights to due process and legal prohibitions against police brutality. White government officials, newspaper editors, community leaders, and voters explicitly exempted some segments of the population from legal guardrails. Their notions of social order and law-abiding citizens included only white Americans. Suspected criminals and dangerous people—African Americans—were not entitled to civil liberties.[26] Cops could beat, torture, coerce confessions from, and shoot African Americans without in any way violating the law or the constitution. "Commonsense justice" dictated that some democratic rights did not extend to these Americans.[27] In the age of Jim Crow—and beyond—racialized police violence operated in the faithful service of the rule of law.

From the distance of a century, the idea of selective, situational constitutional rights and protections seems unimaginable. Recent events, however, also led many Americans to question the boundaries of constitutional rights. According to legal scholars and political scientists, people who genuinely supported free speech and rejected the use of torture in interrogations often wavered about affording such protections to suspected terrorists after the 9/11 Twin Towers attacks, just as many mid-twentieth-century Americans had insisted that communists and suspected spies sacrificed their due-process rights.[28] These more recent examples are not parallel to systemic racial oppression in the age of Jim Crow, but they illustrate the tension between an abstract commitment to constitutional protections and perceived emergencies and crises. Believing that they were under siege from criminals, interwar white Southerners often saw themselves as civilized and fair-minded but demonstrated no reluctance to grant police officers the discretion and authority to beat, bludgeon, torture, and even kill African Americans in the name of law and order and the defense of public safety.

Early twentieth-century Southern whites' willingness to deny fundamental civil rights to African Americans reshaped law enforcement. Because this was the era when police departments expanded and modernized, a racialized construction of criminal justice, complete with race-based limitations on legal and constitutional protections, became normalized. If the mandate of cops was to preserve public order, and if the "public" consisted exclusively of white residents, the police possessed free rein to beat and brutalize African Americans.

Disfranchisement undergirded this formulation of the rule of law. Often relying on nominally race-neutral policies and rules, such as the use of "understanding clauses" and literacy tests, whites systematically suppressed African American voting and monopolized political control. On the eve of World War II, for example, African American New Orleanians comprised 30.3 percent of the population but 0.38 percent of eligible voters. Whites denied them the core rights and privileges of citizenship. In 1944, the sociologist Gunnar Myrdal explained that "just as they are practically voteless in the South, Negroes there have a minimum of what we have called 'legal justice.'"[29] "Southern courthouses," an ethnographer noted, operated as the "bulwark of white supremacy."[30]

Ironically, the brutal, unrestrained treatment of African American residents enhanced police authority and legitimacy in the eyes of Southern whites. Demagogic politicians and criminal justice officials exploited white fears of racial turmoil, reminding them that violent policing safeguarded law-abiding residents from the ravages of African American predators. Likewise, brutal, murderous cops insisted that their methods eliminated dangerous predators and hence protected decent, innocent white residents. When police officers thus argued that their tactics reflected the values and served the needs of white residents, what legal scholars and psychologists call "normative alignment," white Southerners believed that cops were fair, responsible, and had earned capacious discretionary authority, regardless of legal and constitutional constraints.[31] White residents increasingly ceded race control to police officers and supported cops who beat, tortured, and murdered African American suspects—in the name of justice and white supremacy. This perception of enhanced police authority accelerated the shift from individual, civilian, vigilante racial violence to institutionalized police violence targeting African American citizens.

Law enforcers who beat and tortured African American suspects gained a tangible incentive to employ overtly racialized tactics, for such brutality demonstrated their commitment to the protection of skittish white residents, generating white support and funding. City and criminal justice officials, therefore, not only defended but championed the use of violent police tactics to control crime, and sadistic cops who wantonly murdered African American suspects portrayed themselves as heroic guardians of order, decency, and social stability. They boasted about cleaning the streets of dangerous predators and defined racially targeted police brutality as the unmistakable defense of law-abiding citizens. Racial control, crime control, violent policing, and the rule of law blended and blurred in the interwar white Southern worldview.

Such enhanced police legitimacy and discretionary authority unleashed soaring levels of racialized brutality, thinly disguised as preserving law and order. Racial dominance shifted from a mob activity to a state-sponsored mandate. With few legal or constitutional boundaries, cops had virtually unrestrained power to beat and murder African American residents. Early twentieth-century ethnographers observed that every African American Southerner had witnessed, heard about, or endured such violence from law enforcers and felt vulnerable to white policemen.[32] The threat of state-sponsored brutality at the hands of patrolmen and detectives loomed at every moment and developed into racial terrorism masquerading as the rule of law.[33] "The killing of Negroes has become police policy in the United States," one activist concluded.[34]

These attitudes, law enforcement methods, and racial disparities expanded and became nationalized during the post–World War II era, when the Great Migration accelerated and the African American populations of Northern cities swelled.[35] Racial tensions in urban centers exploded throughout the country. A backlash against the civil rights movement, the protest rebellions of the 1960s, particularly the 1964 turmoil in Watts, and the Warren Court led mayors and police chiefs to embrace racialized, militarized law enforcement, create S.W.A.T. units, celebrate "warrior cops," and unleash "shoot-to-kill" policies. Lyndon Johnson's "War on Crime" and Richard Nixon's and Ronald Reagan's "tough-on-crime" platforms amplified these developments and provided capacious justifications for the aggressive policing of African American residents, often deployed in stop-and-search, broken-windows, and more recently in stop-and-frisk practices.[36] But decades earlier, Southern police departments had already announced a "war on crime," launched militarized, rapid-response units equipped with armored assault vehicles, bulletproof vests, army-grade machine guns and sniper rifles, tear-gas grenades, and established racialized stop-and-search mandates and shoot-to-kill protocols. Thus, late twentieth- and early twenty-first-century militarized, violent policing targeting African American residents broadened the law enforcement practices that had been forged and institutionalized in the Jim Crow urban South. Interwar cops in New Orleans, Memphis, Atlanta, Birmingham, and Mobile, in short, constructed the scaffolding for racialized criminal justice in modern America.

. . .

Bluecoated Terror devotes particular attention to police violence in New Orleans for two reasons. First, trends in policing in the city were typical for the region, and remarkably complete police records have survived for New Orleans. Municipal police case reports and court files provide concrete measures of the magnitude of the interwar transformation of law enforcement and criminal justice. Homicide data offer a particularly clear illustration. In 1920, New Orleans cops killed African American residents at 2.8 times the white rate. A decade later, the gap had expanded to 7.6 times higher, and in 1936 it ballooned to an 11.8-fold gulf. Soaring racial disparities in the fatal shooting of the unarmed reveal a similar trend. During the early 1920s, 66.7 percent of white suspects killed by city cops were unarmed, compared with 57.1 percent of African American victims. A decade later, policemen fatally shot unarmed African American residents at quadruple the white rate. Similarly, during the interwar years, the African American homicide conviction rate soared, while the white rate plummeted. Disparities in the use of coercive interrogation methods and execution rates mushroomed as well.

Records from Memphis, Birmingham, Atlanta, and Montgomery indicate that comparable racial disparities in police violence and criminal justice unfolded throughout the urban South.[37] NAACP branch files, FBI archives, Department of Justice sources, and local newspapers chart identical trends in police brutality as well.[38] Furthermore, ethnographic studies from the era reveal the same shifts in law enforcement across the region.[39] Racialized policing, justified in the service of public safety and the defense of law and order, became unapologetically entrenched in American criminal justice during the interwar era and provided the template for the late twentieth-century law enforcement initiatives, including mass incarceration.

The second reason for the local focus is the richness and depth of surviving source material. Extraordinary New Orleans records, such as homicide witness statements and the case files of the Louisiana League for the Preservation of Constitutional Rights, reveal another important facet of the early normalization of police violence.[40] Quantitative data, such as rates of killing by law enforcers and race-based disparities in convictions, incarcerations, and executions, fail to reveal the human, personal dimension behind the numbers, the trauma, and haunting vulnerability endured by survivors, or the purposeful ways in which policymakers and law enforcers formulated, defended, and deployed this violence and institutionalized racial terrorism. This book attempts to strike a balance between charting tangible, measurable trends in criminal justice and exploring the human consequences and purposeful sources of these shifts.

Finally, an explanation of the language used in the book and the scope of my analysis is in order. As much as possible, *Bluecoated Terror* relies on the words of police brutality victims, the perpetrators, their enablers, and white Southerners passively complicit in the racial suppression and uses quotations from brutalized suspects, violent cops, and criminal justice officials, including offensive terms such as "n-----." Sadistic policemen and their defenders and apologists used this and other abhorrent words to convey violence, coercion, and racial dominance. Softening their language risks sanitizing or veiling the vicious intent bound up in their terminology. The book focuses mainly on the police policies and practices that institutionalized racial disparities in law enforcement. Although the actions, protests, and experiences of African American residents receive considerable attention, the analysis concentrates on the behavior and attitudes of white cops and the white New Orleanians who supported their violent methods.

. . .

In sum, *Bluecoated Terror* explores the process through which police brutality became a systemic law enforcement strategy. This largely occurred during the two decades after the Great War, when policymakers and criminal justice officials expanded law enforcement institutions in the urban South and, in the process, blended race control with crime fighting. Police brutality changed from an individual practice by cops to a purposeful, standard departmental strategy. White Southerners, and eventually their counterparts throughout the nation, began to embrace police violence against African American citizens as a normal, appropriate component of law and order and consistent with their understanding of the rule of law.

Racial disparities in law enforcement did not begin during the interwar years but they widened egregiously between the world wars and persist in the twenty-first century. In early twentieth-century New Orleans, city cops killed unarmed African Americans at a slightly lower rate than white suspects. A decade later, they shot African Americans four times more often, and in modern America the gap remains three-to-seven times greater.[41] Differentials in police homicide, convictions, sentencing, incarceration, and executions follow comparable trajectories, surging after the Great War and remaining astonishingly pronounced today.

Modern police brutality is not a new phenomenon and is not the product of the isolated misconduct of a few "bad apples." But neither is such violence a fixed, unchanging practice dating to the seventeenth century. A century ago, most cops were not murderous or sadistic, and this remains true today. Moreover, American racial violence extends to the earliest moments of European colonization. Police brutality—and the threat of police violence—

as a purposeful law enforcement strategy, however, has a more precise history, becoming institutionalized in cities such as New Orleans, Memphis, and Atlanta nearly a century ago. It has not been stagnant, though the continuities are well documented and unmistakable. For many early twenty-first-century Americans, like their early twentieth-century and post–World War II predecessors, law-and-order policing is infused with—mostly—unstated expressions of white supremacy. The recent murders of Tyre Nichols, George Floyd, Breonna Taylor, Philando Castile, Freddie Gray, Tamir Rice, Laquan McDonald, Michael Brown, Eric Garner, and many others reflect policing practices deeply rooted in the nation's history.

ONE

"Any Slight from a Negro Is a Humiliation That Must Be Instantly Revenged"

SHORTLY BEFORE MIDNIGHT, on December 27, 1927, New Orleans police officers Robert McCabe and Louis Dendinger fatally shot Louis Joseph, a fifteen-year-old African American high school student. Both white, Louisiana-born, in their early thirties, from working-class backgrounds, possessing elementary-school educations, and new to law enforcement, the patrolmen killed Joseph in their capacities as white men more than in their roles as police officers, for the teenager had committed no crime and was not evading arrest. Nor did the shooting occur as a part of any criminal investigation. Rather, the schoolboy raced past them late at night on a dark street and refused to obey their command to "halt," which enraged McCabe and Dendinger and led them to shoot him. A bullet lodged in Joseph's abdomen, unleashing the internal hemorrhaging that claimed the teenager's life twelve hours later in the "colored ward" at Charity Hospital.[1]

Before he died, the fifteen-year-old recounted the shooting to police investigators. In a deathbed declaration, Joseph explained that he attended school during the day and sold newspapers at night. Returning from work at 11:30 p.m., he crossed the intersection of Euterpe and Ramparts Streets one block north of his Dryades Street home, when an unfamiliar white man abruptly emerged from a dark garage, shone a flashlight in his face, and demanded that he stop. Frightened, the schoolboy "broke and ran" south on Euterpe Street, toward his house.[2] David Hennessey, the thirty-two-year-old health department investigator holding the flashlight, confirmed Joseph's description of their encounter but added that the African American teenager appeared to be "prowling" near his property, prompting his command.[3] When Joseph fled, Hennessey did not summon the police. Instead, he grabbed his "38 caliber 5 shot revolver" and gave chase.[4] The fifteen-year-old quickly sped away from Hennessey, and, in the process, darted past McCabe and Dendinger, who were patrolling the neighborhood and reported that they heard someone yell "stop the negro."[5] They also ordered Joseph to halt, though he "failed to obey" and continued running.[6] The policemen interpreted the African American schoolboy's behavior as the willful defiance of white men, infuriating them, and they discharged their weapons and shot him in the back. Badly bleeding, Joseph dragged himself home, collapsing on his doorstep and dying a dozen hours later.[7]

Such violence was legion in New Orleans, the sixth most murderous city in the nation in 1927 with a homicide rate quintuple that of New York City, eight times that of Boston, eleven times Minneapolis's rate, and forty-four times Liverpool's homicide rate. New Orleans's white-on-Black homicide rate exceeded the overall murder rates of New York City, Hartford, and Milwaukee.[8] Louis Joseph was the ninth African American resident to die at the hands of white New Orleanians in 1927 and the third fatally shot by law enforcers.[9] As with the other white-on-Black killers, local courts failed to convict the cops. The Louisiana criminal code permitted police officers to employ deadly force against "fleeing felons," but the teenager did not fit this category, having never been arrested let alone convicted of a crime. On May 23, 1928, after twenty minutes of deliberation, an Orleans Parish jury acquitted McCabe and Dendinger of manslaughter charges.[10] Nor did the police superintendent take disciplinary action against the patrolmen, even though department procedures permitted officers to use their service revolvers only in defense of their lives.[11] McCabe and Dendinger had also received repeated reprimands for misconduct and drunkenness on the job, and the latter had also been charged with rape after he stalked and sexually assaulted a young girl and failed to appear at the court hearing, remaining at home and inebriated during the legal proceeding.[12] Dendinger had engaged in troubling behavior since his appointment to the police force and had been suspended on numerous occasions and terminated from the department at least once. Within a month of joining the force, for example, he had been found guilty of drunkenness, disturbing the peace, and "brandishing" his service revolver to menace a local neighborhood, and was fired, only to be reappointed a short time later.[13] In 1920s New Orleans, white-on-Black homicides, especially when African American victims breached racial etiquette and refused to submit to white residents, commanded scant attention in the courts, no matter if the killers were policemen or civilians, with prosecutors bringing only one-eleventh of such cases to trial and securing convictions in just one-fourteenth.[14] To the contrary, white New Orleanians considered such violence appropriate behavior from decent, upstanding citizens.

Popular justice, more than formal law enforcement, secured the racial hierarchy at the core of white notions of social stability in the early twentieth-century South. These residents believed that African Americans lacked the intelligence and emotional self-control to be responsible members of the community and that their intellectual and moral shortcomings posed a constant threat to social order. In a city with over 100,000 such purportedly impulsive, volatile, and potentially dangerous inhabitants, New Orleans's small police force seemed incapable of protecting decent, law-abiding residents. Rather, "respectable citizens," a euphemism for white New Orleanians, shouldered primary responsibility for maintaining stability, and local whites maintained that they must be permitted to employ vigilante violence, even deadly force, to fortify the racial controls that preserved law and order. Prosecutors, judges, and jurors, all of whom were white, as well as voters, virtually none of whom was African American, concurred, as did white newspaper editors, police officials, and municipal leaders.

In such an unstable social environment, Hennessey's reaction to a "suspicious" African American teenager lurking near his garage seemed reasonable and appropriate, at least according to white New Orleanians. Hennessey likely would have shot the fleeing schoolboy, if McCabe and Dendinger had not beaten him to the task.[15] The patrolmen acted in support of the health department investigator and, in this encounter, merely proved more successful in enforcing the racial code, imposing extralegal punishment when Joseph outran Hennessey, who also pursued the teenager with a loaded revolver. In short, law enforcers embraced and exercised white popular justice, eschewing legal niceties, such as the Louisiana Criminal Code and its rules for the lawful use of deadly force. Moreover, the lion's share of whites in the Jim Crow South insisted that even minor transgressions of racial etiquette, such as the panicked flight of a frightened fifteen-year-old who "refused to obey" a command to "halt," represented overt insolence and an assault on white supremacy, which had to be redressed immediately, even with lethal force. As a 1930s sociologist, one of the nation's leading experts on violence, observed, white Southerners typically believed that "any slight from a Negro is a humiliation that must be instantly revenged."[16]

. . .

White Americans, particularly in the South, had long relied on informal mechanisms of racial control, including vigilante violence. Prior to the Civil War, they maintained that legal institutions and law enforcers failed to provide the decisive, rapid responses necessary to prevent slave uprisings and the accompanying bloodbath. Thus, white citizens relied on familiar methods of popular justice to protect—white—civil society and defend its caste system. Non-slave-owning Southern white civilians formed slave patrols, searched for African Americans acting suspiciously, and often exacted summary punishment on those found "out of place."[17] White men could have constructed legal institutions for such tasks, but rather they looked to vigilante justice and treated the informal, extralegal exercise of racial violence as a fundamental component of citizenship.

Municipal officials in late eighteenth- and early nineteenth-century New Orleans, Charleston, Mobile, and Savannah, cities with large African American populations, institutionalized these practices and established the first police departments in the new nation, empowering designated white men to patrol the streets, principally to stop slave revolts.[18] Round-the-clock, armed law enforcers scoured the cities to enforce racial custom, prohibiting African American residents from loitering or assembling and hence reducing the potential for uprisings, racial upheaval, and the mass slaughter of innocent whites. During the early nineteenth century, however, these city police departments were often pulled in other directions. In 1836, when ethnic conflict roiled local society, New Orleans officials eliminated uniforms and weapons for its law enforcers. The parish political machine seized control of the defanged department and used police officers for partisan assignments.[19] Respectable white men and white popular justice reclaimed the mantle of slave control and resumed responsibility for preserving the racial order.[20]

While mid-century Southern cities retained rudimentary police forces, "popular policing" persisted. No clear boundary, however, separated civilian vigilantes from professional law enforcers, but the former constituted the front line of defense against racial disorder.[21] Safeguarding the racialized notion of social stability hinged on the rapid, extralegal, often violent actions of "ordinary white men."[22] Professional policing, therefore, did not conflict with popular policing or even weaken it; the two mechanisms, one formal and the other informal, coexisted and overlapped, and unfettered, extralegal methods maintained white support, providing the most urgent, powerful form of social control in the South. Civilians served as the first responders and the "foot soldiers" for white supremacy.[23]

Such a mandate loomed large during the late nineteenth century and, in the eyes of many Southern whites, garnered even greater legitimacy. Reconstruction, occupation by Union soldiers, political instability, African American suffrage, and demands for racial equality (or at least for due-process protections) challenged white privilege. Paramilitary organizations, such as the Ku Klux Klan and the Knights of the White Camellia, and vigilante violence, particularly night riding and lynching, enjoyed widespread white popularity in countering African American assertions of equality and claims to citizenship. Simply put, white support for extralegal, civilian policing grew stronger through the nineteenth century and continued well into the twentieth century.

The threshold for exercising popular justice and exacting violent summary punishment remained remarkably low. Hypersensitive to racial instability and the perceived threat posed by multitudes of presumably unstable, dangerous people, many white Southerners scrutinized every glance, inflection, conversation, and jostle. Ordinary bumps, collisions, and African Americans' "refusal to obey" white residents became encoded expressions of racial defiance and insubordination, revealing potentially willful political acts, challenges to "caste rules," and assaults on social stability, at least as they defined it.[24] Early twentieth-century ethnographers documented these anxieties and described the resulting violent responses to prosaic, trivial encounters. The sociologist Arthur Raper, for example, explained that "the most ordinary contacts between Negroes and whites" easily assumed "unnatural meaning" and portended a threat to the racial order and the safety of Southern whites. "A glance becomes an insult, a friendly greeting an advance; an effort to ignore becomes insolence—further evidences [*sic*] of insubordination."[25] Another scholar reported that "a Negro may enrage a white man by asking him a simple question in a sneering voice."[26] Other ethnographic studies recounted violent reactions to African Americans "because they forget or refuse to say 'Sir' when addressing a white man" or when African Americans neglected to remove their hats "when talking with a white man."[27]

Such behavior constituted "racial antagonism," explicit defiance, resistance to white authority, and hence demanded an immediate, decisive, unmistakable preemptive response.[28] According to the Swedish sociologist Gunnar Myrdal, writing in 1944, any incidental "break in the caste rules against one white person is conceived of as an act of aggression against white society."[29] Similarly, the sociologist H. C. Brearley reported that "there is always the possibility of more overt conflict, as collisions on the sidewalk, insulting gestures, and minor obscenities."[30] These "antagonistic attitudes" and "unnatural meanings," early twentieth-century ethnographers concluded, make "interracial slayings difficult to avoid," for "any infraction of the accepted race situation may result in mob action."[31] When the skittish fifteen-year-old Louis Joseph failed to submit to the command of white men, his reaction, in their eyes, flouted white supremacy, justifying, indeed necessitating, a violent response.

The mandates of white civilians and law enforcers, particularly with regard to policing race relations, proved fluid, though the former group assumed core responsibility for controlling African Americans. Later in the twentieth century, the police would become the front-line defenders of this foundational notion of law and order. But early twentieth-century Southern whites generally did not expect or rely on police intervention to manage African American residents, believing that unflinching, rapid responses to violations of racial custom entailed a collective and individual obligation. Through the 1920s, civilians committed the overwhelming majority of white-on-Black violence in Southern cities, including most interracial homicides. Again and again, white residents confronted, assailed, assaulted, and murdered African Americans who appeared "insolent," "uppity," or who demonstrated "signs of insubordination," fearing that such micro-breaches in custom exposed larger cracks in the structures that maintained social stability. One observer explained that "even minor transgressions of caste etiquette should be punished" and should be punished immediately and "bodily," if deemed necessary to shore up the racial order.[32]

Incidental transgressions became commonplace and inevitable on the busy streets and teeming sidewalks of early twentieth-century Southern cities, such as New Orleans, Atlanta, and Memphis. Jostles and unintentional bumps occurred constantly, generating abundant opportunities for racial conflict to flare. "The interracial situation is so loaded with explosive prejudices," a sociologist concluded, "that a triviality may easily lead to hostilities," fueling fierce white-on-Black responses and brutal violence.[33] A white mob, for example, nearly lynched an African American New Orleanian on Tuesday, March 1, 1927, in one such "triviality." During the first day of Mardi Gras, in the chaotic thrall of Carnival, two automobiles banged one another in a traffic jam near the city's French Quarter, one operated by a white resident and the other driven by an African American New Orleanian. The damage to the vehicles was modest, though the white man burst into fury that the African American resident had violated his "racial right-of-way." His reaction entailed more than "road rage." Far beyond carelessness or incompetence, interracial traffic accidents implied broader, deeper attacks on social order. By eschewing racial deference, by failing to yield to white drivers, African American vehicle operators, according to early twentieth-century Southern whites, claimed equal access to public space. Or perhaps when they passed, cut off, or collided with other vehicles the Black drivers expressed overt "racial antagonism" and open disdain for white authority.[34] The white driver began beating the African American man, and an angry mob, screaming "kill the n-----," quickly gathered, descended on him, and mauled him. No doubt strangers to the irate, suddenly murderous driver, these white New Orleanians participated in the attack to help fend off an imagined assault on the racial order that elevated their status and maintained social stability.[35] Only the intervention of African American bystanders prevented the mob from lynching the African American driver.[36]

But African Americans witnesses were not always present or able to forestall such violence, and incidental bumps, interpreted as willful, explicit racial breaches, frequently sparked bloodshed and murder in New Orleans and other Southern cities during the 1920s, contributing to stratospheric white-on-Black homicide rates and the larger fragility of Jim Crow social relations. One such minor confrontation sparked two murders on a New Orleans streetcar early on the morning of November 23, 1924. Twenty-eight-year-old Frank DeRocha, a white blacksmith, boarded the vehicle with his brother and a friend and immediately became embroiled in a dispute with Joseph and Ernest Baptiste, African American laborers in their mid-twenties, about the placement of the movable "screen" that segregated Black riders in the rear section of the streetcar.[37] The white blacksmith insisted that "one of the negroes cursed him." DeRocha whipped out his 38 caliber Colt revolver and shot twenty-six-year-old Joseph Baptiste in the right eye and his twenty-seven-year-old brother, Ernest, in the mid-section.[38] Joseph died instantly and Ernest a short time later at Charity Hospital. Sadie Baptiste testified in court that her son's "dying statement" revealed that, immediately before he opened fire, the white blacksmith had announced "I just feel like killing me a n----- tonight."[39]

A comparable spark ignited Andrew Wiebelt's murder of Lilly Johnson, a forty-three-year-old African American housekeeper. The rapid proliferation of automobiles made the streets of American cities contested turf and imbued driving comportment with racial meaning. At 8:35 p.m. on August 23, 1927,

Wiebelt, a twenty-seven-year-old, Louisiana-born white security guard with a seventh-grade education, grew incensed when an automobile filled with African American passengers passed him on Washington Avenue and thus rejected his racial status. The security guard pursued the "insolent negro" driver, caught up with his car, and chastised the vehicle's operator, calling him a "N-----" during the rant. According to Wiebelt, twenty-two-year-old Albert Johnson responded defiantly, shouting from the vehicle "suck my arse, you white mother fuckers [*sic*]," instantly transforming the white man's indignation and sense of grievance into rage and a murderous defense of racial privilege.[40] Wiebelt followed the "insolent and aggressive" Johnson until the vehicle arrived at his Galvez Street home. The white driver leaped out of his Ford brandishing a 38 caliber Smith and Wesson revolver and discharged a hail of bullets at the "saucy and insolent negro."[41] One shot pierced Albert Johnson's foot. A second bullet missed its target, and the third struck the African American man's forty-seven-year-old mother, Lilly, who was seated on the step in front of her house, in the torso, instantly killing her.[42]

Wiebelt's trial focused on Albert Johnson's impertinence, rather than the shooter's deadly conduct. Far from being a rash, reckless act, according to his defense attorneys, the security guard had killed an innocent woman in defense of the city's racial order, as a reasonable, permissible effort to rein in the dangerous, menacing behavior of an "insulting and insolent and aggressive negro."[43] Similarly prosaic disputes and confrontations, freighted with the incendiary baggage of Jim Crow, erupted in other Southern cities as well, contributing to the soaring death toll that white civilians inflicted in response to perceived, often imaginary, breaches of racial etiquette during the 1920s.

Nor were these isolated incidents. As New Orleans and other cities in the region boomed, as their African American populations surged, and as the streets, stores, and sidewalks became more congested, traffic accidents and incidental collisions multiplied. In this volatile, combustible racial climate, white perceptions of defiance and assaults on white supremacy skyrocketed, and white-on-Black violence, ranging from the near lynching of the driver involved in the Mardi Gras fender bender to the murders of the Baptiste brothers and Lilly Johnson, followed and unleashed an explosion of bloodshed.

Rather than discouraging such visceral, impulsive violence, police officers and criminal justice officials supported and endorsed white residents' informal efforts to buttress racial dominance. When O. C. W. Taylor, a prominent African American New Orleanian and the editor of Louisiana's largest Black newspaper, witnessed the white mob attacking the African American driver in 1927, the journalist, who had skillfully navigated the city's racial landscape and moved in the highest circles of local society, summoned the police. A patrolman quickly arrived at the scene of the traffic accident and berated Taylor, threatening to arrest the African American editor for calling the police "merely to keep a Negro from being beaten up."[44]

In other instances, criminal justice officials and municipal law enforcers encouraged white New Orleanians to rely on self-help and popular justice to maintain law and order and police racial boundaries. In December 1924, when fifty-four-year-old Georgina Wilson, a white rooming house operator, expressed racially inflected concerns about robberies in her neighborhood, a New Orleans police officer advised her "to get a gun and use it. I did," the woman boasted to a reporter a month later after fatally shooting Simon Green, a fifteen-year-old African American prowler.[45] A former local district attorney urged "every man and woman" to be vigilant and "carry a good pistol."[46]

In other incidents, New Orleans policemen apprehended African American crime suspects and permitted white residents to beat them, sometimes participating in the assaults. Patrolmen often arrested suspected shoplifters, conveyed them to the backs of the stores where they had been apprehended, and restrained them while storekeepers bludgeoned the accused merchandise filchers. Louis Scharfenstein, a thirty-five-year-old, Mississippi-born white saloon operator, for instance, suspected twenty-year-old Samuel Peebles, an African American college student, of stealing a jug of wine from his barroom. Scharfenstein summoned George Kernan, a forty-two-year-old New Orleans police officer with a seventh-grade education, who held Peebles in the back of the saloon and, along with the barkeeper, beat the college student.[47] Nor was Kernan trying to compel Peebles to confess to the theft. Rather, he joined Scharfenstein in exacting summary punishment on the twenty-year-old. Another New Orleans patrolman arrested fourteen-year-old Samuel Norman after the teenager allegedly "attempted to steal a pair of trousers" in a local store. The policeman confined Norman in the rear of the shop and allowed the storekeeper to bludgeon the young boy.[48]

But even as New Orleans cops endorsed, encouraged, facilitated, and participated in exacting extralegal popular justice, they discouraged large-scale, premeditated, highly visible forms of collective white-on-Black violence, particularly lynching. Political and business leaders sought to tamp down the huge, celebratory, circus-like "spectacle lynchings" that had commanded national attention in the turn-of-the-century South. These prominent men hoped to attract Northern merchants and manufacturers to the region and, by the 1920s, they worried that ritualized, choreographed, extralegal executions sullied the South's reputation and discouraged investment. Thus, they directed police officials to prevent mob violence, fearing that places where bloodthirsty mobs gathered and gleefully tortured and murdered African Americans would not provide appealing sites for Yankee businessmen to build factories and invest capital. Similarly, Southern governors, mayors, and urban boosters warned that sadistic lynchings, where witnesses fought for souvenir body parts and posed for photographs with charred, dismembered corpses, undercut their assertions of white cultural superiority.[49] An elite women's group even issued a statement explaining that lynching "discredits our civilization, and discounts the Christian religion." One after another, Southern political, cultural, and business leaders denounced lynching during the 1920s, at least rhetorically.[50] Small-scale, spontaneous racialized popular justice, on the other hand, seemingly escaped their notice and remained acceptable and desirable measures to bolster the racial order and preserve white dominance.

In short, at the same time that cops in New Orleans and throughout the region encouraged and participated in extralegal, summary punishment to combat violations of racial etiquette, they interceded to forestall lynchings. The local patrolmen who joined civilians in attacking African Americans who bumped or jostled white residents also "rescued" African Americans from murderous mobs. After white dock workers identified John Stephens, a thirty-two-year-old, African American cook, as the assailant in the deadly shooting of John Mercier, a forty-two-year-old white boilermaker on August 2, 1922, they began "shouting 'lynch him.'" Local patrolmen, however, quickly arrived, positioned themselves between the rabid crowd and their intended victim, and dispersed the angry workers.[51] Similarly, the New Orleans police safeguarded Baptiste Hanson Jr.'s family. On March 15, 1925, residents of New Orleans's "Italian colony" learned that the twelve-year-old African American Hanson had killed his eight-year-old, white playmate, Charles Arnona, in a terrible gun accident and began to "talk of lynching" the shooter and his relatives. The city's police department arrested Hanson but also posted a guard at the Hanson's home and then moved his family to custody for "safekeeping" until tempers cooled.[52] Jim Crow race relations proved complicated and riddled with apparent contradiction.

These efforts and especially the wider middle-class campaign to change regional culture—to attract Northern capital rather than to extend legal protections to African American residents—largely succeeded. The lynching of African Americans did not end, but it lost its respectability and decreased sharply, falling by 91 percent between 1900 and 1928.[53] White-on-Black violence, both locally and regionally, however, did not drop during this period. Instead, white New Orleanians and Southerners remained certain that small-scale vigilantism and racialized popular justice provided a legitimate, necessary bulwark for social stability. During the 1920s, while the number of African Americans lynched in the nation, most of them in the Deep South, plunged by 86 percent, New Orleans's white-on-Black homicide rate climbed by 30.3 percent.[54]

Police brutality toward African American New Orleanians occurred in this context and in episodes of popular justice and violent defenses of the racial order. Local cops typically beat, battered, and shot African American residents in reaction to perceived violations of racial convention and in their capacities as respectable white civilians more than as law enforcers. Their occupational status, however, heightened their sensitivity to racial etiquette and exaggerated their responses to seeming breaches in custom. For these low-level public officials, with their enhanced authority to use force, "Negro impertinence" felt especially personal and searing.

The triggers for police brutality closely mirrored the sparks that ignited civilian white-on-Black violence, with local cops invoking nearly identical justifications. At its broadest level, the beatings and murders occurred in defense of the racial hierarchy and thus the white conception of social order. For both cops and other white assailants, two grievances assumed particular importance. First, summary punishment, whether inflicted by civilians or law enforcers, compensated for the impotence of legal institutions. One Louisiana newspaper editor insisted that policemen "are no more brutal than the rest of us." Why then, he asked, were African American suspects routinely "kicked and cuffed and bruised and whipped"? The white journalist explained that "the average policeman is pretty cynical about the courts. He sees notorious rogues go into court and come off scot-free because of the machinations of clever lawyers, the interminable delays of legal procedure, the favoritism of judges, the intimidation of juries or the connivances of unscrupulous court attaches."[55] "In the judgment of the police," Southern ethnographers asserted, "the courts fail to punish Negro offenders properly."[56]

Defensive about the city's towering violent crime rate, New Orleans police-men blamed the courts and invoked a critique of the local criminal justice system to explain the city's sky-high violent crime rate, to deflect attention away from their own institutional shortcomings, and to justify summary punishment and their brutality. "It is extremely difficult to convict a negro murderer," one police official complained in 1924. "The negro is treated too well," he added. "We are just too lenient with them. It is almost impossible to get a jury who will convict a negro."[57] More indifferent to African American murder victims, most of whom died from intra-racial violence, than "lenient" toward the assailants, prosecutors dismissed charges against African American homicide suspects at a higher rate than against white assailants during the 1920s, and jurors, all of whom were white, demonstrated compa-rable apathy and often seemed content to permit African American residents to butcher one another. As a consequence, district attorneys dropped the cases against nearly three-fourths of African American killers and secured convictions in fewer than one-fifth of Black homicides, buttressing allegations that anemic legal institutions proved incapable of combatting Black vio-lence.[58] Police Superintendent Guy Molony asserted that New Orleans's murder epidemic "is due largely to our great negro population" and com-plained bitterly that the courts failed to address the problem.[59]

Faced with soaring crime rates; a dire threat to social stability; lackadaisical, inattentive prosecutors; gullible, disinterested jurors; feckless, indifferent judges; and a failing criminal justice system, white Southerners, and particu-larly the men mandated to protect the social order, relied on popular justice and extralegal punishment. Thus, ethnographers concluded, "the police take it upon themselves to judge and punish criminals" and so "the police beat Negroes as a form of punishment."[60] According to one early twentieth-century observer, "the police often assume the duty not only of arresting, but also sentencing and punishment" disorderly, impertinent African American residents.[61] Informal punishment, or "working over" transgressors, guaranteed retribution for endangering white society. Interviewing local law enforcers, interwar social scientists argued that police officers brutalized African Americans because they believed that the courts refused or were incapable of punishing the people who threatened the marrow of social stability. "Disaffection with formal laws under-lies the use of violence," another sociologist explained.[62]

Reinforcing the quick resort to extralegal violence, early twentieth-century Southerners, and especially their law enforcers, also believed that only brutality and extreme force would deter African American insolence, resistance to the racial order, and the resulting violence. Local and regional commentators emphasized the "animal-like nature of the Negro."[63] Impulse and "sheer primal passions," rather than reasoning and self-control, dictated his behavior.[64] Even if the police made arrests, prosecutors zealously brought criminals to trial, courts operated efficiently, and white jurors returned guilty verdicts, "formal punishment by fine or jail sentence fail to act as deterrents."[65] Instead, "Negroes will respond only to violent methods."[66]

Respectable whites, particularly those specifically entrusted with public safety, therefore, employed informal, violent methods. "The police tend to revert to direct action and to administer punishment themselves," accounting for "much of the beating of Negroes by the police."[67] Frustrated by the combination of anemic courts and African Americans' lack of reasoned self-control, one cop promised that when one particularly intransigent man "raises hell . . . I am not going to arrest him but just 'work him over' myself. That is the only way we can handle some of these troublemakers." Hamstrung by a flaccid criminal justice system and confronting African Americans' "lack of control," 1920s Southern policemen insisted insubordinate Blacks "must be 'taken care of' unofficially," using overwhelming force.[68]

Cops proved to be particularly sensitive to perceived violations of racial etiquette and challenges to the racial order and hence quick to exact summary justice in the name of social order. In New Orleans and throughout the South (and perhaps the nation), working-class men were especially violent toward African Americans. Their material circumstances, often only slightly better than that of African Americans, made them insecure about their social status and desperate to affirm their white status and respectability. More affluent Southern whites had other ways, such as consumption, to perform their authority and privilege. Poor white New Orleanians and other men in the region, by contrast, were often extremely hostile and violent toward African Americans whose inflections, intonations, or behavior appeared to ignore or impugn their racial superiority. Public jostles particularly enraged them because they viewed every encounter as a potential challenge to their status, echoing the remnants of an earlier honor-based culture. Not surprisingly, working-class men, desperate to defend and announce their distance from a group with even lower social standing in white eyes, committed 81.8 percent of white-on-Black homicides in 1920s New Orleans and a comparable proportion of nonlethal interracial assaults. Responding violently to perceived insubordination from African American residents, in short, afforded them a public, unmistakable mechanism to demonstrate their dominance and status as white men.

Law enforcement positions offered working-class men only slightly higher incomes than unskilled labor but abundant opportunities to affirm and perform their racial superiority. "In effect," early twentieth-century cultural anthropologists explained, "the system of law enforcement places in a position of considerable authority members of these classes subordinate in the white social structures," enabling policemen "to officially subordinate persons below them."[69] Sociologists also noted this link between class and racial violence. Southern policemen, they explained, "are poorly educated men usually from 'poor white' backgrounds with a tradition of racial antagonisms toward Negroes and a heavy sense of their special mission of preserving the racial etiquette."[70] The sociologist Charles S. Johnson observed that the "badge of police authority gives lower-class whites freedom to bolster their socially impoverished egos," conferring the power to "punish and even to kill without responsibility. This was been a part of the basic pattern of law enforcement, so far as Negroes are concerned."[71] Describing a "relentless warfare now waged against peaceful, law-abiding Negro citizens," an African American journalist in New Orleans offered the same explanation for police brutality, writing that "Negroes are beaten and killed by the police because the latter have the authority."[72] The prominent sociologist Gunnar Myrdal offered a similar assessment, describing the Southern policeman as "a frustrated man, and, with the opportunity given him, it is to be expected that he becomes aggressive. There are practically no curbs to the policeman's aggressiveness when he is dealing with Negroes whom he conceives of as dangerous or as 'getting out of their place.'"[73] Another ethnologist offered an even blunter assessment, writing "the cop is dumb, uneducated, unreasonable, and is in consequences weighted down by an inferiority complex that demands somebody to be better than."[74]

New Orleans, Atlanta, Memphis, and Birmingham cops brought these powerful race- and class-based sensibilities to law enforcement, and their violence was nearly indistinguishable from civilian brutality toward African American residents, though it occurred at higher rates. The backgrounds of the policemen who beat and murdered African Americans, for example, mirrored those of civilians who committed white-on-Black violence in 1920s New Orleans. Local patrolman, and especially those who beat and murdered African American residents, hailed from working-class families, and before they landed positions in law enforcement, they had typically held insecure, low-paying jobs, usually as day laborers, longshoremen, or "roustabouts" on freighters. Like other unskilled men, they worked in positions where they competed for employment with African American residents. Civilians who committed white-on-Black homicides were similarly concentrated at the bottom tier of the local occupational ladder, and both groups of killers seldom attended school beyond the sixth or seventh grade. Furthermore, civilian and police killers came from the same age group; 38.6 percent of the former, for example, were in their twenties and their mean age was 35.6, whereas 33.3 percent of police killers were in their twenties and their mean age was 35.4. The backgrounds of white Memphis offenders were comparable.[75]

The profiles of victims and the social contexts of the violence tended to be virtually identical in civilian and police killings as well during the 1920s. Of the African American New Orleanians who died at the hands of white civilians, 84.1 percent held unskilled jobs, compared with 90.9 percent of the victims of killer cops. The mean age of the victims of white civilians was 27.6, while the average of those murdered by local cops during the 1920s was 29.8; and 82.2 percent of those killed by civilians and 90.5 percent of the cops were Louisiana-born, with the remainder, in both cases, from surrounding states, particularly Mississippi and Alabama. African American victims of Memphis policemen during the 1920s were nearly identical, with a mean age of 30.4 and 90.3 percent holding unskilled jobs.

The deadly violence also occurred in the same settings, on the comparable days, at similar times, and using the same weapons. The murders usually occurred in the streets, for such public spaces particularly contaminated awkward interactions and discordant verbal exchanges with the "unnatural meanings" that ethnographers described. In New Orleans, civilian and police interracial homicides took place in the same parts of the city as well, with 31.9 percent of the former and 30 percent of the latter occurring in either the central-business district or the French Quarter. Likewise, the violence erupted during leisure times, when white and African American residents interacted and misinterpretations mounted; 30.4 percent of civilian white-on-Black homicides and 31.8 percent of police interracial killers erupted on Sundays, and 24.4 percent of the former and 28.9 percent of the latter occurred shortly before midnight. Nine-tenths of civilian killers and all police killers relied on firearms, typically the identical Colt or Smith and Wesson revolvers.

Most important, similar sparks triggered both sets of murders during the 1920s, underscoring the ways in which lethal police violence mirrored civilian interracial homicide, and Southern cops killed African American residents as a subset of larger popular justice rather than in the capacities as law enforcers. Police and court records documented the same encounters that early twentieth-century ethnographers observed. Perceived slights and imagined expressions of insubordination fueled deadly white-on-Black violence during the 1920s, regardless of whether the assailants worked as lawmen or longshoremen.

Like working-class civilians, New Orleans cops employed violence to defend the racial hierarchy and specifically in response to purported challenges to white supremacy. As police officers, however, local patrolmen more often barked instructions and shouted commands to African Americans residents, increasing the potential for misunderstandings or slow reactions to be interpreted as expressions of de facto racial defiance. Off-duty patrolman James Gagan, for instance, shot Kerny Ellis, a thirty-eight-year-old African American day laborer, after the latter responded lethargically to the former's order to get off the steps of a local grocery store and "move on."[76]

In other acts of police violence, local cops misinterpreted subtler behavior as acts of insubordination. Thirty-four-year-old New Orleans patrolman John Gussoni, for example, fatally shot forty-seven-year-old Albert Colbert on January 25, 1923, in the abdomen with his 32 caliber Colt service revolver, in an exchange sparked by the African American carpenter "using obscene language" in the policeman's presence.[77] In a similar shooting, three years later, a New Orleans cop also shot an African American resident for "using obscene language." According to an African American journalist, "the beating up or the shooting of a Negro by a policeman seems to be the logical thing to do," for such speech, in the eyes of these policemen, constituted racial defiance.[78]

Perceived insubordination led supernumerary patrolman James Cronin to fatally shoot George Simmons on December 27, 1930, as well. Off-beat, in civilian clothes, and inebriated, the twenty-five-year-old, Louisiana-born Cronin passed by a house on Religious Street and heard what he later described as a "disturbance." The cop charged into the residence, where thirty African American New Orleanians stood huddled around a coffin participating in Louis Simmons's wake. Neighbors described the ritual as "peaceful," but Cronin, his 38 caliber revolver in hand, demanded that the attendees "stick up" their hands and "let me search you-all." Thirty-six-year-old George Simmons, the deceased's brother, however, responded slowly. Although other inhabitants of the home quickly revealed that Simmons was "partially deaf" and, as soon as he understood Cronin's command, he complied and raised his hands, the drunken cop, who had also just attended a wake, interpreted the delayed response as insolence.[79] The patrolman barked, "you're a bad n-----huh," and knocked Simmons to the floor with the butt of his gun.[80] Early twentieth-century Southern whites used this epithet to describe insubordinate, dangerous African Americans.[81] As Simmons recoiled from the blow, Cronin fired two bullets at the day laborer, one entering his chest and moving into his abdomen, causing massive bleeding and killing him. Cronin then wheeled around and discharged his revolver two more times, in the direction of the other African Americans in the front room of the house.[82]

Subsequent developments in the case revealed white sensibilities about murderous responses to perceived African American defiance, even when assailants misinterpreted the encounters. Cronin proved too besotted to make a statement after the shooting, and his coworkers delayed interviewing him until the following morning, when he was "sobered up," which they acknowledged in court testimony. In his statements to his colleagues the day after the shooting and in his trial five months later, Cronin insisted that Simmons had been insolent, an assertion at odds with the observations of witnesses and with the police report on the shooting.[83] Even white newspaper reporters, who rarely offered sympathetic depictions of African American residents, described the wake as "a peaceful Negro gathering" and Simmons as an "inoffensive and helpless Negro."[84] The *New Orleans States*, for instance, wrote that the cop had invaded a "peaceable negro wake" with a "big police gun in his pocket and more liquor than he could carry."[85] Yet, Orleans Parish jurors acquitted Joseph Cronin.[86] For these white residents, murderous violence, even when the killer, by all accounts, mistook a slow response for racial defiance, proved permissible. The local district attorney won convictions in 7.3 percent of white-on-Black homicide cases and in no cases involving New Orleans policemen during the 1920s.

For Elmo Evans, a toxic combination of acute, class-based sensitivity to racial affronts and life as a beat cop spawned two decades of violence toward African American residents. Evans believed that police work had exposed him to the dire threat these New Orleanians posed to innocent whites, justifying the wanton, preemptive use of force, ranging from beatings to murder, against any African American resident. Born in New Orleans in 1898 to a working-class family, Evans attended school for eight years and served in the military during the Great War. On June 29, 1921, at the age of twenty-three, he joined the police department as a supernumerary patrolman. Three months later, the department promoted Evans to patrolman and assigned him to the mounted patrol unit, likely because he was obese and struggled to walk a beat. On New Year's Day in 1922, Evans attempted to arrest three African Americans for a minor infraction, one of whom, twenty-year-old Ben Harrison shot and seriously injured him, an incident that shaped his police career and unleashed a torrent of racial violence.[87]

Until he retired from the police force in 1941, Evans attempted to exact revenge on African American New Orleanians, piling up a long list of attacks on these residents, some of which brought sanctions from the police department. It is impossible to know how many such assaults went unreported, but Police Superintendent Guy Molony suspended and then dismissed Evans from the force in 1924, after he beat and shot at twenty-two-year-old Lilly Scales. Battering and attempting to kill an unarmed woman, the police chief determined, qualified as "conduct unbecoming an officer." Evans insisted that the African American woman had "insulted" him. In response, he tethered her to a fence, beat her, and then shot at Scales, though his bullet missed its mark.[88] The twenty-six-year-old patrolman appealed his termination. In his hearing, Evans defended his conduct, testifying that an African American resident had shot him the previous year and that "five policeman had been shot during the past years by negroes."[89] The explanation and justification persuaded the appeal board, which instructed the police chief to reinstate the patrolman. Again and again during the late 1920s, saloonkeepers filed charged against Evans for assaulting African American employees. While on duty, he repeatedly entered African American barrooms, attacked servers, and smashed bottles of liquor.[90] Police supervisors typically ignored the complaints, but the tavern owners filed numerous formal charges against the cop for the destruction of property. Nonetheless, in 1928 Police Superintendent Thomas Healy promoted Evans to detective. His attacks on African Americans and his practice of vandalizing African American saloons, however, continued, and one such episode led to his demotion. In 1930, Evans beat another African American bar employee, a "delivery boy." The assault occurred in front of a young white girl, whose father, an ex-cop, filed charges against Evans, not for the unprovoked violence but because Evans used "obscene language" in the girl's presence. Police Superintendent Hu Myers found him guilty once again of "conduct unbecoming an officer," stripped Evans of his shield, and demoted him to patrolman.[91] The following year, Evans shot and killed twenty-one-year-old Eugene Brown, after the African American laborer called him a "son of a bitch."[92] An assistant district attorney immediately exonerated Evans, who spent another eleven years on the police force, remained a patrolman, and continued to beat and bludgeon

African American residents, exacting protracted revenge for the 1923 shooting against other such New Orleanians.[93]

For Elmo Evans and many other Southern cops, the blend of working-class racial sensibilities, police experience, and the heightened visibility of serving as a uniformed law enforcer increased the potential for the routine use of brutal force against African American residents, though these brutal patrolmen acted out of the same core impulses as white civilians. Even if their formal authority provided freer rein for aggression and enabled cops to engage in higher rates of racial brutality, police violence against African American mirrored civilian violence in every way. One cop succinctly explained that the "policeman is simply the 'channel of the general white hostility against the Negro'" and relied on physical brutality in "acting out what the majority of whites in New Orleans feel about Negroes."[94]

Institutional factors contributed to the similarities between civilian responses to racial affronts and police reactions to perceived racial insubordination. Not only did civilian and police abusers share class and demographic backgrounds, the law enforcers most often had only recently left their jobs at the docks or construction sites and joined the police force. New Orleans had a tiny, unfunded department during the early 1920s, and local cops, by the standards of the era, remained poorly paid. Police expenditures in the Louisiana metropolis ranked fifty-ninth among the nation's sixty-nine largest urban centers, and cops' salaries were the lowest among major US population centers.[95] A postwar spike in violent crime, however, persuaded city officials to expand the unit, which more than doubled during the decade, increasing at seven times the rate of the local population.[96] The police department added new officers so quickly that it hired them as "supernumerary patrolmen." These were essentially emergency appointments, and the "supernumerary" label entailed a kind of probationary status. If the recruits demonstrated basic fitness for the job, the city promoted them, most often within a year, to the permanent status of "patrolmen." Reflecting the meager pay and low prestige of policemen, however, the department could not be rigorous or selective and routinely promoted probationary officers, including those who had been disciplined for violence, drunkenness, and "neglect of duty," such as Louis Dendinger, Louis Joseph's killer.[97] Supernumerary patrolmen were the youngest, least experienced, and most raw men in the department, typically only recently removed from dock work or hod carrying.

At times during the 1920s, white laborers in New Orleans received blue uniforms and service revolvers and exercised law enforcement duties within minutes of leaving jobs on the waterfront. During particular emergencies, such as labor strikes, city officials issued "special police" badges, uniforms, and firearms to civilians. These temporary cops were "not subject to police discipline and control" and underwent no vetting of any sort. Andrew Wiebelt, the 1927 road-rage killer, had held a special police position. A New York consultant hired by a local reform group in 1921 expressed alarm at this "long established practice," explaining that casually providing such men with revolvers and the "insignia of authority" became "the basis of oppressive and coercive" conduct on the streets of the city, as plebian class and racial sensibilities infused and infected the police department.[98]

Nor were 1920s new patrolmen trained after they joined the unit. At precisely the moment when police departments across the nation professionalized and established training classes, city officials in New Orleans, Atlanta, and other Southern cities eliminated training academies.[99] The Louisiana urban center, for example, abolished its instructional program for new officers during the early 1920s, when the city's "Old Regulars" political machine re-established their authority and eliminated the training academy and civil-service rules to consolidate its control over the police department. Although the superintendent mandated marksmanship classes later in the decade, local cops remained otherwise untrained until the mid-1940s.[100] Nearly three-fourths of Southern departments did the same and provided no formal instruction or preparation for new cops, at a time when departments elsewhere in the nation celebrated "scientific policing," and expanded their training programs.[101]

Supernumerary patrolmen, such as Joseph Cronin and Elmo Evans, committed a disproportionate share of police violence against African American New Orleanians. Untrained, only recently removed from dock work, drawn from a segment of the local population particularly anxious about its racial and economic status, possessing enhanced authority to employ force, and supplied with service revolvers, these law enforcers were, not surprisingly, especially quick to perceive slights, to imagine assaults on their social standing, and to respond with fierce, often lethal brutality. Supernumerary patrolmen committed more than a third of white-on-Black homicides in New Orleans during the 1920s and likely a much higher proportion of nonlethal violence against African American residents.

But cops' jobs made perceived slights and fronts even more searing and more personal than the imagined affronts felt by other working-class whites. With their identifiable uniforms, badges, and service revolvers, policemen, especially new patrolmen, saw themselves as symbols of white authority and believed that the most aggressive, most subversive, and most dangerous African American residents—the so called "bad n-----s"—targeted them, viewing public insubordination toward cops as a particular expression of status and as the paramount challenge to white authority. By defying and routing patrolmen on busy streets, these "burley brutes" demonstrated their mettle to their peers and undermined the wider caste system. Thus, for Southern cops, every encounter with an African American resident became a potential test or attack on white authority and backing down or refraining from responding forcefully eroded racial supremacy and brought intense collective and personal humiliation. According to one New Orleans observer, "if he loses the struggle he is through; he has lost everything. So, the police use roughness as a defense mechanism."[102]

Nor was this formulation unique to early twentieth-century New Orleans. Regional ethnographers described the same phenomena—both the defiant, "bad n-----" and the typical patrolman's response to such perceived challenges to his, and therefore to white, authority. Early twentieth-century Southern cops, according to cultural anthropologists, "regard any Negro who resists a policeman as a 'bad n-----,' one who must be 'taken care of' unofficially."[103] "In no field can his heroics and dare-deviltry be so thoroughly appreciated as when he is dealing with 'the law.' The policeman provides for him 'the supreme test of his daring,'" an interwar sociologist explained.[104] A Southern cop, another sociologist wrote, represented the "white man, armed, the embodiment of authority. Whoever gets the better of him has reached the highest goal of the 'bad' Negro," a threat that patrolmen felt acutely and that demanded fierce, brutal, public responses. If this symbol of racial power "does not take the law into his own hands, [he] loses the respect of both Negroes and whites."[105]

Visceral reactions to perceived defiance did not trigger every act of police brutality against African American New Orleanians or Memphians or Atlantans during the early twentieth century. Some violence erupted specifically from cops' duties as law enforcers—after suspects resisted arrest, for example, and attacked patrolmen who attempted to apprehend them. The fatal shooting of twenty-six-year-old Morris Peterson, a New Orleans African American day laborer, reflected a typical mix of informal and formal policing. Just after midnight, on February 12, 1922, Peterson became embroiled in a fight over a dice game in a local saloon—described, according to the linguistic conventions of the Prohibition era, as a "soft drink parlor." Rather than summoning the police, the barkeeper, Edmond Victor, rushed to his room, grabbed his 38 caliber Smith and Wesson army revolver, and fired shots at the African American dice players, one of whom pulled out his gun and fired twice. Victor reloaded and shot five more times. The discharge of the guns awakened supernumerary patrolman William Letten, a World War I veteran and former machinist with a seventh-grade education, who lived across the street from the saloon. With his 38 caliber Smith and Wesson in tow, Letten rushed to North Rocheblave Street, saw two African Americans running, and gave chase.[106] One of the fleeing dice players "cursed and fired one ineffectual shot at the Officer and continued running." In response, Letten shot twice, with one of the bullet striking Peterson in the back and killing him.[107] Such circumstances, when police shootings conformed to state law on justifiable homicide, were unusual, constituting 31.8 percent of the police homicides against African American residents.[108] Instead, minor breaches in the region's racial etiquette more often triggered cop violence against African Americans during the 1920s.

In the lion's share of police beatings and fatal shooting cases, New Orleans (and other Southern) patrolmen employed force in preemptive, spontaneous, brutal defense of white supremacy and the officers' personal racial status. These pressures exaggerated class-based racial antagonisms and made local law enforcers especially quick to respond to perceived disobedience with extreme, often deadly, violence. No slights or affronts seemed or felt trivial to young, untrained, white patrolmen during the 1920s, amplifying working-class racial antipathy and fueling police aggression against African Americans. In short, municipal cops most often beat, attacked, and killed African American residents as an outsized expression of civilian racial hostility. The morphology of cop and civilian violence against African American was nearly identical.

. . .

In sum, 1920s police violence toward African Americans, ranging from street brutality to murder, largely complemented or supplemented civilian extralegal, popular justice. In New Orleans and through the region, vigilantism provided the first line of defense of white supremacy and the Jim Crow caste system, and local law enforcers beat and killed African Americans, usually in response to perceived violations of racial custom, mainly in their capacities as white men, especially white working-class men.

Robert McCabe and Louis Dendinger's 1927 fatal shooting of Louis Joseph was a typical example of police violence against African American residents in the South's largest city. The two New Orleans patrolmen killed the fifteen-year-old high student because he failed to obey them, which they considered an act of racial insubordination, and they shot him in the back in support of David Hennessey, a white civilian, in violation of police policy on the use of guns and state law regarding justifiable homicide. As New Orleans—and other Southern urban centers—grew, its streets became more congested, its sidewalks and stores became more crowded, interracial interactions between strangers multiplied, and the frequency of misinterpreted glances, inflections, and jostles surged, transforming prosaic encounters into imagined challenges to racial etiquette. White-on-Black violence, both by civilians and by cops, rose. Beatings increased, as did interracial murders. During the 1920s, the civilian white-on-Black homicide rate jumped by nearly two-thirds in New Orleans, and during the first half of the decade alone the police rate climbed by 74.1 percent.[109] Nor was this pattern unique to New Orleans. In Memphis, for instance, the rise was even more pronounced, with the rate of police homicide against African American residents swelling by 172.9 percent.[110]

Although a toxic alchemy of racial-, class-, and occupation-based cultural pressures made cops especially quick to perceive defiance and respond with brutality, police and civilian violence toward African American residents remained nearly indistinguishable, with the profiles of assailants virtually identical, the profiles of victims comparable, and the locations, times, weapons, and behavioral triggers mirroring one another. In New Orleans during the 1920s, civilians committed 68.1 percent of white-on-Black homicides and the proportion spiked to 78.4 percent during the closing years of the decade, but there was no boundary between civilian and police attacks on African American residents. The latter erupted as an exaggerated expression of the former, providing a bulwark for white supremacy in the Jim Crow South. Comparable trends unfolded in Memphis, Birmingham, and Mobile during the 1920s.[111] Simply put, cops provided backup for white civilians in the early twentieth-century South, the reverse of the modern construction.

Seemingly skyrocketing breaches of racial defiance during the 1920s, however, appeared to signal an overwhelming assault on social stability. Crime, violence, and racial disorder, in the eyes of white New Orleanians and white Southerners, jeopardized the racial hierarchy, endangering respectable, decent, innocent city dwellers. These residents felt a soaring sense of vulnerability and demanded institutional, systemic protection. Such a perceived collapse of the social and racial order would generate a sharp pivot in policing, and law enforcers would begin to assume a more central, active, and aggressive role in maintaining law and order and especially in defending white supremacy. White popular justice and vigilantism remained normative through the 1920s, though police violence against African Americans would become distinct from civilian violence during the 1930s and would surge, transforming American law enforcement and race relations in the process.

TWO

"At No Time in the History of Our State Has White Supremacy Been in Greater Danger"

NEWSPAPER HEADLINES JOLTED white New Orleanians on the morning of March 22, 1932. Late in the previous evening, two African American men had robbed and fatally shot a forty-nine-year-old white shopkeeper.[1] This was not the first episode of a predatory interracial murder in the city. To the contrary, the violent attack on Edward Melancon marked the latest in a seeming plague of deadly Black-on-white crimes. But the robbery and shooting was particularly cruel and highlighted the surging threat that African American residents appeared to pose to respectable white New Orleanians and the horrific toll of the crumbling racial order. White supremacy had never been entirely secure, and its preservation, which many white residents considered the bedrock of social stability, had always required constant vigilance.[2] All at once, however, the practices, customs, and institutions that sustained the local (and regional) racial hierarchy seemed to be collapsing, unleashing an explosion of African American violence. White Southerners feared that they were losing control of their world, as Melancon's family and a long list of other decent New Orleanians could tragically attest and as residents read, again and again, on the front pages of the city's daily newspapers, and heard from panicked public officials and political demagogues.

The shopkeeper's killers had hatched their robbery plan an hour before they held up the grocery store and murdered Melancon. In a lottery shop near the city's French Quarter, Sanders Watkins, a twenty-two-year-old unemployed day laborer, proposed the heist to twenty-one-year-old Leaval Hubbard, also an unemployed day laborer. The men had known each other for a month and belonged to a loosely organized robbery gang. According to Hubbard, Watkins, alias Zanoo, suggested that they target Melancon's small store, explaining that "it was a good job [and] we could pull it off tonight."[3]

Watkins had heard that the proprietor "keeps a roll [of money] in his pocket." When the bandits arrived at the modest neighborhood grocery, however, they stood outside and bickered about the merits of robbing Melancon. "That man ain't got no money," Hubbard argued, but Watkins insisted that it would be a quick, "easy" stickup and yield a handsome payoff. "Come on," he exclaimed, "let's go make some money."[4]

Hubbard consented and took command of the robbery. He handed his accomplice a dime and instructed him to order a sausage. When Melancon turned to slice the meat, Hubbard would later admit to a police interrogator, "I reached into my bosom and pulled out my revolver and told them [Melancon and two others in the store] to get them up, pointing the revolver at the grocery man."[5] Fourteen-year-old Lloyd Melancon, the proprietor's son, was helping his father in the grocery store that night, and he and an African American customer instantly complied. But Edward Melancon hesitated. This angered Hubbard, who demanded for a second time that he "get them up." Hubbard directed Watkins to empty the cash register, which contained only $1.87. With his 38 caliber revolver trained on Melancon, Hubbard ordered Zanoo to search the grocer's pockets for the rumored wad of money. Humiliated by this indignity and especially by having an African American compel him to submit in the presence of his young son, Melancon balked and instead "stooped to get his pistol underneath the counter." Hubbard immediately pulled the trigger. The bullet pierced the merchant's abdomen, tearing through his small intestine and lodging in the back of his pelvis.[6] Melancon slumped to the floor, bled profusely, and writhed in agony, as Lloyd watched in horror. Hubbard snarled at his partner to rifle the dying man's pockets. Watkins reached into the shopkeeper's trousers, snatched the contents, and the robbers fled, soon to discover that they had murdered a man in a robbery that netted $13.87.

For forty-year-old Lucina Melancon, Edward's widow, and her five sons, three of them under ten, the nightmare had only begun, as New Orleans journalists eagerly detailed. The shopkeeper teetered at the edge of death for two days, before succumbing to his injuries. Creditors quickly foreclosed on the grocery and evicted the family from the property, which included the small apartment behind the store where the Melancons had resided. A "semi-invalid" and unable to work, Lucina rented a tiny, two-room house, and the family of six struggled to survive on the earnings of eighteen-year-old O'Neil, who held a part-time job in a cotton mill and brought home $6.63 per week, more than one-third of which now went to their landlord.[7] Lloyd, who had watched helplessly as Hubbard fatally shot his father and as Watkins plucked the money from the groaning man's pocket, told reporters that the grocery had provided a comfortable living for the Melancons—"not much in the way of luxuries, but the necessities were there."[8] Then "came the night of March 21—and a bandit," Lloyd sobbed. Hubbard's predatory crime left the family "living in want," according to the fourteen-year-old boy.[9] The seventh grader dropped out of school and issued a desperate public plea for work. "I don't care what it is doing, nor how little it pays," Lloyd explained, "but I've got to do something to help O'Neil take care of the family." The other Melancon children would also leave school by the seventh grade, securing jobs as day laborers and remaining in the cramped house to support their "gravely ill" mother.[10]

To white New Orleanians, who remained accustomed to relying on self-help and popular justice rather than formal policing, Edward Melancon's murder graphically illustrated the rapid deterioration of the racial order. But white vigilantism and local custom, core elements of the informal system of racial control, no longer protected respectable residents from African American desperadoes. The viciousness of the crime underscored a new white vulnerability, haunting and terrifying them.[11] And Hubbard's barbarity was not an isolated event. This murder, however, was merely unusually heartless, especially humiliating, and hence copiously covered in local newspapers, as the African American bandit forced a respectable white man to submit and then slaughtered him. Unwilling to abide the shame of being dominated and having Watkins pilfer the money in his pockets as he stood powerless in front of his son, Melancon did what white men in the Jim Crow South were expected to do; he resisted—and was shot down in the process. The degradation continued, however, when Hubbard commanded Sanders to search the dying merchant's trousers. The Melancons' descent into poverty and desperation, gratuitously described in myriad newspaper articles and recounted again at the killers' trial, reminded white New Orleanians of their vulnerability and the looming African American threat.

In short, the crime indicated that white residents' worst fears were being realized. These New Orleanians had worried about the racial order before. But this violence seemed different—more brutal and more wanton. During the late 1920s and early 1930s, local newspapers provided daily evidence of the threat, documenting the crisis with a horrifying and swelling tally of the body count that confirmed white alarm. Far from allaying their anxieties, local officials, including law enforcers, amplified them and expressed similar panic. "At no time in the history of our State," Orleans Parish District Attorney Eugene Stanley warned, "has White Supremacy been in greater danger."[12] Black-on-white predatory violence surged, according to local journalists and prominent residents; the criminals butchered solid, respectable white men, such as Edward Melancon, and preyed on white women as well, rekindling memories of a purported turn-of-the-century rape epidemic.

The African American "marauders" also seemed increasingly bold and merciless, confident that established mechanisms of racial control had become moribund.[13] Their crimes, white observers emphasized, were brazen, even performative, as bloodthirsty African American men "flaunted" their aggressive rejection of racial etiquette and reveled in degrading their white victims.[14] Such overt, violent defiance shocked white residents and highlighted their helplessness, particularly as their efforts to reassert racial dominance often had fatal consequences for respectable men such as Edward Melancon.

White New Orleanians insisted that racial instability had eroded social order during the late 1920s and early 1930s, sparking three chilling changes. First, the Great Migration flooded the community with violent African American newcomers. The tidal wave of migrants seemed to overwhelm mechanisms of racial control and authority. As a consequence, white city dwellers insisted, interracial murder, robbery, and sexual assault skyrocketed.

Leaval Hubbard was typical of a new breed of killers. Born and reared in St. Martinville, a small town in rural Louisiana, he moved one hundred miles to New Orleans and had a history of violent behavior. Hubbard stabbed an acquaintance in a dispute over a crap game, for instance, and served sixteen months in the state penitentiary.[15] Upon his release, he joined a bandit gang that assembled an "arsenal" of weapons and targeted small grocery and drug stores operated by white New Orleanians. Hubbard participated in seven holdups in the months before his deadly robbery of Melancon's shop.[16] African American migrants like Hubbard made New Orleans one of the most murderous cities in the nation.

Second, long-established mechanisms for maintaining racial control faltered during this era, giving free rein to the predators. Not only was custom inadequate, but the crush of migrants transformed the city's social geography in ways that unleashed dangerous "race mixing," exposing white New Orleanians to the ravages of the newcomers. Even white popular justice and self-help now proved incapable of preserving the racial order, a frightening shift accelerated by the proliferation of firearms and "gun-toting" African Americans. These changes jeopardized white supremacy.

Third, the Melancon murder laid bare a crisis in white gender roles, revealing the sudden inability of men to defend themselves, let alone to maintain racial control and authority. Just as his killer typified the dangerous newcomers, the murdered grocer symbolized white masculinity and respectability, and Hubbard and his 38 caliber revolver had easily vanquished him. Hailing from a local, working-class family, Melancon had climbed into the bottom tier of middle-class society. He began his working career in a sugar factory, became a saw mill inspector, and then a plumbing inspector. A few months before Hubbard murdered him, Melancon had acquired the grocery, which generated a modest but stable income. But the shopkeeper could not protect himself or cement his family's status, and his death plunged Lucina and their sons into poverty.

In the years immediately after the Great War, white New Orleanians had been content to ignore African American criminal violence, confident that it remained safety confined within the Black community. During the early 1920s, for example, prosecutors routinely dismissed charges against African American killers and secured convictions in only 14.5 percent of homicide cases. Orleans Parish district attorneys dropped the charges against a higher proportion of these suspects than among their white counterparts and won guilty verdicts at a lower percentage, largely reflecting their indifference toward African American crime and criminals.[17] This quickly changed, however, when migrants flooded the city, race mixing flared, and deadly crime bled across racial lines, seemingly endangering and terrifying respectable, solid residents.[18] Familiar, noninstitutional mechanisms of racial control—custom, civilian policing, popular justice, and vigilantism—suddenly proved incapable of preserving social stability, and the bulwarks of the social hierarchy seemed to be disintegrating. White supremacy, as the parish district attorney conceded, was under siege. Something had to be done to protect the good people of the city.

. . .

The Great Migration unshackled a torrent of social changes that rocked white society and threatened to demolish the racial order. Driven out of the region by Jim Crow, lynching, grinding poverty, and instability in the Southern agricultural economy, nearly a million African Americans fled from rural areas and resettled in Northern industrial centers, pouring into Chicago, Detroit, Cleveland, and other cities. But larger numbers of migrants, most of them young and single, traveled to Southern urban centers. Between 1900 and 1920, nearly 900,000 African Americans moved to Southern cities, compared with 671,292 relocating to the Northern urban areas.[19] Some merely passed through, stopping briefly at local railroad depots on the trip north. Others, however, remained. During the 1920s, New Orleans's African American population swelled by nearly a third, growing twice as fast as the city's white population. Nashville's African American community rose by 20 percent, Vicksburg's by 30 percent, Birmingham's by 41 percent, and Atlanta's by 43 percent.[20] Equally important, in 1930 African Americans comprised one-third of New Orleans residents and nearly 40 percent of Memphis and Birmingham residents, four-to-five times the proportion of Northern cities. Thus, white residents of Southern urban centers felt invaded and besieged by the newcomers, magnifying racialized stereotypes of crime and disorder during the late 1920s and 1930s.[21]

New Orleans's distinctive topography made this migration especially unsettling for white residents. The city was sprawling, covering the third largest area among the nation's urban centers.[22] But the physical dimensions of the municipality were misleading, for bayous submerged much of Orleans Parish and precluded residential development in nearly three-fourths of the city.[23] As a consequence, residents crowded into the patches of high, dry ground, particularly along the banks of the Mississippi River. New Orleans featured a "backyard" or "back swamp" pattern of African American population concentration, with small, dense pockets of these residents clustered close to, behind, and between white neighborhoods.[24]

This unusual social geography left African American areas scattered, surrounded by white residents, and unable to absorb the surge in population without encroaching into neighboring white sections. The increased daily interaction during the 1920s frightened many white New Orleanians, who more often crossed paths with unfamiliar, young African American newcomers. Writing in 1926, the city attorney warned municipal officials of the resulting dangers and insisted that the "races should be kept apart."[25] A local lawyer issued a more incendiary description of conditions in the community, using his weekly radio program to express his horror about "these baboons mixing with white people and being turned loose on the streets of New Orleans to kill people."[26]

Measures to reduce overcrowding and race mixing in the dense, southern portion of the parish created additional problems and deepened tensions. In the late 1910s, the city installed massive electric pumps to drain the bayous and buoy residential development. The project, however, proceeded haltingly and only a decade later did significant construction and demographic expansion begin, affording greater racial separation. But transportation improvements became necessary so that African American factory laborers and longshoremen could travel to work. Affluent white residents who fled to upscale new subdivisions also needed access to the downtown area and especially the business district. In different ways, both public and private transportation developments generated racial friction. Far from shielding white residents from threats, commuting exposed them to greater perils and the evils of race mixing.

Even more than before, white and African American New Orleanians shared streetcars, for example, and perceived violations of racial etiquette became endemic, with the former demanding racial deference in seating and comportment and the latter sometimes balking at remaining crammed into the rear sections of the vehicles. White residents also worried about being attacked on streetcars, and white women traveling alone reported that African American riders made rude, menacing comments and stalked, followed, and sexually assaulted them when they stepped off the cars, particularly at night.[27]

Automobiles brought greater problems as well. As the price of vehicles dropped and the number of cars skyrocketed, whites complained bitterly that African American drivers flouted racial custom, refusing to defer to them at intersections, aggressively passing them, cutting them off in traffic, and displaying aggression and defiance from behind the wheels of their roadsters.[28] These challenges to the local racial code sometimes ended in violent encounters, tinging "road rage" with racial venom. Streetcars and roads became contested terrain in the battle to preserve white authority.

Racial segregation introduced unexpected dangers as well. White New Orleanians worried that African American newcomers were unfamiliar with local custom and that residential isolation left the migrants without sustained contact with respectable residents who could instruct them in the informal etiquette and unspoken codes that maintained racial deference and buttressed social order. Instead, aggressive, racially subversive attitudes and behaviors festered, only to be unleashed in encounters on sidewalks, in stores, on streetcars, and behind the wheel of automobiles. These "unknown miscreants" operated with "impunity."[29] Every effort to protect white New Orleanians seemed to render them less safe.

To the horror of white residents, young African American newcomers increasingly defied local racial custom, according to newspaper accounts and police files, and reports of violent encounters abounded and fed welling anxieties.[30] On January 19, 1925, for instance, George Stouff, a twenty-seven-year-old, white streetcar conductor, died when an African American factory worker reacted to a routine reminder of New Orleans racial etiquette with a deadly assault. At 8:45 p.m., Stouff approached his "sweetheart," nineteen-year-old Thelma Hartman, on the sidewalk in front of her St. Peter Street residence. As they walked closer to one another, the young white woman passed Prince Johnson, a thirty-three-old African American stranger, who made an insolent remark, quipping "Honey do you want some cake and candy?" The police report on the ensuing attack explained that Stouff, like any respectable white man, "resented" the comment, "asked the negro what he meant by insulting the white girl," and ordered Johnson to "move on." Then, the investigating patrolman explained, "without another cause or provocation the negro stabbed Stouff," inflicting a fatal abdominal wound.[31] Again and again, according to white journalists, such prosaic encounters triggered murderous responses from young African American New Orleanians, inciting terror among white residents and signaling an ominous change in the city's racial order.

More assertive white efforts to combat defiance and racial instability proved equally disastrous. Stouff had merely "remonstrated" with Prince Johnson, and he died in the process. Other white New Orleanians resisted African American challenges more forcefully yet suffered the same fate. Civilian policing and manly initiative fell short of restoring white authority and instead revealed the vulnerability of decent, respectable citizens. With dizzying frequency, newspapers reported and police files documented the victimization of solid white men at the hands of vicious African Americans strangers during the late 1920s and early 1930s.

Wilmer Lyons's murder on March 9, 1930, sent shock waves through white New Orleans and garnered statewide attention, providing still more tangible evidence that no white Louisianan remained safe on the streets of the city. Shortly before 9 p.m., the twenty-eight-year-old clerk purchased sandwiches at a grocery close to his State Street home. Lyons paid for the food with a $20 bill. Camped outside the shop, two African Americans watched the transaction through the shop's window, concluded that Lyons was flush with cash, and descended on him. When Lyons exited Fred Gaudet's store, the bandits separated enough for their victim to pass between them on the sidewalk and then pounced on him, one from each side. But Lyons was a strong, powerful athlete, a football and baseball star in college.[32]

He "threw the man on his left off" and ripped free from other holdup man.[33] One of his attackers screamed "give it to him," and the other "negro thug," twenty-one-year-old James Mills, pulled out a handgun and fired.[34] The single bullet pierced Lyons's kidney, colon, the right lobe of his liver, and the lower lobe of his left lung. According to the *Baton Rouge Advocate*, the former star athlete "lay on the ground for 15 minutes, crying vainly for help, and finally dragged himself to his home, a short distance away. He collapsed in his wife's arms" and died a short time later.[35] Accounts of the murder appeared in newspapers across the state, expressing horror that a "vengeful negro, angry at being repulsed," had murdered the former sports star.[36]

Occurring the same week as Wilmer Lyons's murder, George Johnson slaughtered another prominent white athlete, J. Adair Lawrence. This crime was even more emblematic of the wider, deeper breakdown of the racial order and attracted even greater attention from Louisiana newspapers, for it exposed and amplified African Americans' violent subversion of white authority and the migrants' assault on New Orleans tradition, public space, and social order. The twenty-eight-year-old Lawrence belonged to the local elite. A former football star and "campus celebrity" at Tulane University, he attended the institution's medical school after graduation. At the peak of the 1930 Carnival celebration, a truck filled with "Tulane men," most of them former football players and dressed as sailors for the raucous festivities, passed through the French Quarter, where they encountered a "huge crowd of negro Mardi Gras revelers."[37] White witnesses asserted that the African Americans "began to annoy the white men," blocked their vehicle, "cursed" them, and "pulled at the legs of the boys whose legs were hanging from the side of the truck." Refusing to abide such insolent behavior, the "boys on the truck alighted and began to fight back."[38] According to white reporters, the former gridiron stars were "forced into the fracas by the negroes, who were the aggressors."[39]

Lawrence joined his former teammates in the melee, where they defended themselves, determined to reestablish elite, white, masculine dominance on the "impudent" hoard.[40] "Out-numbered by twenty or more to one it was an uneven fight, the negroes using knives, chairs, iron bars and bricks, while the Tulane men had only their fists for protection," one journalist waxed.[41] Towering over the crowd at 6'8" tall and weighing 280 pounds, Lawrence symbolized white manly authority and, relying on his bare hands, began thrashing the brash African Americans. Johnson later told police officials that "I saw a big man knocking negroes down like flies."[42] According to the other

Tulane "boys" and white newspaper reporters, George Johnson then whipped out a gun and shot the unarmed football star in the face from close range.

If Lawrence epitomized white authority and manly honor, his killer fulfilled the stereotype of the African American criminal. Unrepentant, Johnson "readily admitted" shooting Lawrence.[43] Born and raised in New Orleans's southeastern hinterland, he migrated to the city at the age of eighteen and eschewed local racial custom in the regional metropolis. White witnesses to the killing described him as insolent and defiant. Moments before shooting Lawrence, they testified, Johnson announced that African American residents "don't allow any White people on South Rampart street" and promised the white men to "bump you off." He then pointed his pistol at the medical student, bellowing "let me get that White Mother Fucker" as he discharged the weapon.[44] To police interrogators, Johnson boasted that the white men were armed attackers, "but I was a little too quick for them."[45]

African American combatants, witnesses, journalists, and Johnson offered a very different description of the deadly skirmish, though the depictions were not entirely incompatible, and these conflicting images captured the toxic racial climate of the city in 1930. African American participants and bystanders contended that the Tulane men had initiated the fight. "The real aggressors were the whites, as it always is in the southland," an African American newspaper editor explained.[46] While he acknowledged shooting Lawrence, George Johnson maintained that "we didn't bother them."[47] Moreover, the hulking medical student, these witnesses indicated, was hardly an innocent, unarmed victim, for he wielded a knife, had slashed an African American woman, and was attacking Johnson when his shooter, a foot shorter and 130 pounds lighter, discharged his "38 special."

African American residents told journalists and later testified to police investigators that the white men "began the melee by throwing eggs at the crowd of negroes."[48] When the targets of the athletes' fun objected to such treatment, one of the Tulane men announced his intention to "kill all of these negroes."[49] White observers and participants in the fight did not deny these reports, but neither did they consider showering African American residents with rotten eggs to be objectionable conduct or to constitute provocation. Writing shortly after the Lawrence shooting, an African American editor complained that the trigger for the violence was commonplace practice of "bands of young white men" riding through the streets of the city "heaving bricks, rotten eggs—as in this case—and vegetables at all Negroes seen on the streets." The police, the journalist fumed, casually ignored the malicious behavior of these "young southern gentlemen in their pursuit of pleasure."[50] White New Orleanians viewed such conduct as routine, an ordinary, prosaic expression of racial privilege and termed African American objections inappropriate and incendiary. A *New Orleans States* reporter explained that "members of the Tulane party" fought only "in self defense" and that the African American response to being pelted with rotten eggs represented an assault on white supremacy.[51]

Johnson's reaction to racial custom conformed to an alarming trend and confirmed white perceptions that the Great Migration ignited an explosion in violence—in New Orleans and across the country. The local murder rate spiked, as did regional and national rates. Between 1920 and 1925, the US homicide rate swelled by 19.2 percent. Urban murder rates particularly soared, climbing by 30.6 percent, with jumps of 43.8 percent in Detroit and 94.8 percent in Chicago. But the surge in New Orleans dwarfed those increases. The city's murder rate mushroomed by 139.2 percent. By 1924, New Orleans was the third most murderous city in the United States, with rates double Chicago's at the height of Al Capone's reign, four times Detroit's level, and six times Boston's homicide rate.[52] Local observers anticipated that death toll would continue to spiral, with the editor of the *New Orleans Item* terming the situation "intolerable" and warning that "it promises to become worse instead of better."[53] Prominent residents implored respectable New Orleanians to purchase firearms in response to the crime wave. Writing in 1926, a district attorney advised that "every man and women who leaves his home in an automobile should carry a good pistol," a suggestion that likely contributed to the 128.8 percent leap in the city's gun homicide rate.[54]

Local whites attributed the explosion in violence to African American newcomers, a view echoed by newspaper editors and exploited by political officials. The murder epidemic, the *New Orleans Times-Picayune* concluded in 1922, "is all on the side of the negroes."[55] Two years later, Police Superintendent Guy Molony offered a similar interpretation, explaining that "we have a rather high homicide rate but that is largely due to our great negro population. Most of the murders in New Orleans are committed by negroes."[56] He added that "if it were not for the colored murders, New Orleans and the entire South would have an excellent record."[57] The statistician for the municipal board of health concurred, writing that when the "negro rate" is removed from the calculation "New Orleans' [murder] rate is less than the average." Bristling at the suggestion that the city was violent, he insisted that white New Orleanians remained peaceful and law abiding.[58]

"The preponderance of collared-killers [*sic*]," a white editor added in 1926, "is largely responsible."[59]

But African American crime, white residents worried, increasingly leached across racial lines, a terrifying effect of the Great Migration, race mixing, and the newcomers' fierce assault on white supremacy. New Orleans politicians responded by enacting a racial zoning ordinance, passing the statute in 1924 after ten seconds of debate and garnering fulsome praise from relieved white New Orleanians.[60] They insisted that physical separation offered law-abiding white residents the best hope for safety. Local civil rights activists, however, quickly challenged the ordinance, and three years later the US Supreme Court declared the measure unconstitutional, leaving white residents at the mercy of African American criminals, such as Leaval Hubbard and George Johnson.[61]

The Great Migration had flooded New Orleans with "bad n-----s," newcomers who reveled in subverting the racial hierarchy, dominating and humiliating respectable white men, and murdering innocent shopkeepers and other respectable residents. While this stereotype was not new, fears of "bad n-----s" spread as the murder rate surged and became stock images in newspaper accounts of local crime during the 1920s and 1930s. Such an African American resident, according to both local and regional white observers, openly rejected the "racial etiquette defining his sphere and role."[62] But worse, these newcomers were not content merely to rob white merchants. Rather, "their triumph [was] incomplete if they are unable to flaunt themselves in the face of a white man."[63] They degraded and purposefully humiliated their victims, basking in forcing respectable white men to submit and then slaughtering them in order to cement their reputations with their peers. With the city awash with newcomers, "there is always the possibility that almost any one of these strange faces may be the front of a 'bad n-----.'"[64] Inexpensive guns added to the hysteria, emboldening the migrants, according to white observers, and enabling brash, defiant African American newcomers to become savage killers.[65]

Sensationalized newspaper reports and inflammatory rhetoric from demagogic local politicians stitched isolated incidents into a massive crime wave, inciting panic among anxious white New Orleanians while eschewing or distorting quantitative evidence of actual violence. The range and scope of highly publicized accounts of interracial crime magnified the terror and highlighted the perceived failure of custom and popular justice. Two themes, however, commanded particular attention, garnered front-page coverage in local and statewide newspapers, and terrified white residents.

First, white merchants seemed particularly vulnerable, and local editors plastered reports of disastrous efforts to fend off African American robbers on the front pages of local newspapers during the late 1920s and early 1930s. With numbing repetition, the articles described violent encounters strikingly similar to Leaval Hubbard's murder of Edward Melancon. Again and again, according to white crime-beat reporters, African American men entered small shops, requested items from the proprietor, and brandished a weapon when the clerk or proprietor turned to prepare the order for purchase. If the shopkeeper showed any sign of resistance or even hesitated before submitting, the "thug," "marauder," or "negro bandit" bludgeoned or, more often, shot him like a dog.

One after another, African American robbers brutalized and murdered white merchants, crimes emblazoned on the front pages of New Orleans newspapers and reprinted across the state with a contagion-like effect. In an almost formulaic account, local reporters described how the fifty-year-old Ernest Wilbert, a shop manager, "was murderously assaulted Saturday afternoon by a negro who was frustrated in his attempt to rob the establishment." The holdup man entered the store and asked for a bottle of ammonia. When Wilbert "turned his back to wrap up the bottle," according to the *New Orleans States*, "he was dealt a heavy blow on the head with a piece of lead pipe, knocking him unconscious."[66] Likewise, an African American robber shot and killed fifty-two-year-old Peter Capatae, who operated a local restaurant. The criminal "asked Capatae for something to eat. As he turned his back the negro pulled a small automatic and demanded the money." Capatae died from two bullet wounds to his abdomen.[67] In a nearly identical attack, a "negro bandit" shot Julius Schuester "from a distance of only a few feet. Mr. Schuester," a newspaper reported, "was behind the counter when two negroes entered the [grocery] store, and ordered five cents worth of cigarettes. Schuester turned around to obtain the cigarettes and, as he turned back to the negroes, one of them whipped a pistol out of his pocket and ordered him to stick up his hands. Mr. Schuester was slow in complying with the demand and the negro thug, becoming alarmed, fired point blank at him."[68] A few months later, a "negro bandit" shot sixty-five-year-old Leopold Zelenka, who also owned a small grocery. The young assailant ordered a ham sandwich and "without warning drew a revolver and fired a shot," striking the shopkeeper in the shoulder and severing a major artery. According to a Baton Rouge newspaper, Zelenka "tried to reach a gun he kept beneath a counter but his arm was paralyzed by the bullet," leaving him bleeding and helpless.[69]

Reports of similarly murderous robberies, mirroring the Melancon killing, appeared with staccato-like repetition in newspapers across the state and the region, fueling white fears of African Americans, violent crime, and the collapse of white supremacy and masculine authority. According to one New Orleans newspaper, "weekly the negroes have terrorized small neighborhood grocery stores and have awed both owners and customers in the stores."[70] Not only was Black-on-white violent crime seemingly skyrocketing, but the African American assailants obliterated white, masculine authority in every instance, rendering their victims powerless and then murdering them. Virtually identical accounts of "negro bandits" wantonly slaughtering white shopkeepers splashed across the front pages of Birmingham, Atlanta, Mobile, and Memphis newspapers during the late 1920s and early 1930s. In 1930, for example, the *Memphis Commercial Appeal* described an "orgy" of such murderous robberies.[71]

Second, the criminals preyed on white women. Such attacks echoed an earlier Black-on-white crime panic. It particularly terrified them and reinforced notions of a pervasive assault on white supremacy and manhood, as white men proved unable to protect their wives and daughters. No space seemed safe from these "negro thugs," who, according to the *New Orleans Item*, unleashed "a reign of terror by attacking white women."[72]

African American strangers, the white women reported, followed them when they alighted from streetcars at night. As soon as the vehicles disappeared into the darkness, the predators attacked, often dragging their victims into alleys where they robbed and ravaged them. Twenty-three-year-old Frank Williams, according to local newspapers, assaulted numerous white women in early 1930. He traveled "on the same [street]car with them and then followed them on foot when they left the car."[73] Likewise, police officials and New Orleans crime-beat reporters reported that seventeen-year-old Emmit Johnson attacked Mamie Brintell, a fifty-seven-year-old widow who worked as a maid in a movie theater, moments after she stepped off a streetcar, "gripping her by the throat."[74]

In other such assaults, the "fiends" jumped out of bushes or alleys to attack and "criminally assault"—in other words, rape—the white women. A "negro leaped from behind the billboards," seized thirty-four-year-old Bertha Morales by the throat, and dragged her into a vacant lot on November 18, 1928.[75] Similarly, a "negro sprang from the darkness," grabbed forty-eight-year-old Ethel Bennett, knocked her unconscious with "a blow in the face," and hauled her from the sidewalk.[76] In another such attack, an African

American robber and rapist followed fifty-one-year-old Mrs. John Powell "late one night and attacked her in an alleyway near Tulane Avenue," taking her money and sexually assaulting the white woman.[77]

The victims were often middle-aged, respectable women. Two young, "burley," armed African American men, for example, assaulted forty-seven-year-old Clementine Everhart, the wife of a local contractor, and her friend, Mamie Fallo, also forty-seven, as they walked to the St. Francis de Sales church at 5:20 a.m. on December 31, 1928. One pointed "a revolver at the two elderly women," barked "keep still and gimme what ya got," and snatched Everhart's prayer beads and purse. Fallo sprinted into the darkness and screamed, prompting the criminals to flee.[78] Local streets no longer seemed safe for white women.

Not even automobiles provided protection. New Orleans newspapers published numerous accounts of African American mashers attacking white women seated in cars. On May 2, 1929, for example, thirty-nine-year-old Cornelius Martin blocked the vehicle in which a nineteenth-year-old white woman was riding, "dragged the girl out of the automobile into the woods," and criminally assaulted her, a crime reported in every New Orleans newspaper.[79] A few months later, a "negro bandit" attacked twenty-three-year-old Johanna Goldman as she sat in an automobile on St. Charles Avenue, one of the city's busiest streets. According to the newspaper accounts, the "negro thug" hammered Goldman "over the left eye and rendered [her] unconscious."[80]

Nor were homes and bedrooms safe from the criminals, for accounts of African American home intruders attacking women as they slept filled local newspapers during the late 1920s and early 1930s. White readers learned about these predators entering women's bedrooms, usually late at night, presumably intent on robbing and sexually assaulting their victims. A "young negro," for instance, broke into sixty-five-year-old Annie Schling's Gaienee Street apartment in the middle of night, "supposedly in search of money." He invaded her bedroom, "seized her by the throat," and choked her. When Schling resisted his attack and broke free from his grasp, the fiend grabbed a medicine bottle and "struck the woman in the face."[81] Similarly, at 4:45 a.m. on February 21, 1932, an African American man entered Mieralin Cauley's bedroom, "grabbed her, placed a hand over her mouth and dragged her out of bed," according to the *New Orleans States*. As he pulled her across the room, however, the twenty-seven-year-old woman broke free from her attacker, lunged for a dresser, and seized her revolver. Frightened, "the negro leaped through the window which he had entered."[82] Jessie Saunders was less fortunate, local newspapers lamented. A "burley negro" entered her bedroom "rushed up her, slugged her unconscious and tied and gagged her with a bedspread."[83]

Newspaper descriptions of such attacks implied that the criminals routinely robbed and sexually assaulted white women, invoking a familiar "negro rapist" trope. "Before robbing her," for example, sixty-eight-year-old Carrie Wahl's attacker "knocked her down" and "maltreated her. She was found unconscious" on railroad tracks, according to a New Orleans newspaper.[84] Seven other white women identified the same assailant, William Johnson, a twenty-seven-year-old auto mechanic originally from Vicksburg.[85] Local journalists characterized Johnson as a serial rapist.[86] More often, newspaper accounts offered veiled, but pointedly suggestive, references to sexual assaults, describing African American criminals dragging white women into alleys, garages, and vacant lots, and leaving their victims unconscious.

Bold and defiant, these predators even attacked women escorted by their husbands, and the criminals added to the indignity of the robberies and "criminal assaults" by training their revolvers on the men and rendering them helpless or bludgeoning them into unconsciousness. Cornelius Martin, who dragged his victim out of an automobile and sexually assaulted her, first battered her companion senseless, while Leslie Flowers's brazen attacker, who did not even don a mask, confined her husband into another room at gunpoint while he assaulted her.[87] In the summer of 1929, New Orleans police officials warned residents about the "negro bandits" who "had been committing assaults upon white women in various sections of the city, after holding at bay or slugging the escorts of the women."[88] The predators defiled white women, humiliated their husbands, and forced white men, such as Edward Melancon, into powerlessness and submission, subverting the racial hierarchy as they committed their violent crimes. Robbery, murder, and rape blended and blurred.

Sexually assaulting white women and forcing shopkeepers and merchants into helplessness proved especially symbolically freighted. Dominating African Americans, both individually and collectively, formed a core element of racial and gender identity for white men in the Jim Crow South. Thus, the robberies and the sexual assaults of women represented attacks on white supremacy that seemed even more menacing than mere violent crimes and far more unsettling than holdups and sexual assaults by white predators.[89]

The elision of young African American newcomers and predatory violence yoked local anxieties to the social-science scholarship of the era. Reports of

African American men attacking, robbing, and murdering white men and sexually assaulting white women were not new, but newspaper accounts of such crimes and white anxieties increased dramatically during the late 1920s, as the crime panic spread and white fears about the collapse of the racial order mounted. Sociological and criminological studies bolstered and buttressed white New Orleanians' stereotyping.[90] Local officials, for example, often drew upon Frederick L. Hoffman's annual statistical analyses of homicide in America. A vice president and statistician of the Prudential Insurance and the nation's leading authority on violence, Hoffman published a column, complete with a series of tables, each year in the industry's trade journal, *The Spectator*.[91] His annual reports, summaries of which appeared in the leading newspapers, elicited both praise and rage from Southern political leaders, for Hoffman noted the stratospheric homicide rates of African American residents but also identified Southern cities, particularly Memphis and New Orleans, as the murder capitals of the nation.[92] Local leaders applauded and quoted from the statistician's views about race but bristled at his conclusions, insisting that his tables ranking cities according to their homicide rates failed to explain that whites in the region were peaceful and that the high murder rates largely reflected violence committed by African Americans.[93] "The man does not understand conditions here," the police superintendent complained, explaining that the "negro problem was not given the proper attention."[94] Memphis officials became so angry at his reports that they refused to share data with him.[95] Early twentieth-century "scientific" studies of race and violence, such as Hoffman's, mainly enabled Southern whites to couch their familiar assumptions about African Americans in seemingly neutral, scholarly, authoritative terms.

Even these stereotyped images of African Americans, however, became caricatured during the late 1920s and 1930s. City officials, white journalists, local cops, and crime victims invoked formulaic images to describe African American suspects and depicted nearly every assailant as a "burley negro" or a "big burley, black brute." Jessie Saunders, for example, told police investigators that the ravager who invaded her bedroom and bound and gagged her was "a burley negro," while the two church women assaulted in 1929 described their attackers as "two burley young negroes."[96] Such imagery cast African American men as ferocious and beast-like, possessing super-human strength.

Witness testimony and the suspects themselves, however, often belied such characterizations and tropes. Police accounts of his arrest and shooting, for example, depicted sixteen-year-old Willie Gray as a hulking goliath, who physically overpowered two detectives attempting to arrest him and compelling them to shoot the teenager.[97] An African American commentator countered that this was "contrary to fact. The boy is frail, almost a weakling."[98] But the repetition of the stereotypes cemented white perceptions of African American beasts preying on innocent, respectable New Orleanians.

Entirely fabricated descriptions of African American predators drew upon and reinforced these images. Again and again during the interwar period, white New Orleanians invented tales of brawny African American brutes attacking them, using falsified crime accounts to hide a wide range of misdeeds and crimes. Jessie Saunders, for instance, "decided to stage a fake robbery" and sexual assault after she raided her husband's Christmas fund, while thirty-year-old Myrtle Lala invented a similar tale of a "Negro prowler" attacking her in her bedroom in order to "conceal her guilt from her husband" after the woman's adulterous lover battered her.[99] Fifteen-year-old Joseph Garet "told the police that he had been robbed, bound and gagged by a Negro and left helpless in an empty box car" to avoid being whipped by his father for "playing hookey."[100]

In other falsified accounts of African American attacks, the purported victim sought to mislead law enforcers. Eighteen-year-old Martin Sciambra, for example, stole $28 from his employer and then reported that a "negro stuck a pistol into his ribs, ordered him to stand still, and took the money." But police investigators immediately found his "yarn" implausible, and Scambia confessed.[101] Alexander Biri attempted a comparable ploy and went to greater lengths to deceive local cops. After killing his white coworker, the fifty-six-year-old oil station manager fired a bullet into his own knee, summoned the police, and reported that a "Negro bandit" had robbed and shot them.[102] Confronted with contradictions in his description of the holdup, Biri admitted that he had lied and had killed Anthony Vitrano in a dispute over money.[103] White criminals also blackened their faces prior to robbing or murdering their victims.[104] While New Orleans newspapers reported the assaults by "big, burley negroes" on front pages, the recantations usually appeared in tiny articles buried as filler on back pages or not reported at all. The *New Orleans Times-Picayune*, for example, published its correction of Jessie Saunders's attack on page twenty.[105] Therefore, even when they were eventually exposed as falsified, fabricated accounts of African American criminals preying on innocent, respectable New Orleanians mainly buttressed white fears of interracial violence.

National events contributed to the local panic. Across the country, violence soared during the 1920s, and a dizzying number of high-profile crimes, including Leopold and Loeb's 1924 "thrill killing" of fourteen-year-old Bobby Franks, Andrew Kehoe's murder of thirty-eight children in a 1927 school bombing, and the 1929 St. Valentine's Day massacre, captured the attention of Americans. Eager to attract funding for the fledgling Federal Bureau of Investigation, J. Edgar Hoover exploited these events, pioneered public-relations ploys about bandits, and fanned the flames during the late 1920s and 1930s.[106] But regional sensibilities shaped New Orleanians' crime nightmares, racializing the local hysteria. While a handful of major bank heists occurred in the city, white New Orleanians worried most about African American predators and their perceived assault on white supremacy.

Robberies, robbery-homicides, traffic confrontations, assaults, home invasions, and rapes committed by African Americans—reports of such interracial conflicts, rather than the actual crime trends, fueled the white panic, because journalists, political leaders, and criminal justice officials distorted the threat, and white New Orleanians misinterpreted these patterns of violence. Indeed crime mushroomed during the early 1920s, more than doubling, and African American violence particularly spiraled, rising by 155.6 percentage. White violence, however, also spiked. But nearly all of the African American murder remained within the city's African American community, barely affecting white New Orleanians. In 1920, for example, intra-racial conflict accounted for 83.3 percent of African American murders. Five years later, when the rate reached its high-water mark, 94.4 percent of these homicides flared within racial lines. More important, during the late 1920s, at the height of New Orleans's crime panic, the African American murder rate plunged, tumbling by 55.7 percent from 1925 to 1930.

Nor did violence crossing the racial boundary increase, newspaper attention and white panic notwithstanding. Rather, the Black-on-white homicide rate remained virtually flat (see Figure 1). Furthermore, the proportion of intra-racial murders fell. Between 1920 and 1923, Black-on-white killings accounted for 7.7 percent of New Orleans homicides, and during the closing years of the decade these crimes constituted 4.3 percent of murders. Alarm about African American violence, in short, soared as African American crime and interracial homicide plummeted; crime and white perceptions of crime shifted in opposite, contradictory directions.

Panic about African American predatory violence was equally constructed and largely an imaginary crisis. In 1930, at the apogee of the local hysteria, African American holdup men murdered two white New Orleanians, accounting for 2.4 percent of local homicides. In 1932, when Leaval Hubbard

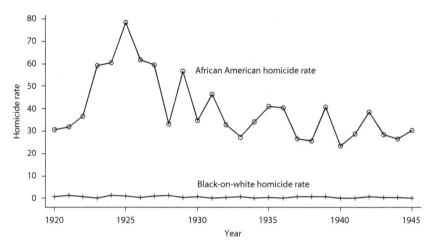

FIGURE 1. African American Homicide Rates, 1920–1945. Source: Homicide Reports, Department of Police, New Orleans.

slaughtered Edward Melancon and sent shock waves through the city's white community, African Americans also committed only two robbery-homicides across racial lines. A white attorney's description of a "bunch of murderous n-----s shooting at people and threatening to kill people on the streets of New Orleans" was wildly exaggerated, though it resonated with white residents anxious about the disintegration of the racial order.[107]

In sum, repeated accounts of horrific Black-on-white predatory violence, amplified and embelished by the inflammatory rhetoric of prominent city leaders, influenced white New Orleanians' views about African American criminality far more than actual assaults and murders, and loomed larger than crime data in inflaming popular perceptions and infusing local politics and public policy. Eugene Stanley, the Orleans district attorney during the late 1920s and early 1930s, skillfully manipulated anxiety about crime and the African American threat to white supremacy to secure reelection and bolster the city's political machine, insisting his racialized law-and-order strategy would rescue law-abiding residents from the jaws of African American killers. For white New Orleanians, the crime panic and the threat to white supremacy, however, felt real, as anxiety-enflamed perceptives trumped empirically based assessments of race and violence.

During the opening decades of the century, civilian policing and formal law enforcement had coexisted and overlapped, with the former assuming primacy and accounting for a higher share of white-on-Black homicides.

Even in their deadly violence, the New Orleans police were largely reactive, typically responding after the fact and employing brutality in their capacities as white civilians more than in the role as law enforcers, retaliating after perceived insults, slights, and other breaches in racial etiquette and challenges to white supremacy, not while trying to apprehend suspects or investigate crimes. Echoed and intensified by city leaders, criminal justice officials, and local newspapers editors, white New Orleanians increasingly feared that informal law enforcement and popular justice could not stem an apparent collapse of the social and racial order.[108] They needed a more active, aggressive mode of policing, one capable of preventing and solving crimes. The *New Orleans Item*, for instance, demanded a more forceful law enforcement system that "protects the white people from the colored killers."[109]

. . .

The Great Migration and its impact on the city's social geography and institutions seemed to erode custom and time-honored mechanisms of racial control during the late 1920s and early 1930s. White, masculine dominance appeared to be in extreme jeopardy and often backfired, as the newcomers slaughtered Edward Melancon, J. Adair Lawrence, and other respectable white men who resisted African American defiance. According to white journalists, municipal leaders, and police officials, the predators also stalked, robbed, and ravaged white women, even when their husbands escorted them. African American thugs, they charged, attacked these innocent, vulnerable New Orleanians on the streets, dragged them from automobiles, and invaded their bedrooms at night. Just as vigilante justice became overmatched, institutional bulwarks failed, with the city's new zoning ordinance overturned and racial restrictions on voting and jury service under siege.

The lion's share of white New Orleanians embraced Eugene Stanley's clarion call regarding the dire threat to racial supremacy. Voters overwhelmingly supported candidates who voiced this apocalyptic vision and campaigned to reestablish white control. Letters to the editor in newspapers magnified such a view, and white residents vehemently supported segregation measures and expressed outrage when the Supreme Court overturned the city's racial zoning ordinance. They also vilified and threatened civil rights activists, both white and African American, and even reformers who advocated for modest changes in the racial hierarchy. To be sure, some white New Orleanians subscribed to contemporary notions of social justice, but such beliefs made them outliers, even pariahs. Instead, most white residents feared African Americans and worried about the survival of white supremacy, which they considered the cornerstone of social stability.

In the 1920s, formal policing in the South served primarily as a backup to civilian policing and was largely reactive. Armed white vigilantes routinely investigated Black-on-white violent crime, apprehended suspects, and tortured them, sometimes coercing confessions and other times murdering the alleged offenders.[110] But, especially in the major cities of the region that received the lion's share of newcomers during the first phase of the Great Migration, this custom of racial control seemed increasingly incapable of countering the perceived collapsing social order. White New Orleanians, Memphians, Atlantans, and their counterparts throughout the urban South demanded a new, more active, and more aggressive mode of policing, one capable of catching criminals, preventing African American violence, and safeguarding respectable residents from the likes of Leaval Hubbard and George Johnson.

The confluence of the Great Migration and a crime surge racialized white anxieties of social disorder in New Orleans during the late 1920s and early 1930s. Similar panics erupted in Memphis, Birmingham, Atlanta, Mobile, Huntsville, Nashville, and throughout the urban South, with the same blend of embellished accounts of African American predators murdering white merchants and raping white women.[111] The *Memphis Commercial Appeal*, for example, reported that "big negroes" attacked ten white women in the city in February 1933, often yanking their victims from automobile and ravaging them.[112] "Action [is] needed," the *New Orleans Item* bellowed.[113] White supremacy and law-and-order policing would blend, blur, and become inseperable in the urban South, eliding in new and stubbornly enduring ways.

THREE

"I Told the Officers to Go Ahead and Kill Me, as They Had Already Half Killed Me"

ON MARCH 9, 1932, Percy Thompson plunged New Orleans into racial upheaval. For two hours, the twenty-eight-year-old African American construction worker violently contested white dominance, surviving a gun battle with two hundred municipal policemen armed with machine guns, sawed-off shotguns, pump guns, sniper rifles, revolvers, and tear-gas grenades. Cops rained volley after volley of bullets, buckshot, and tear gas at Thompson, who suffered a minor flesh wound in the firefight but killed three policemen. The race war that anxious white New Orleanians feared seemed at hand. So many panicked residents called police headquarters during the siege that the department's communications switchboard burst into flames.[1] Local journalists termed Thompson, a recent migrant from Baton Rouge, a "negro madman" and, invoking the language routinely applied to African American residents who resisted white control, insisted the man had run "amuck," "pounced on" municipal law enforcers "without warning" or provocation, and wantonly slaughtered them.[2] National observers offered the same assessment. The *New York Times*, *Washington Post*, and *Chicago Tribune*, for example, described the "negro" as "running amuck."[3] While Thompson fought off a quarter of the New Orleans police force, he roared "come on white folks and get me" and vowed to "get [kill] as many as he could."[4] The violent stalemate ended only when the police superintendent brokered a truce and promised Thompson protection from the small army pounding the station with all manner of munitions and from the enraged, "terrified crowds" that congregated on the nearby streets, chanting "Kill him! Kill him!"[5] Superintendent George Reyer's pledge notwithstanding, the crisis concluded abruptly a short time later when a detective fatally shot Thompson after he purportedly attempted to seize the cop's service revolver.[6]

The events preceding Percy Thompson's two hours of infamy proved to be more complex and exposed the toxic mix of race and criminal justice in the Jim Crow South. Shortly after noon on Wednesday, March 9, New Orleans police headquarters received a telephone report that an African American man "had broken into a house" on South Claiborne Avenue.[7] The desk sergeant dispatched three patrolmen to investigate. They "noticed the negro in question running out Josephine street" and apprehended Thompson, who was carrying two suits of clothing, valued at $60. The police officers transported the suspect to the 12th precinct station for questioning and booking for "petty larceny in the daytime." The precinct doorman and Cornelius Ford, one of the arresting patrolmen, escorted Thompson to a second-floor holding cell, where they interrogated him.[8] Accompanied by William King, a "Negro Trusty" and the station-house janitor, Ford asked the suspect if he had burglarized the residence and filched the clothing. Thompson readily stated "Yes, sir," explaining "I was going to sell them. I was out of work and I was hungry." But when Ford, a thirty-seven-year-old, eight-year police veteran, insisted "I [had] done something else," according to the suspect, "I said, no sir."[9]

Finding the response "unsatisfactory," Ford's demeanor suddenly changed, and he instructed King to "beat him over the head" until Thompson confessed to other home invasions.[10] The trusty began bludgeoning the construction worker, while Ford repeated his demand that Thompson admit to myriad thefts in the white neighborhood. When the hitherto deferential suspect refused to confess to other crimes, Ford brandished his service revolver, held the gun to Thompson's head, and "told me he was going to shoot my brains out." Incensed at the beating and threat after he had been cooperative and certain that Ford planned to kill him, Thompson later explained to Superintendent Reyer, "I knocked the N----- [King] down with my fist" and "grabbed" the patrolman's pistol. Ford "hollered for help," and, as the men "tussled," Thompson discharged the weapon, instantly killing his interrogator.[11] So began the firefight, and Thompson barricaded himself in the cell, crouched behind Ford's body, and fought off the hordes of cops who responded to the patrolman's cry for assistance and the sound of the gun.

The police department summoned every weapon in its formidable arsenal, including tear-gas bombs and machine guns, to reclaim the second floor of the station house and exact revenge on the cop killer. Two hundred officers participated in the attack on Cell Three. Captain Joseph Sonnenberg, the department's marksmanship trainer, mounted "a machine gun in a fire engine station 100 feet away, directly in line with the cell block. He poured round after round of shells at the Negro."[12] Perched on the roofs of other buildings, police sharpshooters sent a torrent of bullets into the second floor of the 12th precinct as well. Thompson expected to die during the siege but refused to submit to his abusers and kept one cartridge in Ford's pistol. "I intended to kill my own self," he later explained.[13] Thompson claimed two additional police victims and suffered only a flesh wound.

Reyer's agreement with Thompson guaranteed that the police would safely convey him to Charity Hospital for the treatment of his injury. After a physician dressed Thompson's wound, however, the construction worker savagely assaulted Detective Vic Swanson in the back seat of the patrol car and attempted to take his sidearm. But the forty-six-year-old officer heroically fought off the cop killer. "He grabbed for my revolver and in the scuffle I managed to get my hand on the trigger of my revolver and fired one shot," the detective recounted, killing his attacker in an act of desperate self-defense. Or so Swanson and the other two officers in the vehicle testified.[14]

In fact, Swanson executed Thompson, but the three policemen constructed an alternate narrative, one that persuaded the police chief and the district attorney, garnered uncritical acceptance from white reporters, and curried favor from anxious white New Orleanians, relieved that the detective had stopped the "negro madman." The cops' testimony, in which they used nearly identical language, constituted a thinly veiled account of a summary execution.[15] Swanson and his colleagues stated that the shooting occurred after they had generously consented to drive their prisoner home to change his bloodstained clothes and that they had refrained from handcuffing or otherwise restraining their cop-killing passenger, who had a lengthy criminal record in Baton Rouge, including convictions for assault, carrying a concealed weapon, and larceny.[16] Casting further doubt on Swanson's yarn, the autopsy revealed that, before shooting Thompson in the chest, the detective had fired a bullet into the prisoner's groin.[17]

The final hours of Percy Thompson's life reflected but also accelerated a core transition in New Orleans policing and criminal justice. News reports of the incident, as well as police records and testimony, depicted the young laborer as murderous, volatile, and uncontrollable. Although Thompson had been arrested for petty larceny and had been docile until King began pummeling him, he posed a dire threat to social order and especially to white New Orleanians, according to accounts of the March 9 violence, justifying, indeed mandating, more aggressive, more racialized policing in the service of public safety. To protect innocent, respectable residents, local cops had to employ rougher, more unflinching methods.

Police officials demanded greater resources, rapidly militarized local law enforcement, and employed more forceful techniques to apprehend and extract confessions and thus to secure the convictions of dangerous African American suspects. Aggressive policing, ranging from adopting coercive interrogation methods, such as using a ratcheting device called the "iron claw," to shooting "suspicious characters," became, according to municipal leaders, acceptable and necessary to shore up white supremacy, preserve public safety, and maintain law and order.[18] Precisely as local and national criminal justice officials denounced third-degree tactics, New Orleans law enforcers and their counterparts in other Southern cities embraced increasing violence against African American suspects, even those apprehended for relatively minor offenses, such as petty larceny in the daytime, for any of these individuals could instantly become "madmen" and "run amuck," like Percy Thompson. Well-documented complaints of sadistic police brutality and the frivolous, unrestrained use of lethal force soared, nearly exclusively targeting African American residents. White New Orleanians viewed such violence as evidence that cops served their interests and had assumed primary responsibility for safeguarding racial control.

Percy Thompson's deadly response to police brutality also provided a chilling cautionary tale for New Orleans cops, underscoring the potential for African American resistance to turn murderous and, hence, reinforcing their use of preemptive force. In their testimony and public statements, police officials insisted that, without provocation, Thompson had slaughtered Patrolman Ford and waged a race war that claimed the lives of Patrolman Albert Oestricher and Corporal George Weidert and injured two civilians. Moreover, the prisoner had responded to Detective Swanson's kind gesture to permit him to change his clothes by attempting to kill the veteran law enforcer. The lessons of the bloodbath seemed clear. Local cops should assume that African American suspects could, at any moment, become violent madmen and that law enforcers could not always avoid employing preemptive deadly force, both for their own safety and for that of all white New Orleanians. In the dozen years before Thompson's onslaught, local cops killed 5.7 African American residents for every policeman murdered by an African American suspect. In the twelve years after the assault on Cell Three, city cops took few risks, relied on more decisive methods, and killed thirty-seven

African American suspects. But no local law enforcers died at the hands of an African American resident, confirming cops' faith in and embrace of aggressive, racialized policing.

For African American New Orleanians, the Thompson upheaval conveyed a different, haunting message. The use of vicious third-degree interrogation methods and Thompson's execution illustrated the perils of arrest and police custody. After a white woman screamed and law enforcers rushed to the scene and fatally shot a fifteen-year-old African American resident who ignored their instructions to "halt," the city's African American newspaper rhetorically asked "why did Jesse Walton run (if he did run), and why do others (if they do) resist arrest and make attempts to escape? Is it because they fear police brutality so much that when stopped or asked to halt, they rather take a chance and run for their lives?"[19] Such a realization was not new, though police brutality and the use of deadly force rose sharply in the wake of the recent crime panic. If the actions of white vigilantes had previously ignited alarm for local African Americans, the police increasingly emerged as the most pervasive violent threat to African American New Orleanians.

African Americans' responses to this surging danger, however, exacerbated the tensions and reinforced law enforcers' inclination to use force. When African American residents fled from police officers, resisted arrest, defied cops' instructions, and tried to avoid confinement in patrol cars and especially station-house interrogation cells, New Orleans law enforcers viewed such behavior as unmistakable evidence of guilt or the prelude to violent noncompliance, justifying their use of force. The spiral and stereotyping became self-perpetuating and abetted brutal police responses.[20] And most white residents expressed a blend of gratitude and relief for increasingly violent, racialized criminal justice in the city. "Negroes are Negroes to police officers," one journalist observed. "All are regarded as potential criminals. Clubs, guns, and public opinion uphold the 'law' in cases of Brutality [sic] to Negroes."[21]

For many white residents, the March 9th carnage revived memories of Robert Charles's 1900 murderous assault on local cops and respectable New Orleanians. After a clumsy attempt to arrest Charles for suspicious behavior in a largely white neighborhood, the thirty-five-year-old African American resident killed two local cops, holed up in an apartment, fatally shot two additional police officers and three civilians, and wounded more than two dozen white New Orleanians before being shot thirty-four times and dying in a ferocious gun battle with city law enforcers. The rampage triggered three days of racial violence in which white gangs roamed the streets and slaughtered at least six innocent African American residents.[22]

The two horrific bloodbaths sparked racial hysteria among white New Orleanians but differed in at least one crucial way. Charles's clash with the police and Southern racial control unleashed a wave of white, civilian vigilantism, while Thompson's triggered an explosion of police violence and generated widespread white support for aggressive, racialized police brutality, including vicious beatings and the use of preemptive force. Between the early 1900s and the early 1930s, the rate of police homicide of African American suspects tripled. White vigilantism did not cease, but during the interwar period the police emerged as the principal enforcers of racial dominance, foot soldiers for white supremacy, and killers of African American New Orleanians.

This shift reflected a far-reaching transformation in the mission of Jim Crow policing and criminal justice in which law enforcers embraced a more central, active, and violent role in racial control, redefining law and order in overtly racial terms. Between the late 1920s and the early 1930s, New Orleans's civilian white-on-Black homicide rate dropped by two thirds, while the police white-on-Black killing rate nearly tripled as white residents ceded the mantle of racial control to local law enforcers. Comparable trends unfolded across the urban South, with police beatings and homicides supplanting vigilante justice.[23] In Memphis, for example, the proportion of African Americans killed by city cops rose by nearly three-quarters during the interwar era.[24]

Police violence, the preservation of racial dominance, and the defense of social stability blurred and overlapped for voters—nearly all-white—and elected officials in New Orleans and throughout the urban South. The change ignited a blistering surge of police brutality against African American city dwellers during the late 1920s and 1930s. One civil rights activist termed it "a reign of terror against negroes."[25] White Southerners overwhelmingly endorsed this violence as a legitimate, necessary public-safety strategy, as long as it targeted African American residents. In New Orleans, voters elected and reelected candidates promising to promote vigorous, aggressive policing to control African American residents and expressed zealous, fawning support for patrolmen and detectives engaging in the most violent conduct—purportedly on their behalf. Similarly, white voters in Birmingham elected Eugene "Bull" Connor as Commissioner of Public Safety in 1936. Police brutality toward African American suspects became so unbounded that in 1934 twenty-four-year-old Vernon Guichard told the New Orleans detectives trying to beat him until he confessed to a murder that he did not commit "to go ahead and kill me, as they had already half killed me."[26]

. . .

For white New Orleanians, and especially for opportunistic city officials, aggressive, violent, unyielding policing filled a vacuum, preserving public safety when popular justice and extralegal vigilantism proved incapable of maintaining order and shoring up white supremacy. Local politicians and law enforcers skillfully manipulated and exploited white racial anxieties to bolster support for their own leadership and for police authority as the core defender of racial stability. This strategy enhanced the hold of the parish political machine and the mandate and perceived legitimacy of city cops. The preservation of white supremacy fused these efforts and tethered white dominance to a particular, racialized definition of law and order.

In the years after the Great War, African American migrants from the rural hinterland poured into New Orleans and other Southern cities and, in the eyes and nightmares of white residents, triggered a crime wave. Although civilian vigilantism failed to stem the surge in local violence, the early 1920s municipal police appeared feckless and corrupt. Aside from providing traffic control and shaking down brothel keepers, city cops mainly supplied muscle for the political machine. According to Stanley Ray, the New Orleans Commissioner of Public Safety, the police department was largely "devoted to blackjacking recalcitrant voters into line." He described the unit as "an effective political club," but "ineffective police force."[27] "No city in America," a former district attorney and the president of the local bar association complained, "has worse protection from the criminal classes."[28] As white racial anxieties multiplied during the late 1920s, a local editor noted the "police department's apparent impotence to protect life and prosperity" in the city.[29] While New Orleans's homicide rate soared during the early 1920s and the city became the third most murderous urban center in the United States, the department ranked in the bottom fifth nationally in police expenditures, and police pay was the lowest among the fifteen largest municipalities in the United States.[30] Between 1922 and 1923, for example, murders jumped in New Orleans by 51.6 percent, yet the size of the police force contracted, shrinking by 18.7 percent. "Unless something is done," the *New Orleans Item* charged, the "situation will become even more intolerable."[31]

But something was done, and ambitious, demagogic politicians seized the moment and leveraged white anxiety into a dramatic increase in financial support for law enforcement—and enhanced support for themselves. Funding for the police tripled during the 1920s, and the force nearly doubled in size.[32] More important, elected leaders and police officials vowed to adopt more forceful methods and make New Orleans a "safe city for respectable people," a thinly masked reference to racial dominance.[33]

Municipal officials militarized the police department during the late 1920s and early 1930s. They purchased faster, more powerful automobiles and in 1928 announced that "explosive gas grenades, gas masks, pistol cartridges with a tear gas charge, nonexplosive gas distributing grenades, and shotgun shells filled with a gas preparation are included in the most recent shipment to arrive in New Orleans for use by police and detectives," promising to employ "advanced warfare" against criminals and vowing to seek funds to purchase airplanes and armored motorcycles. In 1926, Police Superintendent Thomas Healey announced that securing machine guns represented "the first step in a policy of meeting modern crime with modern defense."[34] "Effective immediately," the city's top cop bragged three years later, "each detective will be armed with a sawed-off shotgun."[35] The same year, the police chief unveiled the department's new attack vehicle, an armored motorcycle featuring a sidecar with a Thompson submachine gun, dubbed the "death-dealing machine."[36]

Nearly half a century before the celebrated formation of police "S.W.A.T." teams, Southern city officials had already established specialized, heavily armed, militarized, rapid-response crime-fighting units.[37] In New Orleans during the late 1920s, city officials launched "Go Get 'Em squads," equipped with the "most modern devices of this branch of warfare" and created principally to preserve racial dominance.[38] They deployed these units, whose members carried military-grade weapons, wore bulletproof vests, and drove motorcycles with "left hand accelerators [that] enables the policeman to have his right hand free to wield his revolver" against bank robbers and the African American predators murdering shopkeepers and ravaging white women.[39] Reacting to the same white panic, officials in Memphis, Birmingham, and Huntsville created comparable squads, also dedicated to the twin, intertwined goals of crime fighting and buttressing the racial order.[40]

More important than the creation and arming of these units, city officials dramatically expanded police discretion, authority, and methods. New Orleans mayors and law enforcement leaders vowed that cops would be empowered to do whatever they deemed necessary "to stamp out lawlessness."

City officials pledged that policemen must "meet violence with violence," and the superintendent issued "shoot-to-kill" orders when officers encountered dangerous or potentially dangerous suspects.[41] The policy did not mention race but was applied nearly uniformly against the African American New Orleanians who terrorized "respectable" residents and therefore jeopardized the social and racial order. The police chief also unveiled a mandate for patrolmen and detectives to "learn how to shoot bandits."[42] This instructional program ran counter to recent law enforcement policies in the city. Precisely as departments outside of the South established police academies, New Orleans abolished its formal training program, only to carve out an exception to prepare officers to employ deadly force.[43] Superintendent Ray pledged to ensure that cops could kill robbery suspects. "I don't want police missing bandits as long as I am Chief of Police," he added.[44] Ray and his successors also rewarded patrolmen who killed predators, promoting cops who employed deadly force. Memphis's police chief adopted the same policy in 1931.[45]

New Orleans's white newspapers enthusiastically endorsed this aggressive, silently racialized effort and insisted that respectable residents zealously supported shoot-to-kill crime fighting as well. "The police have to protect themselves and others to maintain order," the *New Orleans Item* editorialized in 1927. "They must occasionally shoot to kill. When they do so, to accomplish any of these things, to protect life and property, they are to be praised as well as exonerated of blame. In such cases, they deserve, and usually receive, not only the support of their official superiors but the approval and support of the people."[46] Prosecutors nearly always dismissed charges against cops who used deadly force against suspects, and when an occasional case progressed to a grand jury or a criminal trial, jurors—still all-white—exonerated and acquitted the killers, without exception.

Arrest protocols and mandates followed the same trajectory, affording New Orleans cops greater discretion and becoming more aggressive, more violent, and more purposely targeting African American suspects. Police officers particularly relied on one local ordinance and one criminal law to preserve racial dominance. City Ordinance 1436 emerged as an especially powerful cudgel for racialized, selective law enforcement. The statute authorized policemen to arrest and detain "dangerous and suspicious characters," permitting cops to hold such suspects "pending investigation." Arrest and detention required neither criminal behavior nor evidence or even a hint of unlawful behavior. Policemen could hold "suspicious" suspects indefinitely without filing any charges. When headquarters received reports of Black-on-white crime, superintendents, precinct captains, and desk sergeants routinely ordered patrolmen to arrest "all suspicious negroes" in the area and hold them as "dangerous and suspicious characters," and police officials increasingly relied on "dragnets," often rounding up hundreds of African American men without any specific reason or evidence.[47] Immediately after Leaval Hubband's murder of the white grocer Edward Melancon in 1932, for example, New Orleans cops used the "D & S" ordinance to apprehend, photograph, and fingerprint more than nine hundred suspects, none of whom proved to be connected to the shooting in any way.[48] Local cops then relied on the files with photographs and fingerprints to justify subsequent arrests, insisting that they had targeted African American men with arrest records, automatically making them "suspicious characters." After detectives beat Aaron Boyd to death, they revealed that he had been arrested twenty-one times, somehow excusing the deadly brutality.[49] Similarly, police officials explained their actions in wrongfully arresting and then beating Ethel Anderson by noting that she had previously been arrested six times and her "photograph is in our [arrest] gallery."[50] City officials, policemen, and white journalists championed the statute, terming it the "most effective means the police have of curbing crime and capturing criminals" and claiming that "law-abiding citizens" held the same view of Ordinance 1436.[51]

Early civil rights reformers challenged the legality of the statute, arguing that it failed to define suspicious behavior, require any evidence of wrongdoing, or even establish any indication of bad character.[52] They found an unexpected ally in city recorders, the judges who presided over the lowest tier of local courts and who hardly defended the civil liberties of African American residents.[53] The jurists bristled at the flood of suspects detained without cause, filling their courtrooms. The Louisiana Supreme Court, however, upheld the ordinance, ruling that "police power extended to the protection of the lives, health, and prosperity of the public."[54] But only white New Orleans belonged to the protected "public." Ordinance 1436 granted policemen virtually complete discretion to arrest and detain any African American resident.

State law criminalizing the possession of concealed weapons operated in parallel ways during the interwar crime panic and was applied almost exclusively against African American New Orleanians. Police officials and prosecutors insisted that African American men embraced the "gun-toting habit," and their volatile, unpredictable natures made this practice "one of the chief menaces with which the police department is concerned in its effort to enforce law and order."[55] Reports of Black-on-white violence, therefore, frequently led law enforcement officials to order patrolmen to "round up all Negroes" on D & S and then search them for concealed weapons.[56] At the same time, local officials opposed the wider enforcement of the concealed weapon prohibition and instead urged white New Orleanians to secure handguns in defense against African American predators.[57] Thus, the D & S ordinance and the concealed weapon law gave local cops the authority to respond to any and all reports of African American criminality and even any unspecified suspicions with mass arrests and detentions, weaponizing fears of racial instability and pandering to white anxiety, under the convenient mantle of maintaining law and order. Race-based differences in arrests widened into huge gulfs.

Metastasizing racial disparities in convictions and incarcerations followed suit. Eugene Stanley, an aggressive young prosecutor, oversaw and directed the racialization of criminal justice in New Orleans. Born in 1894 and the parish district attorney from 1927 until 1935, he focused his law enforcement efforts and his election campaigns on the intertwined goals of waging "a relentless war on crime" and preserving white supremacy.[58] Stanley signed his campaign literature "yours in White Supremacy," and his election and reelection speeches and advertisements emphasized his pledge "to protect white supremacy . . . at all costs."[59] White New Orleanians embraced this clarion call, eliding racial dominance and criminal justice. Stanley won in landslides, capturing 99.8 percent of the vote in his first campaign and similar margins in his two reelection bids.

Although he saw himself as a crusader, Eugene Stanley did not create this racial-control/crime-control linkage as much as he exploited its political value and extended the association into the courts and the wider criminal justice system, translating incendiary, demagogic rhetoric into rapidly growing racial disparities in conviction and incarceration. As the city became one of the most violent urban centers in the nation, Stanley insisted that violent crime in New Orleans "compared favorably with other" cities, "leaving out of consideration the large negro population." Crime was largely a "negro problem," and he vowed to convict, incarcerate, and execute African American assailants.

Judged by this standard, Stanley enjoyed immense success, both at the polls and in the local halls of justice. In his first year as prosecutor, the African American homicide conviction rate doubled, while the white rate plunged by half. The trend persisted for the remainder of his tenure as district attorney, with the African American rate swelling by 74.2 percent and the white rate dropping. The conviction rate in Black-on-white homicide rose even faster during his eight years as prosecutor, leaping by 80.2 percent. When the New Orleans native and Loyola law school graduate became the local prosecutor, the African American and white homicide conviction rates were comparable. One year into his tenure, the African American conviction rate was four times higher. Disparities in capital convictions widened as well. During the 1920s, white killers comprised half of the defendants sent to the gallows. After 1930, however, African Americans made up 87.5 percent of those executed, and between 1934 and 1945 they comprised all of the local killers executed by the state of Louisiana. Under Stanley, prosecutorial discretion and the rule of law worked in the unapologetic, undisguised service of white supremacy.

Stanley transformed an inert court system into a bulwark for racial dominance by largely avoiding trials and bypassing jurors and judges. Like local cops, he distrusted these criminal justice gatekeepers, considering them weak, gullible, and easily manipulated by clever defense attorneys. Rather, Stanley partnered with aggressive cops and relied on the confessions that they secured and the plea bargaining he then imposed, buoying his conviction rates and fulfilling his campaign promises.

Violent policing changed dramatically during the interwar era and especially during Stanley's tenure. Throughout this era (and beyond), New Orleans cops brutalized suspects, inflicting sadistic, almost unimaginable abuse. Police violence, particularly targeting African Americans, had occurred for decades. But law enforcers—and white civilians more generally—had typically employed such beatings as informal, extralegal punishment rather than as a systematic, purposeful tool for securing confessions and plea bargains and operating in the guise of the rule of law. The same pivot occurred in Memphis, Birmingham, Mobile, Atlanta, and throughout the urban South during the 1930s and early 1940s.[60]

Coercive interrogation methods were illegal in Louisiana. The state's 1921 constitution prohibited "any treatment designed by effect on the body or mind to compel confession of crime."[61] Beatings during interrogations, however, persisted, occasionally as punishment and more often as a result of police indignation when suspects defied them or became intransigent—rather than to extract confessions. Because the abuse usually occurred entirely as extralegal punishment, rather than as a part of a legal process, such violence operated outside of the bounds of court control and constitutional protections. The publication of Herbert Hoover's Wickersham Commission reports, however, shone a bright spotlight on police brutality and the use of "third-degree" tactics, triggering a national scandal. Report 11, entitled *Lawlessness in Law Enforcement*, detailed a lengthy catalog of "grilling" methods, including beating suspects with rubber hoses, steel cables, and pipes, shocking prisoners' genitalia with electrodes, inflicting the 1920s version of modern waterboarding, and staging mock hangings.[62] Detectives routinely bludgeoned and tortured prisoners. Judges, legal reformers, and police administrators across the nation quickly denounced such practices, and municipal law enforcers, among them New Orleans police superintendents and prosecutors, prohibited these extractive interrogation techniques and insisted that they no longer occurred in the city. But throughout the nation, and especially in the South, practice lagged behind rhetoric, and cops continued to pummel and maul prisoners.[63]

Interrogation methods in New Orleans abruptly changed in May of 1932, when Detective William Grosch beat Ross Palumbo to death. On May 9, police headquarters received a complaint about three white men behaving suspiciously. When the patrolmen arrived on the scene, one of the men fired a wild shot in their direction, and the cops arrested him and two friends, one of whom was Palumbo, a thirty-two-year-old Italian grocer. Policemen transported the suspects to the 12th precinct station, the site of the Percy Thompson upheaval two months earlier, and the patrolmen summoned detectives to question the prisoners. Shortly after Grosch began interrogating Palumbo, other prisoners in the precinct heard the detective crowing to another cop that he planned to "club up" Palumbo and "beat that Dago's belly off." Then Palumbo began howling in pain, crying "stop kicking me in the stomach. You're killing me. For God's sake stop," followed by Detective Grosch snarling, "Now I guess you'll talk." A short time later, another policeman found the merchant dead in his cell. Grosch's report stated that Palumbo had sustained his injuries from "a fall" prior to his arrest.

George F. Roeling, the parish coroner and typically a reliable ally and staunch defender of the police, found unmistakable evidence that the prisoner had been beaten to death in the 12th precinct station, dismissing Grosch's explanation as "preposterous."[64] From head to toe, welts and contusions covered Palumbo's body. Blood filled his abdominal cavity, and his internal organs were ruptured and shredded. Local newspapers expressed outrage, public opinion turned against the police, the Italian consulate launched an inquiry into the death, and District Attorney Stanley took the case to a grand jury. Police Superintendent George Reyer suspended the veteran cop. Although the grand jury returned a "no true bill" verdict against the detective, prompting Stanley to drop the charge and police officials to restore Grosch to active duty, public anger and criticism persisted, leading city and criminal justice officials to vow to eliminate coercive interrogation methods. Local cops largely abandoned the use of third-degree techniques.

But the protocols banning brutal, violent interrogation methods applied only to white suspects, and white newspaper editors, prominent citizens, and prison reformers roundly ignored or even championed the beating of African American suspects. White New Orleanians more generally echoed this exception to constitutional protections against coerced confessions. Simply put, these residents believed that African Americans' violent, volatile, predatory ways placed them outside of legal protection. African Americans, they insisted, posed a threat to law and order and to respectable New Orleanians so profound and so dire that they failed to qualify for constitutional safeguards. White policymakers and writers generally saw no contradiction in demanding the end of third-degree interrogation methods and endorsing sadistic police brutality against African American prisoners. "To the ordinary policeman," an early twentieth-century sociologist explained, "justice is the process by which people keep the country safe from 'n-----s.'"[65]

Although city, police, and criminal justice officials typically avoided explicit references to race in their selective support for coercive practices, they invoked language that unambiguously reflected the belief that respectable—that is, white—New Orleanians must not be subjected to abusive treatment, but those seeking to overturn social stability would not be afforded constitutional protections from the techniques necessary to maintain law and order. A group that constituted an imminent threat to white public safety was exempt from the benefit of due process. This was "commonsense justice" in the Jim Crow South, and white New Orleanians bristled at any suggestion that legal safeguards should protect dangerous predators who "exercise their fiendish desire on law-abiding citizens."[66] "Murderous thugs," the *New Orleans States* argued in 1938, should not be coddled. Rather, criminal justice officials needed to "give due reflection to the right of the public to set up its defense against the wanton taking of human life."[67] Mrs. F. I. Williams, the chairperson of the local League of Women Voters, made a similar argument, defending the savage beating of an African American teenager in 1933. After insisting that "I am opposed to third degree methods," Williams then added, "but the Mims boy got what he richly deserved."[68]

New Orleans cops, political leaders, and white newspaper editors repeatedly denounced violent policing and coerced confessions yet carved out exceptions to due-process protections. Immediately after the Palumbo murder, for example, one editor explained that "we are not of those who believe that criminals of the vicious type developed since the war and prohibition should be coddled and treated with an excess of gentleness. If they were, many a major crime against society would go unsolved and unpunished. We believe, therefore, there should be some license conceded to the authorities in their effort to protect themselves and the community from the bandits, gunmen, murderers and their like."[69] Similarly, in a 1933 editorial entitled "Against Third Degree," the *New Orleans States* stated that "where habitual and murderous criminals are picked up as suspects in violent crimes against society, the public is usually disposed to turn its head in the other direction if the police have to use some coercion in extracting confessions from them."[70] Private citizens often expressed the same view of third-degree methods, though in less guarded terms. A short time after the post-Palumbo repudiation of police violence, one white New Orleanian responded to the notion that local detectives who brutally beat an African American teenager during an interrogation be disciplined by bellowing that "it is an outrage to prosecute two white men for beating a 'N-----.'"[71] A journalist added that the "reaction of Southern white people to cases of abuse of Negroes by officers is irritation. If they get into trouble with the law[,] they are to blame."[72]

African American residents denounced this idea, fumed about the unending "sadistic horseplay of the officers of the law," and offered ungarnished descriptions of the selective rejection and embrace of police violence.[73] Reacting to police repudiation of third-degree methods after Palumbo's death, the editor of the city's (and state's) largest African American newspaper quipped that the "furor" occurred only "because a white prisoner is alleged to have been beaten."[74] In other cities in the region, white residents and police officials applied the same selective, racialized standards. Cliff Davis, Memphis's police commissioner, for example, defended and cleared six cops who beat an African American loitering suspect to death during a 1933 interrogation but two weeks later fined a patrolman for "slapping a white prisoner."[75]

Nor was the violent, brutal interrogation of African American suspects unusual. Police violence against African American suspects increased and well-documented complaints skyrocketed during the interwar period. Victims lodged protests, and their attorneys, civil rights reformers, and African American journalists gathered photographs of bruised, battered bodies, assembled medical records and autopsies showing the effects of vicious beatings, and filed affidavits and testimony from other prisoners who observed the routine infliction of sadistic police violence against these suspects. Hundreds of similar descriptions of sustained torture and brutality appeared in complaints filed with district attorneys, in testimony offered by the victims' relatives, in the records of local civil rights organizations, in interviews published in African American newspapers, and in legal appeals of convictions secured with coerced confessions.[76] During one three-week span, less than a year after the Palumbo scandal, a New Orleans prison reform organization received more than two hundred such complaints, and in a 1939 survey, the American Civil Liberties Union ranked the city in the bottom 1 percent for third-degree brutality and related violations of legal safeguards.[77] "The Rights of Negroes are more commonly violated than those of any other race or class," the report concluded.[78] An investigator of police methods termed "brutality a standard procedure, especially, but not exclusively, in the handling of Negroes" in New Orleans.[79] "Hitler's brown shirters," the editor of the *Louisiana Weekly* remarked, "would turn pale with envy if they were acquainted with the procedure of some of the members of the local police department," a parallel noted by other observers as well.[80] "No worse condition could exist even under Hitler and Nazi Germany," a local civil rights activist remarked, while another writer concluded that New Orleans cops employed "Gestapo methods" and that "such outrages" were "condoned by the higherups."[81] All the while, city officials, police administrators, and parish prosecutors denounced third-degree interrogations and claimed that local law enforcers did not use them. A white editor explained that "the cry, 'third degree,' is the usual refuge of criminals and it is most frequently shouted by lawbreakers with long records of thuggery."[82] Thus, many white New Orleanians viewed third-degree complaints from African American suspects as indisputable evidence that the victims of the beatings were guilty.

One after another, African American suspects recounted horror tales of vicious abuse in police holding cells. Detectives typically questioned the suspects without charging them with any crime, insisting that legal and constitutional safeguards did not apply until formal charges had been filed.[83] The interrogators demanded confessions, and pummeled suspects who refused to admit their guilt. Policemen repeated this cycle again and again, sometimes beating African American prisoners to death. Henry Hauser, a twenty-five-year-old longshoreman, succumbed to the injuries sustained during his interrogation after being arrested for public drunkenness, dying from the effects of a perforated ilium. Before being rushed to the hospital where he subsequently died, he described his ordeal to Lottie Williams, his common-law wife. "I'm beaten to death," he told Williams, explaining that "the police beat me yesterday evening and last night; when one of them knocked me out, they threw a bucket of water on me to bring me to, then they beat me some more with their fists, a rubber hammer and kicked me. They beat me mostly in the stomach. After they brought me to, one policeman told me to stand up but my stomach was hurting so much I could not straighten up. As I was trying to stand up, one policeman ran at me and kicked me in the eye; when the other shift came on later at night, they beat me again."[84] Edward White told a reporter that he had been "beaten with gun and black-jack [*sic*] and kicked on the leg and groin," while Floyd Washington, a forty-one-year-old local chef, described how two cops had "man-handled" him. "One hit me in the stomach and jumped atop of me, when I fell and began stomping me. After a while, others pulled him off and said, 'wait a while, give him a chance to confess and if he doesn't you may start again!'" By the time that the detectives discovered that Washington had no connection to any crime, they had broken his jaw, knocked out his six of his teeth, and fractured his ribs.[85] William Drummond, an African American tile setter, detailed a similar beating at the hands of New Orleans detectives. "They took me to 'school,'" he told a journalist, and "beat me and whipped me with their fists and pieces of rubber hose. One of them hit me in the stomach with a baseball bat. They did everything but kill me."[86] In one case, the victim testified that thirty-four different officers abused him.[87]

The deployment of such violent interrogation methods to secure confessions became so commonplace that it gained its own euphemism. New Orleans cops dubbed it "ice cream and cake," so called because detectives promised African American suspects ice cream and cake if they confessed—and often rewarded those who admitted their guilt with such treats.[88] After interrogators beat three African American teenagers until they confessed to murdering a white tamale vendor in 1941, for example, Detective Grosch served them "a plate of ice cream and a piece of cake apiece."[89]

In the wake of William Grosch's murder of Ross Palumbo, the coercive interrogations became increasingly racialized. Not only were nearly all of the abused African American men being questioned for Black-on-white crimes, but the precise form of the brutality became racialized. Police interrogators staged mock lynchings to extract confessions from African American suspects. When eleven-year-old Eddie Johnson failed to implicate another young African American in a crime, "police placed a belt around his neck and threatened to hang him if he did not say that Williams, the accused, was the guilty man."[90] Similarly, Charles Johnson's 10th precinct interrogators wrapped a rope around his throat and "lifted him up for about ten minutes, beating him while suspended in the air."[91] New Orleans ethnographers labeled the practice "symbolic 'legal lynchings.'"[92] Arthur Raper, a sociologist who collaborated with Gunnar Myrdal, found the same coercive technique employed throughout the South during the 1930s. In a St. Petersburg, Florida, case, for example, he noted that two sixteen-year-old African American boys had been rushed "to a hospital after having been hanged from a rope to scare them into a confession."[93] Twenty-one-year-old James Pillows described how Memphis detectives "would beat him and put a rope around his neck and hang him up unless he confessed, and how he was so afraid until he signed a confession."[94] Raper lamented that "there is no limit to the type of third degree methods which may be invoked."[95] "Negroes especially, and sometimes we think solely, have been given a too intensive diet of ice cream and cake," a Louisiana African American editor concluded in 1939.[96]

Typically suspected of committing violence against white New Orleanians, African American teenagers and young men comprised the overwhelming majority of prisoners beaten and tortured during interrogations.[97] Vernon Guichard recounted a typical third-degree ordeal in 1934. After the fatal shooting of Harry Chaison, a twenty-five-year-old white, public works employee, patrolmen arrested Guichard, a twenty-four-year-old African American carpenter. Certain that he had committed the murder, the police, according to Guichard, "took me to the 5th precinct and there they began to abuse me. I was hit over the head with billies, and one of the police hit me in the eye, blacking it. Each time they hit me they asked me to admit to the killing of Chaison." Policemen then transported Guichard to the 1st precinct, where the abuse began anew. "My sweater was opened so as to expose my abdomen. The detectives began cursing me calling me all kinds of vile names and beat me in the stomach with broom sticks until I fell to the floor. Each time I was hit the men said, 'You did kill that white man, where is the gun?' I denied all of these accusations and was beaten until I fell to the floor. The detectives kicked me and told me to shut up." The beating stopped when a police clerk informed the detectives that another man had confessed to the shooting.[98] "While the American law is to the effect that a man is innocent until proven guilty," an African American journal explained in 1939, "the attitude in New Orleans and surrounding communities is that a Negro is guilty until he is proven innocent, and that anything may be resorted to to make him 'admit' guilt."[99] Policemen throughout the urban South embraced the same methods and attitudes during the 1930s.[100]

Police interrogators, however, also brutalized African American New Orleanians suspected of committing minor offenses. Harold Lee, a Tulane University philosophy professor and the president of the Louisiana League for the Preservation of Constitutional Rights, complained that the "New Orleans police use the third degree rather freely; and not only in cases of major criminals ... but also in cases of petty crimes and misdemeanors."[101] Some of the most brutal violence occurred when detectives sought confessions for minor offenses. They bludgeoned Henry Hauser to death for drunkenness, tortured Edward White to make him confess to loitering, Wilbert Patterson for petty theft, and Percy Thompson for stealing two suits. One of the most high-profile cases of the era occurred after detectives arrested fifteen-year-old James Mims for being "a dangerous and suspicious character" and for possible involvement in a home invasion. They transported him to police headquarters and, supervised by the chief of detectives, handcuffed the teenager, stuffed paper into his mouth "to keep him from screaming," and bludgeoned Mims on the head and torso with a steel cable for five hours.[102]

African American women did not entirely escape the violence, though they made up a modest share of local abuse victims. Hotel maids or domestic servants suspected of filching small sums of money or household items comprised the vast majority of the women enduring beatings to coerce confessions. Detectives suspected twenty-year-old Ethel Anderson, for instance, of purloining cash belonging to a guest at the hotel where she worked as a housekeeper. Interrogators punched and kicked her, only to learn that the victim's wife had taken the money.[103]

In other cases involving brutal, sadistic police interrogations, detectives tortured African Americans to secure information. Detectives staged the mock lynching of an eleven-year-old boy, for example, to pressure him into identifying a suspect fleeing from a crime scene and beat fourteen-year-old Flora Mae Taylor to force her to reveal her mother's whereabouts.[104] According to one ethnographer, the use of third-degree brutality in such cases "rests squarely on the assumption that police officers and court officials have the right to use such methods as are necessary to secure from the accused the type of statement wanted."[105] In short, police assertions that heinous crime justified the selective suspension of legal protections were situational, hinging on the race of the suspect and his or her willingness to provide "satisfactory" responses to their interrogations.

Although detectives presented coercive methods as a crucial tool in securing confessions and evidence against dangerous African American predators, such purported explanations often lapsed into justifications for humiliating prisoners or punishing defiant suspects. Policemen frequently stripped prisoners of their clothes, interrogating and beating naked suspects. They particularly did so while questioning women, and detectives reveled in the "paddling of prostitutes," not to make them confess but to degrade them.[106] When suspects refused to admit their guilt, cops escalated the brutality, as Cornelius Ford did while questioning Percy Thompson. Frustration spiraled into rage, and interrogations and levels of violence and sadism soared. Because Alcide Bacchus and John Bagneris, suspected "Negro stick-up men who have robbed various grocery stores" in 1937, "refused to confess to the robberies of which they were later proven innocent," detectives brutally beat them for three consecutive days.[107] Recounting a familiar description of 1930s' police abuse, another wrongfully accused African American suspect explained that as soon as the detective "saw that I was not going to be punched into confessing something I had not done, he began stomping and kicking me until one of my ribs was broken."[108] The sociologist Gunnar Myrdal concluded that "it is part of the policeman's philosophy that Negro criminals or suspects, or any Negro who shows signs of insubordination, should be punished bodily, and that this is a device for preventing crime and keeping the Negro is his place. . . . In this setting," Myrdal added, "the application of the 'third degree' to get 'confessions' from Negro Suspects easily becomes a routine device."[109]

Extracting confessions became inseparable from asserting racial dominance. The rule of law provided the justification for either or both. For all of the rhetorical emphasis on crime fighting and protecting respectable white New Orleanians from African American predators, policemen beat and tortured these residents anytime they so chose, relying on vague arrest pretexts, such as the "dangerous-and-suspicious character" ordinance, and virtually limitless discretion during interrogations. Eliding law and order with white supremacy, in short, created an unbounded landscape of vulnerability and terror for "Negroes so unfortunate as to be caught in the toils of the law or the long arms of policemen."[110] Cops in Mobile and other cities employed the same methods and comparable justifications.[111]

New Orleans city and police officials and detectives alleged to have engaged in brutal, sadistic interrogations simultaneously denied employing third-degree methods and crowed about extracting confessions from the most vicious African Americans and thus protecting the—white—public. Admissions of guilt enabled prosecutors, especially the fiery Eugene Stanley, to secure convictions without depending on gullible jurors and judges even vaguely attentive to the rules of evidence and constitutional safeguards. Police brutality and prosecutorial complicity yielded tangible rewards as well. Police officials leveraged their zealous efforts to protect respectable New Orleanians into swelling white endorsement of enhanced authority and law enforcement power. Voicing fulsome support for the use of third-degree methods to extract confessions, a self-described "business woman and mother" reminded *New Orleans States* readers in 1939 that "we depend entirely on the police department for protection, and if the police department will treat a criminal as a hotel guest, then we should do away with the police department."[112] For his part, Stanley missed no opportunity to brag about his surging conviction rate and the residents his methods protected. His 1929 tally "breaks [the] record" for convictions, he told the *New Orleans States*, and his 1931 figures constituted "the most successful year in the history of his office."[113] Stanley exploited this crime fighting–white supremacy nexus to cruise to reelection for second and third terms as parish district attorney.

Spearheaded by Stanley, the racialization of criminal justice redefined policing and racial dominance. As New Orleans policemen embraced these practices, civilians ceded primary responsibility for enforcing white authority to cops. Early twentieth-century sociologists discovered that comparable shifts occurred throughout the urban South. "The policeman is delegated" to preserving "the caste order," Myrdal explained.[114] The change institutionalized law enforcement brutality, under the banner of the rule of law, a trend that would endure through the remainder of the twentieth century and into the twenty-first century.

An abrupt shift in violence against African American residents starkly demonstrated this process. New Orleans patrolmen and detectives assumed responsibility for racial control, and their violence largely supplanted white vigilantism. Police white-on-Black killing soared, while civilian white-on-Black homicide plunged. During the late 1920s, the rate of white civilian homicide of African American New Orleanians was nearly quadruple the police rate, and non-policemen killed three-fourths of the African American residents who died at the hand of white residents. By the early 1930s, however, the proportion committed by civilians had fallen by half, the rate plunging by 57 percent. The share of white-on-Black homicides by local cops nearly tripled and the rate climbed by 138.5 percent. In 1928, the civilian rate was 4.1 times the police rate. Four years later, the police rate of homicide of African American residents was double the civilian level, and cops committed two-thirds of the homicides. In 1940, policemen accounted for all of these homicides. A sea change in racial violence and racial control rapidly unfolded.

In other cities in the region, white-on-Black violence changed in comparable ways, as civilians throughout the urban South looked to the police to impose and enforce racial dominance.[115] Between the late 1920s and the early 1930s, the number of African Americans who died at the hand of policemen climbed 3.4-fold in New Orleans and 3.5-fold in Memphis.[116] The same shift occurred in Birmingham. In 1933 a civil rights group petitioned the city commission to protest the "very high and shameless rate" of African American residents "being killed by Officers of the Law [sic], and not the killing of Negroes by [civilian] whites."[117] Increasingly, local cops committed interracial violence and, under the mantle of maintaining law and order, a jarring shift took place that entailed the preservation of white supremacy through a transformation in the scope and focus of policing and criminal justice.[118] By the early 1940s, policemen account for nearly four-fifths of white-on-Black killings in New Orleans and Memphis.[119]

In the eyes of most white city dwellers, state-sanctioned racial brutality, ranging from sadistic interrogation methods to wanton murder, became necessary and legitimate. Percy Thompson's execution reflected the shift in policing and white sensibilities regarding racial control. After the construction worker challenged the racial order, according to local journalists, city cops responded with lethal force, much to the relief of white New Orleanians. Though a huge white mob demanded the summary execution of the "murderous negro," the task fell to Detective Vic Swanson, and white residents celebrated his heroism and insisted that the shooting had protected the "respectable," law-abiding residents of the city. Summary executions, like coerced confessions and the plea bargains extracted for Eugene Stanley, preserved social order and safeguarded white supremacy in the age of Jim Crow. A new law enforcement mandate, blurring racialized police violence and law and order, emerged during the interwar years. The change simultaneously relied on the rule of law rather than civilian vigilantism and bolstered the status quo in race relations.

Stanley shaped this transformation in New Orleans, and local patrolmen, detectives, jurors, and judges imposed and enforced it, though similar shifts, directed by a comparable assortment of prosecutors and other criminal justice officials, occurred in other Southern urban centers. Racialized police brutality, particularly coercive interrogation methods, became endemic and overlapped with notions of law and order, while white civilian vigilantism, including lynching, persisted but became less frequent, especially in cities. Early twentieth-century ethnographers, criminologists, and sociologists, charted this process and noted its regional scope, trends also documented in police, court, and civil rights records.[120]

. . .

The late 1920s and early 1930s crime panic exposed the limitations of civilian racial control and forged a capacious new police mandate, one that dramatically expanded cops' authority and enhanced their legitimacy among white New Orleanians. In the Louisiana metropolis—and elsewhere in the region—white voters increasingly looked to the police to safeguard white supremacy, and local leaders vowed to employ "any means necessary" to buttress racial dominance. They armed cops with machine guns and sawed-off shotguns, stockpiled tear-gas grenades, purchased faster patrol cars and assault vehicles, unveiled armored motorcycles, such as Police Chief Ray's "Death-Dealing Machine," and lobbied for funds to secure police airplanes and other military equipment. With the vehement support of white newspapers and white voters, law enforcement officials extended greater discretionary authority to cops to employ preemptive force, issued shoot-to-kill orders to patrolmen, launched racially selective arrest dragnets, established specialized, militarized crime-fighting squads, and encouraged detectives to extract confessions from African American suspects, even if they relied on sadistic, unconstitutional, third-degree methods. Buoyed by their surging public support and elevated status in the community as the guardians of racial order, New Orleans cops embraced the new mandate and a warrior ethic. Reflected in a tidal wave of police brutality complaints and an explosion of police shootings, these cultural and institutional pressures redefined both law enforcement and notions of law and order during the late 1920s and 1930s. City officials, police chiefs, and cops throughout the urban South adopted parallel changes, including creating specialized, militarized squads, conducting dragnets of "suspicious negroes," employing racialized interrogation practices, and implementing shoot-to-kill protocols. "Police brutality," a Mobile civil rights activist lamented, "goes unchecked."[121]

White New Orleanians demanded and, in their capacities as respectable citizens, criminal-court jurors, and especially voters, supported such shifts, as in other Southern cities.[122] Parish prosecutors, spearheaded by the opportunistic Eugene Stanley, explicitly pledged to use local legal institutions to preserve white supremacy, oversaw coercive interrogative techniques in order to secure confessions from African American suspects, and relied on the resulting plea bargains to increase the conviction rates of African American defendants at the same time that rates for white offenders tumbled. White vigilantism dropped as police violence soared; jurors more often supported recommendations for capital verdicts for African American defendants, even as they eschewed such sentences for white defendants; and the most zealous proponents of racialized criminal justice rode their crusade for white dominance to landslide victories in elections.

This white support reinforced police certainty that they could employ violence against African American residents with impunity. The "flagrant abuse of police power," a New Orleans civil rights reformer concluded, became routine "because the police think that when it is against Negroes nothing will ever be done about it."[123] To the contrary, racialized brutality bolstered white support for law enforcement. A local sociologist argued that "the police behave toward Negroes the way they think white New Orleans expect them to behave." One local cop explained that the "policeman is simply the 'channel of the general white hostility against the Negro.'"[124] New Orleans law enforcement had ample evidence for such a perception and received nearly unequivocal support for their racialized violence from above and below. Voters cast their ballots for office seekers promoting this view; police leaders encouraged racialized methods and practices; coroners prohibited physicians from examining the suspects and prisoners held in police custody and nearly always accepted cops' explanations for battered bodies; prosecutors ignored the testimony of African American abuse victims and witnesses of such police abuse; jurors disregarded evidence of police violence; and judges typically excluded photographs of beaten suspects and testimony from tortured African Americans defendants but accepted the statements and testimony of cops, even when they included numerous accounts employing identical language and implausible explanations. African American observers in other Southern cities witnessed an identical, chilling transformation in policing and racial control. According to an outraged Birmingham writer, "such police actions apparently are justifiable in every instance."[125]

Falling rates of African American homicide bolstered white perceptions that law-and-order policing and the brutalization of African American bodies reduced crime, managed disorder, and protected them, even though the drop in violence preceded the most explicit forms of selective law enforcement. They hinged on a solipsistic view of police brutality, constitutional and legal rights, and public safety. Between 1925 and 1932, African American homicide dropped by more than half. During the same span, however, the rate of lethal police violence against these residents increased by 159.5 percent, the conviction rate for African American homicide suspects rose by 54.7 percent, and the rate of capital verdicts against African American suspects more than doubled. White New Orleanians perceived clear and obvious causal connections between these figures, certain that aggressive, unrestrained policing controlled African American criminality, reinforcing white residents' faith in police authority and their belief that the rule of law protected white supremacy.

The disfranchisement of African Americans anchored this system, largely eliminating the guardrails against the most extreme forms of racial police brutality. Local politicians recognized that racial demagoguery mobilized white voters. Between the mid-1920s and the mid-1930s, the African American population of New Orleans grew by 20.9 percent, and in 1935 they comprised 29.8 percent of local residents. Yet their share of registered voters contracted sharply. In 1935, these residents comprised 0.53 percent of local voters, and by 1940 they made up 0.37 of those eligible to cast ballots. Between 1920 and 1940, the African American share of registered voters dwindled by 88.1 percent. African American New Orleanians and local civil rights activists decried police brutality, but their formal political muscle remained modest, giving local white supremacists virtually free reign in city elections, in formulating public policy, and in the operation of criminal justice institutions.

In short, the police secured the political mandate and institutional authority to translate racial custom into legal action. And, for most white New Orleanians and other Southern whites, cops' brutality toward African American residents demonstrated their responsiveness to the voters' values, priorities, and needs. Rough justice was reborn and refocused in the form of violent arrests, coercive police interrogations, the discretionary use of lethal force against African American suspects, and growing racial disparities in conviction and execution. Police brutality assumed a race-specific definition for white New Orleanians.

Racialized policing and violence served the cultural needs of white New Orleanians as well, accelerating this shift. Reliance on police violence, rather than civilian vigilantism, outsourced racial control. White residents simultaneously empowered and encouraged such racial violence and celebrated their restraint, civility, cultural superiority, and nobility.[126] They no longer lynched their African American neighbors nor systematically roamed the streets and wantonly murdered these residents. Instead, they relied on the municipal police to engage in vicious violence. Disguised and masked as the rule of law, police brutality allayed white racial anxieties and bolstered white dominance, making the preservation of white supremacy the core mission of the local—and regional—criminal justice system. Such white perceptions and electoral actions enabled them to ignore the beating of Percy Thompson and to view him as a "murderous negro" who "ran amuck" without provocation, and to accept, indeed laud, the sadistic methods that police detectives employed to coerce Vernon Guichard into confessing to a murder that he did not commit, leading the twenty-four-year-old African American carpenter to tell his interrogators "to go ahead and kill me, as they had already half killed me."

FOUR

Buttercup Burns, Bulldog Johnny
Grosch, and the Killer Twins

IF EARLY TWENTIETH-CENTURY New Orleans had a serial killer, it was Willie Grosch. In one of the nation's most murderous cities, Grosch stood alone in his violence. Between 1932 and 1941, he committed seven documented homicides and likely had additional victims. Grosch beat one person to death and fatally shot the others. Many were executions in which he forced residents into his vehicle, transported them to an isolated setting, and shot his victims in the head. Grosch also participated in another handful of killings as an accomplice. Although he boasted about his violence, Grosch was never punished in any way. But he was not a gangster, bandit, or criminal predator. To the contrary, the killer was a highly respected New Orleans police detective.

Most New Orleanians did not consider Willie Grosch a rogue cop—or a proverbial "bad apple." Many proclaimed him a hero and guardian of law and order, and city officials showered Grosch with praise, counting him among the police elite. In 1934, for example, the superintendent of police identified Willie Grosch as the "cream of the crop" among municipal law enforcers.[1] Not all New Orleanians, however, shared this view. African American residents saw him as a sadistic beast who targeted members of their community, insisting that suspects often mysteriously died in his custody and that his homicides constituted an explicit tool of racial oppression. The city's leading African American newspaper, for instance, charged that "whenever there is a questionable killing, the shooting of handcuffed prisoners, the use of the third degree, whenever there is brutality and murder by the New Orleans Police Force [sic], look for the 'killer twins' and there will be Grosch and Arnold," his longtime detective partner.[2]

Grosch's murder of Charles Handy on November 25, 1937 featured the signature law enforcement methods that led white New Orleanians to lionize the detective and African American residents to vilify him. The forty-four-year-old cop from a hardscrabble background considered Handy, a diminutive, eighteen-year-old African American day laborer, the principal suspect in a series of sexual assaults of white women. Over the course of a week, seven women reported being attacked by a young knife-wielding African American man, who roamed the city at night "seeking prey." According to the victims, the predator abducted them from downtown streets, steered them into dark alleys, snatched their purses, and then raped them.[3] Early on Thanksgiving Day, November 25, a state trooper apprehended Handy, who roughly fit the victims' descriptions of their attacker, and delivered him to police headquarters, where Grosch and his partner interrogated him. Handy quickly confessed, the detectives reported, admitting to raping two white women and attempting to sexually assault five others.[4] Shortly after noon, Grosch took the serial rapist on a journey he dubbed "the ride." He and his partner drove Handy to a rooming house purportedly to search for the stolen purses and the cap he wore when he assaulted the women, even though the suspect had already signed a confession, admitting to multiple capital offenses.[5] According to Grosch, the 145-pound rapist broke away from the detectives and tried to escape, tossing his partner against a wall and compelling the detective to fire a bullet into the side of Handy's head from close range.[6]

To many white New Orleanians, Grosch eliminated a vicious predator, dispensing with a protracted, unpredictable trial, and hence the detective had instantly secured justice for the city's white women and respectable residents. Police and criminal justice officials defended the shooting, terming it a "justifiable homicide," and swiftly closed the case, ignoring protests from local civil rights organizations. But the Handy killing did not occur in isolation. Again and again, Willie Grosch committed virtually identical acts of lethal violence, often inexplicably transporting suspects to a remote setting just outside of the city and shooting those he considered menacing criminals. During a decade of soaring police violence, Grosch, by himself, committed at least one-sixth of all homicides by New Orleans cops. Over a dozen suspects also filed brutality complaints against the detective, charging that he tortured them and threatened to take them for a ride and kill them if they refused to sign confessions. African American New Orleanians comprised the lion's share of his victims. Such methods enhanced Grosch's power and bolstered police authority and legitimacy, inspiring respect and gratitude from jittery white residents and trepidation from African American New Orleanians. For many white city dwellers, Willie Grosch's brand of summary justice safeguarded the racial order and buttressed public safety during an era of social turmoil. He shouldered the burden for performing the unpleasant, dangerous tasks that enabled decent, white residents to remain secure.

Although his unflinching tactics and death toll were extreme, even by New Orleans standards, Willie Grosch belonged to a small group of detectives who routinely beat African American suspects and committed nearly half of the city's police homicides. Commanding fawning headlines in daily newspapers, holding high positions in the department, and receiving adulation from white New Orleanians, the detective squad set the tone for law enforcement in the city. During the late 1920s crime panic, local policemen became aggressive crime fighters, and the small detective unit evolved into the most visible, forceful defenders of law and order. Their high-profile campaign against violent predators, particularly African American criminals, became the public face of police authority in interwar New Orleans. Fierce and fearless, they pursued the most dangerous offenders and refused to submit to legal niceties and technicalities in their zeal to protect respectable residents. At the height of the crime hysteria, Police Chief Thomas Healy promised to "personally" maintain a detective squad "that'll make Scotland Yard look like a bunch of Shubert [*sic*] chorus boys."[7] In the age of Dick Tracy comics and Eliot Ness, these detectives blended older expressions of street justice with distinctive notions of professional policing and the rule of law. Spearheaded by this elite group, a new model of aggressive law enforcement emerged in New Orleans and enjoyed gushing support from white residents. Comparable units, methods, practices, and killer cops, however, surfaced throughout the region; every department seemed to have a small cadre of hard-boiled detectives who tackled the toughest cases and refused to coddle depraved criminals, risking their lives and bloodying their hands to save white lives. Police brutality developed into a form of crime fighting that employed violence in the service of white supremacy and operated as state-sponsored racial terrorism.

. . .

In the years after the Great War, the New Orleans police department remained tiny, underfunded, and amateurish. Residents relied mostly on civilian vigilantes to preserve public safety, and temporary, or supernumerary, policemen dominated the patrol force. These short-term, emergency cops barely investigated crimes, and few suspects went to trial, even for the most heinous offenses. During the early 1920s, less than one-seventh of murderers were convicted. Killers who glowered over their bloodied victims routinely avoided arrest, indictment, and punishment.[8] While city cops were often violent, civilians committed the largest share of the brutality against African American residents, particularly interracial homicide. Moreover, the cops employing lethal force tended to be young, inexperienced, skittish supernumerary patrolmen, who panicked during encounters with "suspicious characters" on local streets.

But both policing and police violence shifted abruptly during the second half of the decade, when white fears of an invasion by "bad n-----s" and a crime panic redefined law enforcement in New Orleans. Municipal officials poured resources into crime fighting, and the police department depended less on temporary patrolmen and relied more on permanent, veteran cops to maintain law and order. With the expansion and militarization of law enforcement and the emergence of elite, aggressive detectives, crime fighting, rather than traffic control, became the lifeblood of local policing.

The new crime-fighting mandate fueled a surge in police homicide and transformed the morphology of police brutality in the city. Between the late 1920s and early 1930s, the rate of police homicide rose 51.4 percent, and the proportion of killings with African American victims leaped by two-thirds. Moreover, cop violence, ranging from beating suspicious loiterers to fatally shooting suspects, increasingly occurred as a part of crime investigations or police interrogations, rather than during prosaic street encounters. Tasked with solving crime, particularly African American crime, older, experienced, high-ranking detectives assumed responsibility for catching the most vicious offenders and questioning suspects in the most serious cases. In the process, they became more aggressive and the city's most violent law enforcers, a shift that Willie Grosch exemplified.

Changes in police homicide revealed the magnitude of the transformation. Between the early 1920s and the early 1930s, the share of killings by supernumerary patrolmen fell by 81.6 percent, while the proportion by detectives more than tripled. By the mid-1930s, no African American suspects died at the hands of temporary cops, and detectives, who comprised 5 percent of the police force, accounted for almost half of homicides, reflecting both the shifting composition of the department and a growing embrace of aggressive crime fighting. Similarly, 55.6 percent of killer cops were in their twenties during the decade after the Great War, compared with 13 percent during the 1930s. Between the early 1920s and the early 1930s, the mean age of New Orleans policemen who killed African American suspects climbed from 24 to 34.8.

Police homicide increasingly focused on African American New Orleanians and became more purposeful. Nor did killer cops hide their brutality. To the contrary, police violence against African Americans became a badge of crime-fighting acumen and an instrument of fear or a source of security, depending on the race of the resident. Even though police brutality retreated from busy city streets and the crowded, raucous French Quarter to department headquarters, precinct interrogation rooms, and remote sections of New Orleans, it became more visible and publicized, for aggressive detectives bragged about their crime-solving prowess. They pandered to the anxieties of white residents and boasted to African American residents as a form of intimidation and racial control. Willie Grosch missed no opportunity to remind the former of his value in protecting them and to attempt to cow the latter with bluster about wantonly killing suspects. For white New Orleanians, the combination of more racialized and more violent policing made the city safer and thus enhanced the department's value and legitimacy. In the eight years after homicide reached its high-water mark, in 1925, the local homicide rate tumbled by 52.8 percent, the African American rate plunged by two-thirds, the new model of law enforcement took root, and its architects claimed credit, even though the drop in murder reflected a national trend.

At least rhetorically, police violence centered on crime fighting rather than violations of racial custom, though cops and white New Orleanians in general viewed crime in racialized terms. Detectives insisted that they employed the methods required to protect good—white—citizens from predators such as the serial rapist Charles Handy. Interwar policemen believed that trials and court proceedings failed to safeguard respectable residents. In 1930, a Louisiana newspaper editor explained that the "average policeman" recognized "that arresting criminals is much easier than convicting them. He knows there are often wheels within wheels in his city's legal machinery. So it has become a police axiom that the case against a suspect is hardly complete without a signed sworn confession."[9] Given the mandate to preserve law and order, New Orleans detectives deployed every means to secure confessions from suspects and therefore to make the streets safe, insisting that they dealt with the most menacing criminals in the city and had to be aggressive. And if savage predators refused to confess, more extreme measures, even executions, became necessary, for the ends justified the means. Top city officials concurred and instructed detectives "to preserve law and order in New Orleans at any cost."[10] These cops were not "Shubert chorus boys," and their efforts enabled white residents to sleep at night.

When they encountered African American suspects, detectives enjoyed unfettered authority, relying on their own discretion and whim and knowing that police officials, the courts, and most white New Orleanians supported their methods.[11] In an era when African Americans faced nearly total disfranchisement and complete exclusion from juries, detectives could beat, torture, and even murder them with impunity, and they flaunted this power.[12] Interwar civil rights activists charged that cops exploited such autonomy and "framed" African Americans to promote themselves and placate whites desperate to be protected from dangerous criminals. One NAACP observer, for example, argued that policemen "must do something to allay the rage of the wild beast that lurks in an 'outraged' public sentiment. Negroes, because of poverty, ignorance, traditional prejudice, and their own sad lack of organized co-operation, offer the most convenient sacrifices for such purposes."[13] It is impossible to know if New Orleans detectives, such as Willie Grosch, believed they were preserving law and order or if they scapegoated African American residents out of overt racism and crass opportunism.

Their expansive crime-fighting mandate and working-class, Southern attitudes toward African Americans also inclined interwar detectives to anticipate resistance and rely on aggressive methods during interrogations and crime investigations. Third-degree techniques for questioning African American suspects, according to a 1941 observer, became "almost synonymous with the Detective Bureau of the New Orleans Police Department."[14] Grosch and his colleagues routinely tortured the prisoners during interrogations, certain both that such methods were necessary to secure confessions and that "the higher officers of the Department" fully supported their actions.[15]

Again and again, African American suspects charged that beatings and the fear of death at the hands of vicious interrogators led to extracted, false confessions, with elite detectives accumulating bulging files of complaints from bloodied, battered victims. These coerced confessions, however, only burnished their reputations as department "specialists" renowned for their success in closing high-profile cases and thus cleaning up the streets.[16] "Fear of physical violence," an African American journalist wrote in 1939, "makes many men 'confess' to any crime, just to know a second's respite from rubber hose, clubs, and fists. And while the American law is to the effect that a man is innocent until proven guilty, the attitude in New Orleans and surrounding communities is that a Negro is guilty until proven innocent, and that anything may be resorted to to make him 'admit' guilt."[17]

Detectives viewed suspects' unwillingness to confess as defiance, rather than an indication of innocence, prompting them to become more aggressive and more sadistic. Their use of increasingly violent methods yielded false confessions and contributed to soaring rates of African American conviction and incarceration, bolstering stereotyped images of race and crime and seemingly confirming the claims of police officials about the magical impact of aggressive law enforcement. Subsequent developments, however, sometimes revealed that the admissions of guilt had been secured through coercion and that the detective had wrung confessions from innocent suspects. For example, in 1933 two New Orleans detectives brutally beat a fifteen-year-old African American boy until he signed a confession. According to an African American reporter, "it was proved in this case as in many other cases that the police in order to extort forced confessions from suspects, do subject them to merciless beatings, and the latter to avoid torture reluctantly admit participation in crimes of which they know nothing."[18] The detectives "stuffed paper into his mouth, tied a handkerchief over his face and then beat him with a wire cable about three feet long" until he confessed.[19] The suspect's white employer, however, corroborated the teenager's claim of innocence, testifying that he had been working at his pharmacy at the time of the crime and compelling police authorities to release their prisoner.[20] But prosecutors, juries, and judges typically ignored such inconvenient, conflicting evidence, convicting defendants based on forced confessions. Detectives conducting the interrogations employed greater and greater brutality to extract confessions, the cycle of beatings that triggered Percy Thompson's violent resistance to third-degree methods.[21]

New Orleans detectives' perceptions of race and criminality also fueled the preemptive use of deadly force. Some cops fabricated accounts of threatening behavior to justify deadly violence, but others may have misinterpreted ambiguous movements or even imagined that the suspects they encountered undertook motions that endangered them and employed extreme brutality and lethal force. As detectives interrogated suspects in the most heinous cases and investigated serious crime, these circumstances "primed" them to anticipate and then perceive resistance and threatening actions. Hyper-surveillance made the stereotype of violent African Americans self-affirming.[22]

Ecological changes magnified this priming effect. As massive electric pumps drained local bayous during the late 1920s and early 1930s and more of the land within New Orleans became suitable for development, racial segregation increased. New construction led to the displacement of African American New Orleanians, who were forced out of small, "backyard" pockets close to white residents and concentrated on the eastern side of the city. The 1930s construction of an enormous, racially segregated housing project accelerated this process. Detectives investigating reports of African American crime more and more often searched for suspects in the city's 12th police district, the emerging racial ghetto. As white cops in an African American neighborhood, detectives believed themselves to be entering hostile territory and in constant danger, contributing to their exaggerated scrutiny of residents and preparing them to anticipate dangerous resistance. They became hypersensitive to ambiguous behavior and quicker to respond preemptively to perceived and imagined threats.[23] The proportion of deadly police shootings of African Americans in this section of New Orleans quadrupled.

Again and again, killer cops described identical circumstances preceding fatal encounters. Detectives shot African American suspects who appeared to be reaching for weapons—or engaging in a "hip-pocket move." Detectives testified that they shot to protect their lives. A police officer killed Dave Hughes in 1930 when the day laborer appeared to be "putting his hand in his left hand pants pocket."[24] In other cases, cops testified that they shot a "suspicious character" who "made a movement" to his pocket, "reached in his back pocket," "made a motion as if to draw a weapon," "made a move with his right hand towards his front trousers pocket," "attempted to reach for something in his pocket," "reached for his back pocket," and "reached towards his hip pocket in a threatening manner."[25]

Such hyper-scrutiny frequently triggered the preemptive use of deadly force against unarmed African suspects. In 1939, for example, Detective Edward Duthu shot fifteen-year-old Thompson McCormack when the teenager, a suspected bicycle thief, "placed his hand in his right pocket as though he was going to pull something out." The detective, however, found no weapon in McCormack's trousers.[26] Similarly, Milton Battise died when the twenty-one-year-old laborer attempted to dispose of a bottle of hooch during Prohibition. Two cops saw Battise make "an attempt to pull something out of his right hip pocket, and, thinking it was a weapon, they both pulled out their revolvers and each firing one shot at the fleeing negro, one of the bullets taking effect in the back of the negro's head."[27]

These policemen insisted that African American suspects' ambiguous movements placed their lives at risk, justifying the resort to deadly preemptive violence. "I fired these shots because I believed my life was in danger," one New Orleans cop explained.[28] Another police officer stated that "thi[nk]ng that his life was in danger drew his revolver and fired two shots at the negro," killing William Forest, while another municipal law enforcer, "fearing that his life was in danger" when larceny suspect Harold Martin "placed his hand into his right pocket," discharged "one shot at the negro from his service revolver."[29] Detectives insisted they shot in self-defense, an explanation that police supervisors and parish prosecutors always accepted at face value.

This use of preemptive lethal force in response to furtive or ambiguous movements had two devastating effects. First, it exaggerated suspects' inclination to flee from policemen. As the African American sociologist Charles Johnson explained in 1943, "there are few Negroes in the South who have not either experienced or witnessed" such "violence on the part of these guardians of the law."[30] A New Orleans writer noted that African American residents were accustomed to municipal cops' "quick resort to firearms," and therefore "it is not to be wondered at that the average Negro boy or man runs when approached by either uniformed or plainclothed [sic] officers."[31] The result was a staggering number of police homicides, for when suspects ran, it amplified cops' certainty that the African American New Orleanians they targeted were guilty, posed threats, and must be dealt with aggressively.[32] Why else would the suspects run? The *Louisiana Weekly* lamented the "amazing regularity with which Negroes get shot to death for 'resisting arrest' and making 'attempts to escape.'"[33] After a New Orleans cop fired three bullets into the back of Russell Williams, a thirty-year-old railroad section hand, an African American writer described the killing as "merely the 'familiar' police report of an arrested Negro trying to escape and being shot to death."[34] In another fatal shooting, the murderous law enforcer told an assistant district attorney that his "only reason for shooting the youth [was] that that he heard a white woman scream and saw the boy running," leading the prosecutor to label the killing of the unarmed teenage boy "a routine matter" and a justifiable homicide.[35] Civil rights activists in Birmingham and other Southern cities observed the same behavior and deadly reactions.[36]

Second, the use of preemptive force when New Orleans policemen perceived "hip-pocket moves" resulted in the disproportionate killing of unarmed African American suspects. The cumulative weight of a crime panic, stereotyped perceptions of African American residents as violent predators, the emergence of detectives as the main crime investigators, and increasing residential segregation contributed to a surge in the proportion of unarmed victims killed when they seemed to reach for nonexistent revolvers. Between the mid-1920s and the early 1930s, as fears of African American marauders exploded and local detectives garnered white support for the quick resort to deadly force, the share of unarmed African Americans killed doubled. By the early 1930s, two-thirds were unarmed. Yet, killer cops testified that African Americans threatened them and compelled them to shoot in self-defense.

Hyper-scrutiny activated and weaponized stereotyped perceptions of African American suspects and widened racial disparities in criminal justice. Because New Orleans policemen typically did not perceive white residents to be dangerous, they rarely interpreted vague movements toward pockets as menacing and seldom shot unarmed white suspects, even when they actually possessed weapons.[37] While the percentage of unarmed African American victims soared, the proportion of unarmed whites killed by local cops plunged. By the early 1930s, African American victims of police homicide were five times more likely to be unarmed than white victims—a disparity that persists into the twenty-first century.[38] Racialized perceptions of criminality and the racialization of police violence became intertwined and self-perpetuating, an alchemy that erupted throughout the urban South. In Alabama, cops killed nineteen African American suspects and one white resident, while their Atlanta counterparts fatally shot twenty-five African American and one white suspect, most of them unarmed.[39]

Some New Orleans detectives exploited the hip-pocket explanation. Shooting unarmed suspects because they allegedly made ambiguous body movements offered the most aggressive, murderous cops plausible deniability. Killer detectives recognized that it was impossible to disprove events that hinged on purported inflections or to establish whether the victims actually reached for their pockets. Criminal justice officials deferred to the discretion of the "guardians of the law" in all such cases.[40] Not every New Orleanian, however, concurred. African American residents and local civil rights activists frequently charged that detectives fabricated explanations to justify summary executions. The editor of the Louisiana Weekly, for instance, discounted most hip-pocket reports as "too thin for well thinking persons of either color" and noted that local detectives "require no training for shooting

Negroes for misdemeanors, but somehow or other they lose the art of shooting altogether whenever they fire at white bandits."[41] He dismissed the explanations as "flimsy pretexts."[42] In a letter to the editor of a city newspaper, another observer called "the supposed facts" in such killings "ridiculous and absurd," while a civil rights reformer similarly concluded that police killers employed deadly force "at the slightest provocation, and sometimes with no provocation at all."[43] Criticism of this thin patina of plausibility, however, fell on deaf ears and failed to persuade police authorities or district attorneys, who remained eager to deploy detectives' use of preemptive violence as a balm for white residents' anxieties about racial stability and law and order. Police homicide served an important political purpose for municipal officials and a powerful institutional role for Jim Crow law enforcement leaders.

At least in part, interwar cops invoked contrived explanations, often unmistakably manufactured and employing identical descriptions of the events prompting the use of deadly force, to generate public support from frightened white residents. Many of the African Americans who died under questionable, murky circumstances were suspects in interracial crimes. Few white New Orleanians fretted about procedural fairness or the precise legal definition of justifiable homicide when Detective Vic Swanson shot the cop killer Percy Thompson or when Detective Willie Grosch executed the serial rapist Charles Handy "without the formalities of a legal accusation or court trial."[44] To the contrary, respectable residents—the local electorate— expressed relief and gratitude, sentiments that reflected white New Orleanians' growing faith in granting discretionary authority to municipal cops. Paradoxically, detectives' violence fortified the legitimacy of the police.

Such public support gave detectives free rein to impose their own standards of justice and kill the suspects that they personally most reviled. White journalists, prosecutors, and city residents deferred to Grosch's statement that an implausible movement "forced him to shoot" a prisoner who had killed a police officer a decade earlier, just as residents blithely accepted another local law enforcer's explanation that he fired in self-defense when he fatally shot a thirty-eight-year-old African American suspected of having burglarized his own home.[45] Stubborn, noncompliant African Americans enraged crime investigators, and the suspects subsequently made the ambiguous movement that provided plausible deniability and justifiable homicide determinations from parish prosecutors. On November 2, 1935, Grosch claimed such a self-defense explanation after he and his partner fired ten bullets into the body of Haze Howard, a thirty-four-year-old burglary suspect who had been slow to raise his hands upon command.[46] Describing another wantonly violent episode by the detective and his partner, the *Louisiana Weekly* declared that they had hands "dyed with blood."[47] The *Chicago Defender* labeled one of Grosch's justifiable homicides a "lynching" and a "streamlined lynching."[48] For Willie Grosch and other city detectives, the license to employ preemptive force—to beat and kill suspects—became increasingly capacious, as long as the victims were African American. One critic of police violence likened New Orleans detectives to the "Brown Shirts of Germany."[49] A local civil rights activist made a comparable comparison in 1941, charging that "no worse condition could exist even under Hitler and Nazi Germany."[50]

Seven municipal cops, nearly all part of the city's detective unit, committed almost half of the police homicides during the 1930s.[51] These local law enforcers, along with one precinct commander, inflicted the most brutal, sadistic beatings during suspect interrogations as well. Far from being rogue cops who embarrassed city authorities, they constituted New Orleans's elite crime fighters, and police superintendents selected them to serve on the highest visibility specialized squads and assigned these men to investigate the most serious crimes and interrogate the most hardened criminals. They were the most influential, revered cops in the city—the "cream of the crop"—and included chiefs of detectives, special advisors to the police chief, and acting police superintendents. The toughest, most fearless cops in New Orleans, they shaped law enforcement and criminal justice in the city.

Again and again, members of this small group served on the special units assembled to make the streets of New Orleans safe. When the crime panic began, they formed the "Go Get 'Em squad" and during the 1930s comprised the "vigilance squad" empowered "to clean up the town."[52] Top police authorities actively supported their methods, heaping praise on these elite, murderous detectives and rewarding them with promotions and high salaries. Willie Grosch's salary, for instance, was nearly double the mean for city detectives. The most sadistic interrogations also routinely occurred in police headquarters, in rooms adjoining the district attorney's office, and in other settings overseen by leading officials. Police chiefs and prosecutors boasted about their detectives' brutality and violent methods. "Obtaining confessions" from vicious criminals, city authorities crowed in 1937, was "baby play for these fellows."[53]

Some of these cops had signature methods for extracting confessions. James Burns achieved particular notoriety and infamy during the early 1930s.

Municipal officials and parish judges knew Burns as a jovial, self-deprecating police captain with a colorful, flamboyant personality, though they also recognized that he possessed almost magical powers to secure confessions from the fiercest suspects.

Born in 1878, the child of Irish immigrants, Burns grew up in working-class New Orleans and joined the police department in 1902 as a supernumerary patrolman. Two years later, the superintendent made him a permanent officer, and Burns rose through the ranks. In 1928 police officials promoted him to captain and commander of the department's 12th precinct station. He also became a local celebrity. Though standing five feet seven, Burns weighed more than three hundred pounds, making him the "heaviest man on the police force," and he competed in the department's yearly "fat man's race."[54] During the 1910s, he gained particular renown, however, acting in the department's annual minstrel show. Each year, the rotund Burns donned a short white dress and a wig with flowing curls and "gamboled about the stage as a song and dance entertainer" in a performance of "Pinafore," earning him the moniker "Buttercup Burns."[55] His colleagues and local journalists called him the "funniest policeman in America," and Burns became well known for his "amiable disposition and kindliness."[56]

With this public persona, the dancing captain's remarkable prowess at securing confessions from crime suspects especially amazed city authorities, but African American New Orleanians encountered a very different cop in the 12th precinct's interrogation room. To compel these residents to confess to crimes, Buttercup Burns routinely instructed his officers to remove suspects' clothing, heat an iron stove poker, and sodomize the prisoners until they admitted their guilt. During one such session, he ordered a patrolman to "burn the n----- until he tells where he stole that watch."[57]

Burns's methods were an open secret, particularly well known to African American New Orleanians.[58] Under his leadership, the station house was dubbed the "damnable 12th," and Burns routinely commanded his officers to secure confessions with the aid of a heated stove poker.[59] According to one journalist, this interrogation method was "much in vogue at the Twelfth Precinct."[60] Through their defense attorneys, the ostensibly affable commander's victims charged that their confessions had been extracted using methods "so revolting that a newspaper account cannot be given."[61] But judges dismissed the complaints, insisting that the jolly captain could not have acted with such cruelty. In one case, Judge A. D. Henriques declared allegations of torture inconceivable, stating that "I have known Captain

Burns for years and I know him to be one of the kindest-hearted men I've ever met."[62] African American residents apprehended as "suspicious and dangerous characters," however, recoiled in terror when patrolmen threatened to deliver them to Burns's precinct for questioning. Buttercup Burns's interrogation methods yielded rapid confessions, contributing to surging racial disparities in criminal justice. Murder suspect Eli Terrell, for example, told a judge that he confessed "only after he had been tripped to the 12th Precinct police station and threatened with a red hot poker."[63]

Even more brutal and menacing for African American suspects were the Grosch brothers. No one considered William Grosch and his younger brother, John, kindhearted or funny, but these detectives, each employing a signature method, orchestrated a campaign of racial terror in interwar New Orleans and exercised commanding influence over policing and race relations in the city and the region. They formed the core of the department's "royal family," according to other cops, received "rapid" promotions into leadership positions, and enjoyed immense support from white New Orleanians, top city officials, and even state legislators.[64]

The Grosches grew up in rough-hewn, plebian New Orleans, the sons of a day laborer and grandsons of German immigrants. William was born in 1893 and John two years later. They completed six years of schooling, and both entered the workforce by their eleventh birthdays. The young boys initially found employment as "doffers" at a New Orleans cotton mill and then worked, most often side-by-side, in a wide range of unskilled jobs—as pile drivers on the city's docks, sailors on Lake Erie cargo freighters, railroad hands, and longshoremen. They each served in the navy during World War I. After the military, the Grosches returned to their former positions on the New Orleans docks. During the 1920s, they joined the police department, John in 1921 as a supernumerary patrolman and William seven years later as a supernumerary doorman. Both became permanent patrolmen within a few years. In 1925, on the same day his "boyhood buddy," neighbor, and then patrol partner, George Reyer, became the chief of detectives, John was promoted to detective, and five years later, Reyer became police chief and immediately appointed the younger Grosch to succeed him as the chief of detectives, a post he held for the next fifteen years.[65] In announcing his close friend and longtime partner's promotion to this leadership position, Reyer declared that "I don't know another man on the force who merits it more than he does."[66] Shortly after becoming the chief of detectives, John elevated his older brother to detective and gave him plumb assignments in the department.

The Grosches quickly established reputations as the city's most feared, violent detectives, though they specialized in different methods of brutality. Willie's unrivaled tally of summary executions notwithstanding, he gained even greater public attention for an interrogation ritual he called "the ride." Again and against during the 1930s and early 1940s, Willie Grosch informed African American suspects that unless they confessed and signed the documents he drafted, he would transport them to a particular isolated location on the Air-Line Highway half a mile outside of the Orleans Parish boundary and kill them, claiming that he had shot in self-defense because they had assaulted him, attempted to escape, and made hip-pocket moves. After pulling the police vehicle onto the shoulder of the highway, he once again demanded a confession, usually punctuating the request by holding his service revolver to the handcuffed suspects' heads.

Nor was this mere bluster. Grosch repeatedly murdered African American suspects on this section of the highway. Far from hiding these executions, the detective missed no opportunity to "boast" about them.[67] He reminded suspects that he had killed noncompliant crime suspects in the past, even mentioning his previous victims by name as he posed the threat.[68] The city's African American newspaper disclosed in 1937 that Willie Grosch had been "bragging about it [executing Charles Handy] in the streets."[69] Four years later, after another African American suspect died in the same spot on the Air-Line Highway, civil rights activists "demanded an investigation by state and city prosecutors because Grosch had killed several Negroes under similar circumstances."[70] A white reporter also wrote that "stories circulated in the Negro sections that he [one of the cop's victims] had been beaten, then assassinated" by Grosch.[71] In one of the executions, he crushed the skull of a handcuffed suspect with the butt of his gun and then shot him in order to support his claim that he killed in self-defense.[72]

The detective's testimony explaining these murders ranged from implausible to absurd. Grosch claimed that he took his prisoners to this setting to search for evidence, failing to indicate why all the suspects had presumably stashed evidence in precisely the same remote setting or why gathering the cap worn by a rapist mattered after the predator had confessed. In one killing, he insisted that his prisoner, who had allegedly already signed a confession, was leading him to the location of a gun used in a crime a decade earlier.[73] Grosch routinely testified that handcuffed suspects attacked him or that prisoners who had been searched and interrogated at police headquarters reached for imaginary weapons, compelling the detective to shoot in self-defense.[74] He made little effort to construct even vaguely plausible narratives for his repeated homicides, all committed "in the line of duty."

African American suspects frequently insisted they signed false confessions to avoid the fate of previous victims of the infamous "ride." Both the forced confessions and the summary executions burnished Willie Grosch's reputation with white residents and city officials and underscored his expansive, unrestrained authority. As long as his victims were African American, white New Orleanians, including parish prosecutors, accepted his fabricated explanations and celebrated his vigorous actions to preserve racial order and public safety. Grosch extracted confessions and killed suspects in the next parish to avoid close scrutiny. Although white New Orleanians applauded the detective's efforts to protect them from dangerous criminals, Grosch likely worried that his methods, such as bashing in the skulls of handcuffed prisoners or shooting them in the genitals, might be less palatable, and he knew that Jefferson Parish officials would defer to outlandish explanations for the preemptive use of deadly force, conduct superficial autopsies, and quickly release bodies for immediate burials.[75]

Though less murderous than his brother, John Grosch was interwar New Orleans's staunchest, most public, and most unapologetic defender of police violence, coercive third-degree interrogation methods, and the racially selective suspension of legal and constitutional protections for crime suspects. He believed that maintaining public safety and preserving law and order sometimes required cops to employ violent means. Legal safeguards undermined this mission, compelling policemen to coddle vicious criminals, jeopardizing social stability and public safety. Grosch would abide none of this and openly rejected such constraints, often telling defense attorneys and even judges that he would not submit to constitutional restrictions. No cop in interwar New Orleans or the lower Mississippi Valley became more closely identified with the third degree, more brazenly rejected legal and judicial boundaries on the treatment of suspects, or more stridently embraced police brutality in the service of law and order. White New Orleanians, but also white Southerners and white Americans overall, celebrated John Grosch's efforts and his violence. During the 1930s, a Baton Rouge newspaper called him "one of the outstanding police officers in the South," and a nationally renowned crime journalist offered even more fulsome praise, declaring Grosch "one of most outstanding detectives in America."[76] Ironically, the New Orleans detective's fierce public embrace of violent interrogation methods and police violence, and his acclaim for such a position, occurred in the wake of the publication of the Wickersham Commission's denunciation of the third degree and cop brutality.

Even more than most early twentieth-century cops, John Grosch distrusted lawyers, jurors, and judges, believing that their maudlin sensibilities, gullibility, and slavish submission to formal law endangered public safety. Law and order could only be ensured when suspects confessed, and policemen must use any means necessary to protect citizens—white citizens—from violent criminals by compelling them to admit to their depredations and face punishment. Whereas his brother argued that such a view justified the summary execution of African American predators, John Grosch focused on extracting the confessions that yielded convictions, imprisonment, and "lawful" executions. For him, flouting legal protections and defending the rule of law somehow coexisted, resulting in savage, unabashed, illegal police violence in order to preserve law and order.

Although Grosch secured his position in the New Orleans police department as a consequence of his friendship with his former partner, Superintendent Reyer, the head detective garnered public status for his seemingly uncanny ability to secure confessions from the most defiant suspects. By the early 1930s, white New Orleanians dubbed John Grosch "the best third degree artist in the United States."[77] Local defense attorneys and civil rights activists concurred, though they used the label to convey their searing criticism of his routine use of illegal interrogation methods. Reformers referred to him as "Third-Degree Grosch," argued that the chief was "notorious" for his "third degree methods," and called him "Bulldog Johnny Grosch" for his dogged commitment to violent, unconstitutional interrogation practices.[78]

John Grosch reveled in his reputation as a "third-degree champion" and defended his brutality with undisguised pride and bravado.[79] During a 1933 trial, he crowed that "I have secured over 300 confessions, and the facts show that I have almost a 100 per cent [sic] record for introducing these confessions into evidence," describing himself as a "hard-boiled detective."[80] He also maintained that these violent methods were "the only way to handle criminals."[81] Grosch added that "only the guilty" received such treatment.[82] He employed "the third degree because they [criminals] deserved it."[83] This was the "best policing" and "curbed crime," making the streets of New Orleans safe, Grosch bragged.[84] "The greatest thrill I get is when I hear a criminal say, 'Yes, I did it.'"[85]

For more than two decades, John Grosch threatened, beat, and tortured suspects, and during his fifteen years at the helm of the detective unit he unapologetically brutalized prisoners. In one interrogation, he used the butt of his gun to knock out the suspect's teeth, jammed the barrel of his service revolver into the prisoner's mouth, and "said he was going to kill him if he didn't talk." The following day, after a prisoner was found dead in an adjoining cell, the suspect testified that "when I heard that, I knew he meant business" and signed a confession.[86] In another case, a twenty-six-year-old African American robbery suspect told a grand jury that the chief of detectives had "slugged him until he confessed" to a crime he did not commit.[87] Other suspects described the same methods, testifying that Grosch had bludgeoned them until they signed false confessions. "Chief Grosch punched me in the head and knocked me to the floor. Then I got punched all over. I was knocked down several times."[88]

One after another, for two decades, suspects leveled comparable charges that Grosch beat them until they confessed, the brutality often committed in his office at police headquarters. Frank Silsby, a robbery suspect, testified that the detective threatened that "if he did not make a statement" admitting to the crime "it would be 'too bad' for him," after which Grosch repeatedly kicked him in the genitals. "To avoid being crippled to life," Silsby relented, screamed "yes," and signed the statement that Grosch had drafted. When he appealed his conviction, alleging that the confession had been coerced, Silsby testified that "my groin was three times the natural size," and "I told Chief Grosch, then and there I told him I will say 'Yes' to anything you want me to say."[89] Similarly, Grosch, his older brother, and his son pummeled a robbery suspect in the chief of detective's office. "The cops beat me so hard," the convicted prisoner testified in his appeal, "that I thought I was going to die. So I confessed."[90] During his tenure as the department's top detective, hundreds of the suspects that Grosch interrogated signed confessions, but he also accumulated dozens of sworn complaints identifying similarly coercive interrogation methods. But he treated the allegations as badges of honor and characterized the victims who lodged brutality charges and appealed the convictions based on their confessions as criminals merely "trying to beat the rap."[91]

John Grosch openly crowed about his strategic, selective violence, claiming that these methods preserved law and order. In 1939, at a Rotary Club luncheon, he insisted that he had made New Orleans safe for respectable people. "If it were not for the 'third-degree' methods by which I have forced legal admissions in which cases where I had every reason to be sure of guilt," Grosch gushed, the city would be "delivered over to organized rackets and brutal crime as New York, Chicago, and other cities are."[92] Although his "spirited defense" of illegal practices elicited shock and outrage from civil rights activists and some white newspaper editors, white New Orleanians, including those attending the luncheon where Grosch "glorified" the use of torture, lauded his practices and credited him with protecting law-abiding residents. One Rotary Club officer agreed with the detective chief that "in dealing with hardened criminals, we can't get confessions by offering them ice cream and cake."[93] A self-described business woman and mother offered an even more full-throated endorsement of Grosch and his policing methods, stating that "Chief Grosch should be highly commended for any tactics he may use to rid the city of filth and the underworld that will attempt to congregate in New Orleans—and continue to make New Orleans a city safe and proud to live in."[94] "During my incumbency," Grosch boasted, "our good women and little children could safely walk the streets of New Orleans."[95]

Despite his public, open admission of routinely employing illegal, unconstitutional methods, Grosch's Rotary Club speech, according to one newspaper, produced only "a little stir in the city."[96] A few Rotarians refused to comment, while others asserted that Grosch's speech had been misinterpreted but they shared the detective's sentiments. The group's president suggested that Grosch had merely emphasized "making it uncomfortable . . . for hardened criminals."[97] For white New Orleanians, the chief of detectives was a hero.

Amplifying his public stature, Grosch was so committed to serving the interests of decent New Orleanians that he openly defied judges, publicly flouted judicial mandates, and explicitly rejected constitutional safeguards that he believed imperiled law-abiding residents. When newspaper reporters, defense attorneys, judges, and even Justice Department officials asked how he justified employing patently illegal law enforcement methods, New Orleans's chief of detectives defiantly barked "because I want them to" and explained that he "had no intentions of changing his methods."[98] He beat suspects, detained them without filing formal charges, held them in secret, undisclosed locations, denied them access to attorneys and relatives, and refused to seek warrants whenever he considered it necessary in order to preserve law and order. "Constitutional rights?" a forty-year-old New Orleans barber wondered. "Sounds like a foreign language to Chief Grosch."[99] Nothing, the city's top detective bragged, would prevent him from "catching murderers and thieves."[100]

White residents, persuaded by such bluster, credited Bulldog Johnny Grosch with safeguarding public safety and reducing crime. During his tenure as the chief of detectives, the murder rate fell by 27 percent, earning him praise from city leaders and white New Orleanians and reinforcing support for his methods. The *New Orleans Times-Picayune*, for instance, declared that he "made gangsters a bullet-marked legend in New Orleans."[101] Local residents seemed unaware that the national homicide rate plunged by 35.2 percent during this span.

But the politics of race infused both Grosch's crime-fighting mission and popular support for his methods. Most white New Orleanians applauded Grosch's philosophy, averring that violent predators and other dangerous characters, particularly African American criminals, sacrificed their constitutional rights and were not entitled to exploit the legal system to jeopardize public safety. The Louisiana legislature weighed in on the debate and unanimously commended Grosch and his selectively illegal law-and-order measures. "Unless drastic steps are taken at once," according to their 1938 formal resolution expressing "moral support" for his efforts, "white supremacy will be endangered."[102] Not even repeated allegations of corruption or indictments for fraud and bribery, including huge payoffs from vice lords and expensive gifts from local gangsters, such as a "Cadillac limousine," dampened white support for John Grosch and the racialized policing practices he championed.[103] Much like District Attorney Eugene Stanley, John Grosch perceived crime and guilt in racial terms. Both men used their positions and authority to institutionalize this view, conflating law and order with racial control, seeing themselves as guardians of law and order, rather than champions of racial custom. Nonetheless, during the 1940s, Grosch established a "civil organization" committed to the "cause of white supremacy," echoing Stanley's worldview.[104]

Chief Grosch also encouraged his men to employ violent methods. He promoted the fiercest, most aggressive cops into the detective unit he headed and rewarded them with pay raises and high-profile assignments, including his brother and son. Patrolmen who employed deadly force often immediately joined the detective force. All at once, New Orleans detectives became the department's elite crime fighters, and members of the unit emerged at the most violent, homicidal law enforcers in the city. These unflinching specialists tackled and cracked the toughest cases, extracted confessions from the most terrifying predators, committed an enormous share of police homicides, and claimed credit for the city's plunging violent crime rate, legitimizing and institutionalizing violent law enforcement.[105] Outraged by the unit's record, one local attorney termed the detective squad "Grosch and his armed thugs."[106]

Grosch normalized such practices, which then extended beyond the department's detective unit and gave other interwar cops, confident that department officials supported such behavior, license to imitate his violent methods.[107] One young cop explained prominent detectives established "brutality to be a general practice, and that he just followed the lead of the older men."[108] Some patrolmen, who fully qualified as "rogue cops," copied the Grosch brothers, routinely brutalized suspects, boasted far and wide of their sadism, and gleefully tortured African American residents, accelerating the racialized definition of the rule of law.

Lawrence Terrebonne belonged to this group. Born in 1895 in working-class New Orleans, he dropped out of school at the age of ten, served in the military during the Great War, held a variety of unskilled jobs, and joined the police in 1929 as a doorman, assembling a checkered service record. Terrebonne survived numerous complaints—for brutality, drunkenness, and disorderly conduct.[109] He repeatedly beat and threatened to execute African American suspects.[110] Like Willie Grosch, Terrebonne also bragged about his brutality.[111] But unlike the infamous detective, Terrebonne's bluster was largely hyperbolic. On one occasion, Terrebonne shot a suspect and then bellowed that his victim was "very lucky that he did not shoot him twice. It is not my custom," Terrebonne announced, "to shoot a 'N-----' once and stop. I always follow the first shot with a second one, and the second shot means another dead 'N-----'; I've killed three 'N-----s' already, and you're lucky you're not the fourth one."[112] Neither police nor coroner's records support his Willie Grosch–like claims, however. He used the braggadocio as an instrument of racial terrorism, reminding African American residents that he could kill them under the cover of police authority.

Though even more violent, David Marks's career mirrored Terrebonne's, complete with bravado about killing African American suspects, myriad complaints for brutality and reprimands for violations of departmental procedures. But police officials defended the patrolman, actively misleading the courts—and the public—about Marks's record. The lifelong New Orleanian joined the department in 1924 and walked the same beat for two decades. Marks fatally shot an African American burglary suspect and an African American prowler in Willie Grosch–style executions, even asserting that he fired in response to hip-pocket moves and in defense of his life. Before killing the unarmed thirty-six-year-old Clarence Thompson, who had raised his arms to surrender, Marks screamed, "Halt, you black son-of-a-b----h." According to numerous witnesses, the patrolman, from a distance of ten feet, shot Thompson "like a rat."[113] The victim's neighbors told reporters that well before the murder, the fifty-eight-year-old police veteran had bickered with Thompson at a local vegetable stand, had threatened to kill "that n-----," and had "boast[ed] that he had already killed thirteen Negroes."[114] During the hearing to investigate the death of Clarence Thompson, Police Superintendent George Reyer, the Grosch brothers' benefactor, described Marks as a fine officer and testified that Marks "had been a member of the department for 17 years and had never been charged with any infraction of police rules," overlooking his suspensions for the neglect of duty, disobedience, conduct unbecoming an official, and forcing young girls into his patrol car.[115] After fifteen minutes of deliberation, a grand jury ruled the killing "justifiable homicide" committed in the line of duty.[116] Much like Lawrence Terrebonne, David Marks was volatile and unpredictable, gloated about shooting African American residents, and borrowed Willie Grosch's methods.

The Killer Twins, Bulldog Johnny Grosch, and Buttercup Burns's influence, however, extended beyond the racial brutality of Terrebonne, Marks, and a handful of other erratic, sadistic cops. Some policemen imitated the Grosches' practices, even transporting African American suspects for "a ride" to Willie's Grosch's favorite spot on the Air-Line Highway, beating or shooting them and then fabricating narratives to justify the preemptive violence. On August 6, 1941, James Smith, a fifty-year-old sergeant, for example, forced a witness into a patrol car, drove him to the specific secluded site of Grosch's executions, quickly became frustrated with Charlie Sims, shot the twenty-nine-year-old day gardener, and then claimed—successfully—that he had acted in self-defense.[117] But cops such as Smith were outliers on a police force with over eight hundred officers. Members of the small, elite detective force committed a disproportionate share of police homicides and the egregious police brutality.

Most New Orleans cops carried their racial sensibilities to the streets and treated African American residents with disdain, though their embrace of Southern racial custom did not typically produce extreme violence. The majority of municipal policemen refrained from shooting or beating African American residents or publicly extolling such practices. Nonetheless, the horrific brutality of New Orleans detectives buttressed so-called good cops' authority and haunted every encounter with African American residents. Detectives' violent methods and other policemen's nonviolent interactions with these residents comprised different layers of a single, larger system of racial control in which an implicit threat of violence always existed, even when it was not invoked or employed.

African American residents knew that any encounter with a policeman could land them in the "damnable 12th" for interrogation with a cop wielding a heated stove poker, at detective headquarters being tortured by John Grosch, in Willie Grosch's vehicle, or in the clutches of the other vicious detectives, for patrolmen routinely called in—or threatened to call in—specialists, the department's "expert technicians," when high-profile crimes occurred on their beats, when African American residents refused to reveal potentially relevant information, expressed reluctance to provide testimony, were not fully compliant, or for no reason at all.[118] "Where the Negro is involved," an African American journalist explained, they "treat their victims as they please, with no thought or fear of the consequences."[119] One resident noted that African American New Orleanians routinely "witnessed the unmerciful beating and kicking of negroes by the police."[120] Detectives' law enforcement methods always loomed, generating unabating vulnerability for African American New Orleanians.[121]

Although interwar cops focused their crime-fighting efforts on young, poor African Americans—the newcomers who comprised the imaginary invading army of "bad n-----s"—older, wealthier African American New Orleanians might also, without any explanation or logic, be delivered to the most loathsome, feared interrogation rooms or, worse still, to remote settings on the Air-Line Highway. "Who knows just who will be the next victim of police brutalities," an African American journalist asked in 1934.[122] "No classes of Negroes," another observer noted, "are wholly exempt."[123] In response to this omnipresent danger, many African American New Orleanians either fled from cops, which seemed to confirm cops' notions of their guilt and justify more aggressive actions, or these residents nominally cooperated with policemen. The former option often yielded horrific results, but the latter operated as a subtler form of racial dominance. Patrolmen discovered that African Americans on their beats sometimes turned in offenders, voluntarily provided information and witness testimony, and in other ways cooperated with them as these residents cultivated the goodwill of cops as a hedge against the "toils" of detectives.[124] "Even when they are not violating the laws," a New Orleans detective explained, "Negroes are very, very scared and afraid of the police."[125] "All [African American] citizens," Leon Lewis lamented in 1938 in the *Louisiana Weekly*, were "at the mercy of a band of blood-thirsty police."[126]

The influence, infamy, and crime-solving acumen of New Orleans detectives, especially John Grosch, also reached beyond the city during this era. Just as local patrolmen invited detectives to extract confessions in tough cases, small-town sheriffs throughout the lower Mississippi Valley also turned to Grosch to interrogate uncooperative African American suspects. In 1933, for example, Thomas Magee, the Bogalusa police chief, transported thirty-eight-year-old Allie Mae Purvis from Washington Parish to New Orleans so that Chief Grosch could interrogate her and an eighteen-year-old African American suspected accomplice in the woman's husband's death. Using his renowned "'third degree' methods," Grosch was able to "wring confessions" from both.[127] Likewise, Sheriff O.L. Meador of Harrison County, Mississippi, brought Grosch, whom he considered an "expert on extracting confessions," to his local jail house to interrogate a robbery suspect. According to Elliott Shaw, the New Orleans detective "sat him in a chair and gave him five minutes to confess." After the time had expired, Shaw testified, Grosch and a colleague "beat him in the stomach and on the back of his head with their fists. He said he fell to the floor and was pulled up by his hair." Another man, however, would later confess to the robberies.[128] "Grosch and his thugs" achieved celebrity status as crime fighters and beat, bludgeoned, and tortured African American throughout the Gulf region, though the shift from civilian to police racial control occurred more slowly in rural areas.

The Grosches, James Burns, and members of the New Orleans detective squad were distinctive but not unique. Every Southern city had comparable "expert technicians," who employed signature methods to extract confessions, executed African American suspects, and imposed racial domination in the name of law and order. In a neighboring Louisiana city, William Stander assumed this role and murdered six African American suspects "in the line of duty."[129] Interwar Memphis had Jack Crumby, a grizzled detective, who killed at least five suspects, and Alfred Clark, a detective who fatally shot at least six African American suspects.[130] One cop in Helena, Arkansas, tallied six African American victims between 1934 and 1939.[131]

Early twentieth-century ethnographers described policemen with comparable records and reputations throughout the urban South. Social scientists studying Natchez, for instance, reported that "one policeman spoke of another policeman with professional admiration: 'We pick up anyone who acts suspicious and turn them over to Joe, who questions them. He certainly knows how to find out what they know, and by the time he gets through, they tell everything they know.'"[132] In his analysis of another city in the region, sociologist Arthur Raper discovered that two policemen served this role. "One of these officers has put notches on his gun for five Negroes he killed, while the other with even more notches has exhibited 'a fine lack of racial discrimination.' These two officers take especially hard assignments, however, [and] are called into situations when somebody 'needs to be killed.'" Atlanta's police department included a four-time killer of African American residents, usually complete with Willie Grosch's references to hip-pocket moves to justify murdering unarmed suspects. In the Deep South, the sociologist explained, "a common explanation is that the man was reaching for his hip pocket as if to get a gun or knife. Sometimes knives are planted on dead men to make peace officers appear the more defensible, while in others such subterfuge is not even considered necessary. The mere statement by the officer that 'he reached as if to get a gun' or 'refused to halt' suffices."[133]

The Grosch brothers' and Burns's counterparts in other Southern cities employed similar methods to extract confessions from African American suspects during the 1930s and early 1940s as well. Using the comparable interrogation practices as New Orleans detectives, policemen throughout the interwar South extracted false confessions. An Atlanta policemen, thirty-six-year-old Warren Sutherland, adapted Burns's interrogation technique and used a heated tacking iron to secure confessions.[134] Memphis detectives preferred John Grosch's method and maintained a "whipping room" in police headquarters, complete with a "torture chair." Interrogators tethered African American suspects, threatened to kill them, and beat them until they confessed.[135] Moreover, just as sheriffs in the lower Mississippi Valley turned to the New Orleans chief of detectives to interrogate defiant prisoners, their mid-South counterparts relied on Memphis third-degree specialists.[136] Appeals of the resulting convictions poured into state courts, and defense attorneys and local civil rights activists flooded the national office of the NAACP seeking legal assistance with their cases.[137] Buttercup Burns and the Grosch brothers had larger-than-life personalities, but their law enforcement methods were more typical of interwar Southern cops than distinctive. Systemic police brutality, disguised as the rule of law, infected race relations throughout the region.

. . .

When law and order fused racial control with crime control, policing evolved into a bulwark for white supremacy. Spearheaded in New Orleans by John Grosch and his handpicked "cream-of-the-crop" detectives, a multilayered system of racial violence infused, permeated, and poisoned law enforcement, employing both explicit and subtler forms of dominance. His small cadre of depraved cops and nearly a thousand relatively nonviolent policemen operated as a single, interconnected department. The potential for brutality hovered over every aspect of law enforcement and every African American resident of the city. Detectives, however, committed the most purposeful acts of racial brutality, accounting for much of the police homicide and cop brutality during the 1930s and early 1940s. Their notion of protecting white New Orleanians from the threat posed by African American residents fueled a 62.6 percent hike in police homicides between the early 1920s and the early 1930s, most often in circumstances similar to Willie Grosch's 1937 execution of Charles Handy.

But the impact of such violence proved to be still greater than the numbers would suggest. Even at its early 1930s level, the victims of cops' use of deadly force accounted for only 6.6 percent of the city's African American homicide victims. Yet the threat and vulnerability haunted daily life for African American New Orleanians, and municipal cops used this vulnerability to garner support from white residents, to enhance police legitimacy, and to buttress racial dominance in the age of Jim Crow. Detectives, but other New Orleans law enforcers as well, trumpeted and embellished reports of police brutality against African American suspects. They not only boasted about such savagery committed in the name of law and order but also counted on reports of such violence circulating freely in the city's African American community. Killer cops expected the relatives of their victims to recount suspects' final moments to friends and neighbors and wanted African American residents who saw beatings or heard about police executions to serve as witnesses to the power and unbridled authority of the police. Murderous detectives in other cities employed comparable campaigns of terror to maintain racial dominance, casting themselves as selfless public servants, assuming the dangerous, unsightly work to protect white society.

The ferocious brutality of interwar detectives served multiple and overlapping purposes. It tapped and exploited white racial anxiety in ways that amplified voters' perception that they depended on men such as the Grosches to maintain law and order. Ironically, detectives' savage, murderous practices enhanced white support for expansive police authority and legitimacy. Concentrating police brutality in the hands of the detective squad also separated white civilians and most cops from the violence that provided the foundation of their status.[138] "Respectable" New Orleanians, and their counterparts throughout the region, could affirm their rejection of mob justice and their belief in white cultural superiority. Similarly, most municipal law enforcers both assumed the role of "good cop" and maintained the explicit capacity to unleash violence against African American suspects. Cream-of-the-crop detectives shielded white residents and patrolmen from the institutional sadism that preserved white privilege and bolstered police authority. And the nearly complete disfranchisement of African American city dwellers ensured this system of systemic racial oppression translated into political power, remained self-sustaining, and operated both within and outside of plain sight—for white residents and municipal cops.

The egregious, sadistic methods of Buttercup Burns, Bulldog Johnny Grosch, and the Killer Twins informed and contaminated every encounter between New Orleans cops and African American residents. "Each [police] slaying to no small degree terrifies entire Negro communities," one observer explained, "for that is its purpose."[139] Detectives beat and murdered suspects specifically as an instrument of domination, deployed to control the larger African American community. Policing fortified white supremacy and evolved into a haunting form of state-supported racial terrorism in New Orleans, throughout the urban South, and subsequently across the nation.

FIVE

"Negroes Are Willing to Die Rather Than Submit to the White Man's Terror"

"THE LAW IS WHITE," sociologist Arthur Raper observed in his 1940 analysis of race and police violence in the South. "So too are the officials who administer it."[1] In New Orleans, every elected city official, police officer, prosecutor, assistant prosecutor, juror, and judge was white, as was nearly every registered voter. Not all white New Orleanians applauded police violence against African American residents, but most embraced white supremacy, feared that African Americans threatened social stability, and believed that racial control provided the bedrock for law and order. Thus, they granted law enforcers expansive authority to employ virtually any means necessary to preserve racial dominance. Emboldened by this capacious mandate, some New Orleans policemen beat, tortured, shot, and murdered African American suspects, doing so at will and with impunity. Violent cops who engaged in egregious acts of racial violence and even executed African American New Orleanians faced no legal consequences for their conduct. City leaders, voters, and criminal justice officials tolerated, encouraged, and ignored police brutality masquerading as the rule of law. The most sadistic, aggressive detectives, led by the Grosch brothers, bragged about their methods and reaped handsome rewards for their violence, ranging from public acclaim to bloated salaries.

African American New Orleanians recognized their vulnerability to police brutality and racial terrorism and knew that they had little legal or political recourse. They did not, however, submit to such attacks. Despite widespread white support and complicity for such brutality and court endorsement of coercive, even deadly treatment, African Americans resisted, challenged, and denounced police brutality in myriad individual and collective ways. Nor were they without some white allies in this crusade. A small group of white civil rights and labor activists shared their outrage and joined them in protest, often becoming targets themselves. African American resistance cast a glaring light on illegal police conduct, making it impossible for city officials, jurors, prosecutors, voters, and white newspaper readers to deny being aware of systemic, institutionalized police brutality. But protest in any form came at a high price. It triggered a ferocious backlash and unleashed even more horrific violence, greater police repression, and more frantic white support for police methods. Cycles of resistance and retrenchment infected race relations in ways that persisted long after surviving victims' wounds healed and scars faded.

In many ways, Willie Gray's 1936 ordeal and the ensuing fallout typified this toxic spiral. A sixteen-year-old, diminutive, African American high school student, he committed no crime, came from a respectable family, and had never been arrested. But this did not prevent Gray from becoming a victim of police violence. On March 14, fifty-two-year-old Alice Gray gave her son $1.50 and instructed him to purchase a pair of trousers. Willie visited a South Rampart Street clothing store and discovered that the pants would cost $2. He then walked a short distance to the shop where his eighteen-year-old brother Lawrence worked as a porter. The younger Gray borrowed fifty cents from Lawrence and learned that his brother would soon complete his shift and return home. Willie bought the trousers, after which he strolled through the neighborhood, killing time while he waited for his brother. William Drewes, a fifty-one-year-old detective with a fifth-grade education, and his partner, thirty-six-year-old John Walsh, saw the high school student and demanded to know the contents of the package in his hand.

Frightened by the unexpected encounter, Gray nervously explained that it contained pants he had just purchased and "tore open the package and showed" the detectives.[2] The cops, however, insisted that the teenager had stolen the clothing, deemed him a "suspicious and dangerous character," and, according to Gray, "told me to get into the automobile."[3] In 1936, every African American New Orleanian knew about the infamous "ride" and how it often ended, and the sixteen-year-old panicked, dropped his parcel, and ran. Drewes ordered two young, white seamen on the sidewalk to grab the teenager, screaming that he "had been breaking into places." Tommy Kane and Dick Marks complied and held young Gray. Drewes reached them and mauled the teenager. "The negro wasn't doing anything and the cop began twisting his arms behind his back," Kane and Marks told reporters. "They kept walking the negro up and down, twisting his arms behind his back and finally they put him in an automobile and drove off." Drewes also battered his young prisoner's head with the butt of his gun. Terrified, Gray leaped out of the moving vehicle, prompting Drewes to shoot him as a dangerous, flee-ing criminal.[4]

The veteran cop's formal report, however, offered a very different narra-tive. Gray, he explained, behaved in a "suspicious" manner, "failed to give a good account of himself," tried to escape, and defied his instructions to halt. But, with the help of the sailors, he apprehended the suspect. While Walsh drove to the 1st precinct, where they intended to question Gray, described by classmates as "frail, even rather cowardly," the teenager viciously attacked them.[5] "He suddenly punched me in the face," Drewes wrote, and "the negro grabbed Walsh around the throat almost wrecking the car and he kicked me in the groin. I shot him in the stomach as he was getting out" of the vehicle. The report omitted that Drewes fired his revolver twice, one bullet hitting Gray and the other striking a white bystander. Walsh conveyed the bleeding teenager to Charity Hospital, where he lapsed into "critical" condition. Police Superintendent George Reyer posted a cop at the hospital to guard the dangerous prisoner.[6]

Henry Gray demanded justice for his son. The following day, Reyer announced "that he will make no formal investigation of the shooting because he is convinced that 'the boy kicked one of the officers. I have only the statement of the boy against that of the two officers and I do not think the boy's statement is sufficient to warrant an investigation,' he said."[7] Gray's fifty-three-year-old father, the longtime pastor of a local Methodist church, turned to his ministerial colleagues for support. Forty-five African American ministers, "representing more than 50,000 communicants," quickly drafted a petition "protesting the increasing brutality on the part of the city police," requesting a meeting with Reyer and demanding an investigation into the shooting. The superintendent grudgingly agreed to speak with the clergy-men. The meeting, however, went badly, with Reyer expressing his unquali-fied support for Drewes and closing the case. "I grant you that the boy might not have been doing anything wrong," Superintendent Reyer stated, "but in the opinion of the officers he was acting suspicious [sic] and after he was arrested, I can't understand why he should have put up such a fight. I can't blame the officers for what they did. If my own brother would grab me around the neck when I was arresting him I think that I would shoot, too. You see if that boy had gotten the officer's gun then they would have been in a bad way themselves."[8] "If he had done nothing that he was afraid to have been confronted with, why did he put a fight with these officers?" the police chief added.[9] Reyer concluded that "the negro prisoner had made such an attack upon the arresting officers as to justify their shooting him."[10] The superintendent then chided the ministers for focusing on Willie Gray and ignoring the cases of "several negroes recently arrested for criminal assault on white women."[11] Reyer's comparison of Gray's case and rapists somehow implied that brooking no resistance from an innocent African American teenager protected white women.

Frustrated by Reyer's response, the clergymen called for a mass protest meeting. A group of white reformers, labor leaders, and child-welfare activists, ranging from the Louisiana Society for the Prevention of Cruelty to Children to the New Orleans Teachers' Association, rallied to the minsters' support. They endorsed the pastors' plan to stage a public protest against Gray's treatment and police methods more broadly.

Reyer reacted quickly and decisively. First, he urged his police officers to exercise caution in their use of deadly force, not because Drewes had nearly killed an innocent teenager but rather to avoid the "danger attached to shooting at a prisoner because an innocent person may be seriously wounded by a stray bullet," a reference to Clarence Alker, the white bystander who suffered a "superficial wound" in the Gray shooting.[12] The superintendent then reaffirmed his support for Drewes and "banned" the protest meeting, warning that the police would "break it up" and framing the demonstration as a ruse. "The negro element," he declared, "is trying in some way to cause trouble, which in my mind may result in a race riot here. This thing has gone far enough."[13] Police officials also warned the ministers that they would not tolerate "any criticism of the police or the city administration" and would not permit any protest gathering.[14] Perhaps because of reports about the recent Harlem race riot, Reyer announced that he would flood the site of the proposed gathering with cops to forestall racial violence and preserve law and order.

The police superintendent acknowledged that Gray might have engaged in no unlawful or menacing behavior, conceding to the ministers that "you are probably right" about the teenager, but the incident underscored the threat that African American New Orleanians posed to white residents and social stability as well as the necessity for detectives to defend their own lives and safeguard the rule of law, pandering to the racial anxieties of local voters.[15] White newspapers also conceded that a "mixup" prompted Drewes to shoot Willie Gray and that his official account was "garbled." Nonetheless, the reporting emphasized that the detective discharged his weapon in self-defense after being assaulted.[16] Thus, in both the formal police response to the incident and white newspaper coverage of the shooting, Gray, instantly transformed from a "frail" teenager to a powerful, ferocious attacker, had provoked the use of the deadly force. The police became the victims, and protesters endangered public safety. Again and again, this cycle repeated itself in interwar New Orleans and throughout the region. African American resistance to abuse, allegations of police brutality, and protest efforts produced conflicting public responses. Police violence mobilized the African American community, energizing the civil rights movement across the South.[17] But the resulting African American reactions triggered a backlash, replete with police denials, reminders that African Americans preyed on whites, and vehement reaffirmations of white support for racialized policing as a prescription for law and order. Protest signaled dangerous subversion, an overt challenge to the racial hierarchy and hence to social stability, necessitating rapid, violent repression from law enforcers.

. . .

Every African American New Orleanian (and Southerner), particularly young men, feared the approach of a cop. Some suspects had committed or witnessed criminal acts, though the lion's share had not, yet they worried that they would be beaten and perhaps murdered by the "guardians of the law."[18] And so the reflex, even for African Americans who had done nothing wrong, was to avoid being arrested, forced into a police car, shuttled to a precinct house, such as the "damnable 12th," for questioning, or, worse still, taken on "the ride" to the Air-Line Highway. Evading apprehension took many forms.

Fleeing constituted the most common reaction. African American New Orleanians defied cops' commands that they "halt" and ran. In an editorial entitled "It's Happened Again," the *Louisiana Weekly* analyzed a series of deadly police shootings. When policemen see a "Negro boy running" from them, the editor lamented, they assume "he had committed some dastardly deed . . . terrible enough to be shot without a chance." Given this ugly reality and the frequency of cops responding with deadly force, why did they flee?[19] In one such lethal police shooting, a fifteen-year-old, 110-pound "suspect" died from a bullet wound in the back after he "failed to heed the officers' call to halt to question him concerning a scream by Mrs. Charles Camp," a thirty-seven-year-old white woman who heard "loud noises in the street," and ran.[20]

Charles Jones, the policeman who killed the teenager, acknowledged that his "only reason for shooting the youth [was] that he heard a white woman scream and saw the boy running."[21] Willie Gray, and countless others, anticipated being beaten (or worse), chose to flee, and suffered horrific consequences when the arresting cops assumed that flight indicated guilt of some sort and employed lethal force. Such police behavior reinforced African American New Orleanians' instinct to run. Civil rights activists throughout the urban South reported comparable responses. "Why should not Negroes tremble in fear of their lives when called to submit to arrest," a Birmingham NAACP official asked.[22]

Other suspects resisted more forcefully, ripping themselves free from the cop's grasp, shoving the arresting officer away to avoid apprehension, or striking their abusers to facilitate their escape. They knew from experiencing brutality, witnessing police violence, hearing neighborhood accounts of savage beatings and summary executions, or from the self-congratulatory bluster of Willie Grosch, Lawrence Terrebonne, or other sadistic cops that law enforcers "regard any Negro who resists a policeman as a 'bad n-----,' one who must be 'taken care of.'"[23] Some, such as Percy Thompson, expected to die when they refused to submit, and used deadly force to defend themselves. Writing in 1943, one sociologist described similar episodes throughout the South. Charles Johnson explained that some police-brutality victims felt compelled to battle for survival. "He will fight and take no thought of consequences because he has no recourse to either whites or Negroes for protection of his person. He is his own and only protection."[24] The editor of the city's *Louisiana Weekly* grumbled that "Negroes who are willing to die rather than submit to the white man's terror, are said to 'run amuck.'" These men "are not 'running amuck,' but have chosen what they think to be the best way to defend themselves, hence, fighting it out is the better part of valor with them."[25] Local cops shot dozens of brutality victims when they offered even token resistance, though the threat to the policemen, which provided the legal justification for the use of preemptive force, was largely chimerical. Between the Thompson turmoil in 1932 and 1945, New Orleans cops killed twenty-two African American suspects, but no policemen died at the hands of an African American suspect. Nor was the pattern different in other Southern cities.[26]

Survivors of police brutality often responded after the fact, hoping to receive justice from the courts or at least discourage such conduct by exposing the rampant violence to public scrutiny. They filed complaints with prosecutors and police superintendents, disclosed their mistreatment to their attorneys, contacted civil rights organizations, testified during their trials, and reported the beatings to local newspapers. One local prison reform group received so many abuse complaints that the organization urged the district attorney to require the parish coroner to conduct physical examinations on "all prisoners signing confessions."[27] Similarly, a New Orleans civil liberties organization reported receiving stacks of such complaints each week.[28] At the urging of defense attorneys and reformers, battered suspects frequently gathered testimony from witnesses, statements from relatives who saw their bruised, disfigured bodies, and affidavits from physicians who tended to their injuries. Victims also secured photographic evidence of their wounds.[29] During their trials, often the product of coerced confessions, many prisoners removed their shirts and displayed their mauled, maimed bodies to jurors and judges. The attorneys for Cornelius Brown and Louis Foley, for example, told the trial court judge and jurors that Lawrence Terrebonne and Willie Grosch had beaten them until they confessed to the 1937 shooting of a white shopkeeper. The lawyers then instructed "the two negroes strip to the waist and exhibit [the] scars and bruises on their backs, shoulders, and legs."[30] Similarly, the relatives of African Americans who died in police custody or were fatally shot while fleeing or resisting New Orleans law enforcers obtained copies of autopsy reports and shared these files with district attorneys and newspapers. This evidence documented the abuse and exposed the "whitewash" that filled police accounts of the arrests and interrogations.[31] "The public," an African American journalist groused, "however skeptical, cannot refute the evidence as offered by men's bruised and scarred bodies."[32] Simply put, the victims and relatives of police-brutality victims did not submit or suffer in silence.

A few survivors of vicious beatings found creative ways to support their allegations. On trial for burglary in 1940, forty-two-year-old Maurice Ruttman testified that detectives had bludgeoned him until he confessed. When the prosecutor claimed that his confession had been entirely "voluntary," Ruttman's attorney directed the judge to examine the confession statement more closely. The clever defendant had signed it "Maurice H. Duress Ruttman," compelling A. D. Henriques to order the document "thrown out."[33]

African American responses to surging police brutality assumed other forms as well. Many employed strategies to reduce their vulnerability. Some feigned cooperation as a form of risk aversion, manipulating patrolmen into viewing them as "good negroes" and hence shielding themselves from the "bad n-----" label and the suspicion, arrests, interrogations, and violence that too often ensued. They provided information to beat cops, offered witness testimony, and even revealed the locations of suspects, thus ingratiating themselves to the police officers.[34] "Good n-----s often secure protection," a sociologist explained in 1940, "by voluntarily reporting to the police the presence of questionable strangers or lawless persons."[35] Nominal compliance with individual policemen occasionally yielded tangible benefits. On trial for murder and possessing an extensive criminal record, Milton Pierce, for example, summoned Captain William Bell to testify as a character witness on his behalf. The officer told the court that the suspected killer "has never given me any trouble," adding that "I have always known him to be a quiet negro."[36]

African American New Orleanians, particularly women, occasionally confronted murderous cops in public settings. After Patrolman John Licali fatally shot twenty-nine-year-old Felton Robinson for making an ambiguous motion, the officer failed to find the weapon that the victim was supposedly grabbing. Licali and other cops scoured the Robinson home in search of the imaginary gun that would corroborate the cop's self-defense account. As policemen and neighborhood women crowded into the Robinson's living room, the victim's sister-in-law asked, "Which one of you shot him?" Embarrassed and seemingly cowed, Licali and the other cops abruptly fled from the house.[37] Such conduct did not reduce brutality, but it represented another way in which the African American community refused to submit passively or silently.

As brutality complaints and killings skyrocketed, African American community leaders and community activists acknowledged the futility of these individual efforts and urged more collective, strident protest, calling for mass meetings to demand accountability, justice, and reform. Between the early 1920s and the early 1930s, the police homicide rate climbed by nearly two-thirds, and the number of brutality allegations and complaints swelled even faster.[38] "Hardly a day passes but that some Negro man, falling into the toils of the law, has a story to tell of unnecessary man-handling on the part of the arresting officers," an African American journalist lamented.[39] Nonetheless, "as far as some white juries are concerned," he thundered, "the killing of innocent Negroes by policemen is no graver an offense than killing a rat or an insect."[40] In 1933, the editor of the *Louisiana Weekly* declared that "nothing will be done until the Negroes get up and do something themselves" and issued a "call to arms."[41] The president of a local civil rights organization concurred, conceding that "there is very little that anyone can do to curb such brutality other than protesting."[42] Shortly after William Drewes shot

Willie Gray, one community leader called on local ministers "to arouse Race members in a definite manner and to build up public sentiment against increasing police brutality."[43]

The tidal wave of police violence transformed African American activism in interwar New Orleans and throughout the South. Demands for protest redefined the local branch of the NAACP, for example. From its 1915 founding until the late 1930s, the organization had been cautious, its presidents reluctant to criticize city officials. Elite, high-born Creole leaders, anxious to preserve their ties to the white power structure, refrained from confronting municipal officials and hence reacted tepidly to police-brutality cases.[44] Again and again, African American New Orleanians complained that the president of the local chapter dismissed demands for concerted action. Instead, he chided them for making such requests unless they were dues-paying members.[45] The chapter president also refused to investigate brutality complaints if victims had prison records, determining that only allegations from the most sympathetic, nonthreatening suspects would be considered.[46] One African American editor became so incensed that he termed the New Orleans chapter "dormant."[47] Complaints poured into NAACP national headquarters. This hue and cry spearheaded the emergence of younger, more radical leaders, and, by the end of the decade, the chapter became a forceful critic of municipal law enforcement.[48]

Demands for police reform grew louder and more insistent, sparking a sea change in African American activism and the civil rights movement in New Orleans. Allegations of "rampant" police brutality unified the local community across class lines and generational lines.[49] In response to the shooting of Willie Gray and similar cases, religious leaders became especially active. Such violence ignited mass protest gatherings, and calls for police reform became more frequent and more difficult for city officials and police authorities to ignore.

White New Orleanians reacted to allegations of racialized policing and systemic brutality in divergent ways. A tiny group of activists consistently voiced outrage and joined forces with African American civil rights leaders in protest. Harold N. Lee, a philosophy professor at Tulane University, became the most irascible and visible white critic of police brutality. The Ohio-born scholar established the Louisiana League for the Preservation of Constitutional Rights in 1937 and led the organization through the interwar era. Mirroring the wider civil rights movement in the city, Lee became an increasingly committed to exposing and denouncing police violence.

From its inception, the Louisiana League had condemned police brutality, charging that local cops "willfully disregarded" core "provisions of the Constitution of Louisiana and the constitution of the United States."[50] But early on, the organization took a cautious approach. Although Lee challenged the use of third-degree interrogation methods, he focused the League's efforts on "educational activities," informing the press and city officials about complaints that police officers routinely violated the civil liberties of African American residents and employed illegal, constitutionally prohibited arrest procedures and interrogation methods.[51] He also urged the superintendent and the district attorney to investigate abuse allegations and discourage detectives from using coercion to extract confessions. But Lee avoided confrontational clashes with city leaders, and the League initially excluded African American New Orleanians.[52]

By the end of the decade, however, the philosophy professor waged a more combative campaign against racialized policing. Jettisoning his previous respectful, almost lawyerly tone, he launched piercing denunciations of the "flagrant use of arbitrary and dictatorial methods by the police" against African American New Orleanians and asserted that the behavior of detectives "is closely parallel to the way Fascism arose in Italy and Germany."[53] Frustrated by city officials' unwillingness to rein in sadistic cops, Lee employed increasingly incendiary strategies, exploiting political fights to intensify the pressure on municipal officials. New Orleans mayors had long battled with state leaders over patronage jobs on the docks, and the League began to report brutality cases to the governor and attorney general, urging them to investigate abuse complaints in order to embarrass city officials and undermine their political authority in Baton Rouge. Similarly, Lee revealed police abuses to Department of Justice officials as Washington policymakers bickered with New Orleans politicians about New Deal projects, specifically control over federal funds and the jobs that they generated. He urged the Civil Liberties Division of the DOJ, for example, to scrutinize municipal law enforcement practices and "prosecute" violent cops "under federal laws."[54] Unabashed about his motives, Lee explained, "I think we are now in a position to make the police in New Orleans more or less acutely uncomfortable on the score of brutality and illegal arrests" and argued that "we have them on the run through two channels, the State Attorney's office and the Federal authorities. Both of these channels are easily available to us now because the political scandals have so greatly stirred everything up."[55]

But Lee persuaded few city officials or white New Orleanians and became a pariah. Mayors and police superintendents typically ignored his demands, and hate mail poured into the reformer and his organization. Some included threats, unmistakably invoking the language and methods of Willie Grosch. One unsigned, handwritten 1939 letter addressed to "N----- Loving Harold Lee," for instance, began with, "If ever there was a man that needed the living Hell beat out of him, that man is you—And let me warn you that one more crack out of you in regard to all this (n-----) protection, we'll run you out of this city." The writer advised Lee that "we better not hear another word from you, one way or another, in regard to (n-----s) or we will take you out for a ride + I'll guarantee you'll never mention (n-----s) again."[56] Membership in Lee's League peaked in 1940 at just 271 in a city with half a million residents and a well-documented reputation for police violence.[57]

Some labor organizations vociferously protested police brutality against African American residents as well. The United Transport Workers, the National Maritime Union, Workers Alliance Association, and the Congress of Industrial Organizations were reliable allies of civil rights activists, as was the International Labor Defense division of the Communist Party, though these were smaller groups locally and perceived in New Orleans's white community as disreputable extremists. City officials most often ignored such critics but sometimes explicitly mentioned them in order to discredit police detractors and enhance white solidarity with law enforcers and support for their methods.[58]

Women's and child-welfare organizations also occasionally partnered with the African American community, Lee's League, and labor unions to protest police brutality. These alliances, which bridged racial and class divisions, however, tended to be fragile, short-lived, and formed only when specific reform interests "converged" with calls for racial justice.[59] Elite white activists mainly joined anti-brutality protests when cops targeted and beat very young suspects, and they were always quick to qualify their support, emphasizing that they objected to the mistreatment of children rather than to aggressive, violent police methods in general. "Negroes and whites are interested" in the Willie Gray beating and shooting, Susan Gillean, the forty-nine-year-old executive secretary of the Children's Bureau of the Louisiana Society for the Prevention of Cruelty to Children indicated, "because they see trouble ahead for all youths unless the police are put under such pressure as to bring to a stop their uncalled for brutality."[60] Reacting to another police assault on a child, she insisted that the "third degree is barbarous enough when it is used on grown men, but when children are clubbed, slapped, beaten with hose and wire, it is time that something be done."[61] Explaining her organization's enthusiastic participation in protests against Willie Gray's assaulter, she explained that "in this instance racial barriers are forgotten."[62] Another reformer offered a similar parsing, declaring that the abuse allegation "is not a question of color in this case but the protection of the youth of our city."[63] White reformers demanded the humane treatment of children, not racial equality or the end of racialized, violent law enforcement.

Despite their conditional, selective criticism of police brutality, white women often voiced the most pointed, searing attacks on violent cops and their apologists. Racial convention encouraged African American activists to remain respectful, though their occasional allies in the battle felt no such constraints and tore into the city and police officials who justified police violence against children. One elite white reformer, for instance, responded to Superintendent George Reyer's elision of a sixteen-year-old African American abuse victim with a confessed rapist by denouncing his transparent effort "to becloud the real issue in the case of Willie Gray, the brutal beating and shooting of the boy." Reyer, Susan Gillean roared, was "drawing a red herring across the trail" to protect his vicious detectives.[64] The fierce child advocate warned Superintendent Reyer after yet another incidence of horrific abuse against an African American child that "I hope that there will be no whitewashing of the police in this case."[65]

But interracial alliances were rare and fleeting, and even when the victims were children, white reformers sometimes failed to harness their racial sensibilities and dismissed or minimized the brutal beatings of African American teenagers. Mrs. F. I. Williams, the child-welfare chair of the Orleans Parish League of Women Voters, for example, rallied to the defense of the detectives who battered an innocent fifteen-year-old African American, arguing "the boy appeared older" and implying that all African Americans were criminal predators. As a consequence of his race, his brutality claim constituted "much ado about nothing."[66]

Local religious leaders divided along similar lines. African American pastors often organized and led protests against endemic police brutality, and the white ministers of small, racially progressive churches frequently joined their colleagues to challenge beatings and shootings. New Orleans's religious establishment, however, demonstrated less interest.[67] In a city with an overwhelmingly Roman Catholic white population, the local archbishop remained silent on the matter and ignored efforts to enlist him in protests. Archbishop Joseph Francis Rummel, for example, did not even acknowledge his fellow clergymen's petition to investigate Detective Drewes's 1936 shooting of sixteen-year-old Willie Gray.[68]

Most white New Orleanians either shared Rummel's indifference or hailed aggressive, racialized policing, believing that cops had to possess wide discretion to preserve public safety. They seldom criticized the mistreatment of African American residents and usually applauded police methods to combat crime, credited aggressive, unrestrained tactics with reducing violence, and heaped praise on the city's most brutal detectives as the guardians of law and order. In a 1938 editorial in the *New Orleans States* expressing support for the cops who coerced confessions from violent criminals, the writer captured white public opinion. "Of course, the police should not use brutality, even when dealing with such brutal and inhuman young toughs," the journalist averred, yet "nor should murderous thugs be treated with cream puffs and lollipops. But, whatever methods they use, we note that Superintendent Reyer and Chief Grosch have pretty well broken up major crime in this city."[69] Another white writer argued that cops must be afforded wide discretion "to maintain order," and "Department and city officials, and public sentiment, will support policemen who are compelled to kill in the line of duty."[70]

White New Orleanians openly and unapologetically defended violent, even deadly racialized policing. In one of the most egregious cases of the era, where two detectives beat and battered an innocent thirteen-year-old until he signed a confession, a white New Orleanian interrupted the court hearing and declared "it is an outrage to prosecute two white men for beating a 'N----.'"[71] The homeowner whose house was burglarized in this case, expressed only gratitude to the detectives, though the young suspect they coerced into confessing was not the thief. W. E. Gilthorpe, a twenty-nine-year-old white customs official, told a reporter, "I appreciate the efficiency of Detectives Thomas Whalen and Louis Martinez in trying to incarcerate the offenders."[72] In an exposé to the Department of Justice, Harold Lee recounted the comments of grand jurors in one instance of "flagrant abuse of police power." During the court hearing, they announced that "this was case of a policeman shooting a 'n----,' and that was all right."[73] Again and again, in editorials, letters to the editor, courtroom testimony, private correspondence, and elections white New Orleanians affirmed their support for aggressive, violent, racialized policing, insisting that African Americans were so dangerous that, as a group, they should not be protected by constitutional safeguards or legal constraints on law enforcers. "The due process principle," Harold Lee lamented in 1939, "is an empty farce where the third degree is used."[74] Especially for New Orleans's top cops and prosecutors, safeguarding public safety trumped civil liberties, a stance that became an article of pride for them.

Other cops, particularly the veteran detectives who committed the most extreme violence against African American suspects, shared this view and followed Grosch's lead, certain that white residents endorsed and demanded racialized policing. Local policemen insisted that their methods reflected the desires and served the interests of the city's white residents. According to one New Orleans law enforcer, "the policeman is simply the channel of the general white hostility against the Negro." The cop told a sociologist that the "police behave toward Negroes the ways they think white New Orleanians expect them to behave."

Contemporary ethnographers of the region offered similar interpretations, though they emphasized that voter suppression undergirded this view. According to a 1940 study of Southern law enforcement, "an ordinary policeman has no conception of democracy, justice, or even law and order. (Democracy means white voters going to a democratic primary, while justice is the process by which white people keep the country safe from n-----s, communists, and other dangerous people.)"[75] Another interwar scholar reached the same conclusion. "Police officers and court officials," he wrote, "merely point to local values and prevailing practices; they know they are the public agents of the dominant element in the community—and the smaller the number of people in this 'dominant element' and the more completely race and class groups are excluded from responsible participation in community affairs, the more certain will be mass arrests, police brutality, short trials, chain gang sentences, and third degree confessions."[76]

Both Grosch's enduring popularity among white New Orleanians and district attorney Eugene Stanley's landslide election and reelection victories underscored the link between racialized policing and the disfranchisement of African American residents. A reliable supporter of abusive, violent cops, Stanley repeatedly warned white residents of the necessity for preserving racial barriers to voting to safeguard social stability; permitting African Americans to cast ballots "threatened [the] destruction of white supremacy."[77] Police brutality and voter suppression worked hand in glove. Between 1920 and 1940, the number of African Americans registered to vote plunged by 77.3 percent, and the proportion of African American voters tumbled by

88.8 percent. During the same span, the number of these residents killed by the police climbed by 100 percent. On the eve of World War II, African American residents comprised 30.3 percent of the city's population but 0.37 percent of eligible voters and 75 percent of police homicide victims.

In this political climate, and fanned by the inflammatory rhetoric of influential officials, racialized policing buttressed white support for local cops. When detectives pursued racialized law enforcement methods, such as extracting confessions from African American suspects and shooting "suspicious and dangerous characters," whites felt safer, and thus voters ceded greater discretion and legitimacy to local cops. Believing that African American predators "infested" the city, white New Orleanians argued that these residents, as a group, jeopardized social order and therefore "surrendered the civil liberties" enjoyed by other Americans.[78] To the horror of civil rights activists, especially Harold Lee, white city dwellers believed that African American residents could and should be denied constitutional protections in the name of law and order. There was no contradiction between racialized policing and the rule of law. To the contrary, preserving law and order dictated that political and civil rights could not be extended to African American residents. Legal constraints on law enforcement must be selectively ignored. In 1938, the Louisiana legislature explicitly endorsed this view, voting 99–0 to "support" John Grosch's methods.[79]

In short, white New Orleanians overwhelming considered racialized policing, including brutality and the preemptive use of lethal force, legitimate and necessary because African Americans posed a dire threat to their definitions of social stability and law and order. The effects of this attitude were self-sustaining. As cop violence increasingly targeted African American residents, white residents, largely shielded from such law enforcement practices, believed that "their" police operated in appropriate, entirely lawful ways.[80] In their experience, cops, even the Grosch brothers, were fair, reasonable, dedicated to preserving law and order, and committed to the public good—or at least their conception of the public good. They did not fear local detectives or tremble when cops approached them.[81] Nor did they associate precinct houses with sadistic violence. And New Orleans cops did not perceive their ambiguous movements to be menacing and rarely used deadly force in response to furtive motions from white residents. Thus, police conduct seemed increasingly legitimate and professional in the eyes of most white residents just as it became increasingly contaminated by racism and brutality for African American New Orleanians. In the interwar South, municipal cops faithfully served the public interest in the minds of whites because these city dwellers defined the "public" and the "public good" in racial terms.

Some early twentieth-century observers, however, maintained that "law-abiding white citizens" tolerated violent law enforcement because they were "unaware" of the widespread "brutality to Negroes."[82] But such ignorance was unlikely. Cops too often bragged about their mistreatment of African American suspects, and white newspapers provided copious coverage of police homicides, including Willie Grosch's executions on the Air-Line Highway, acts that typically elicited approval from white commentators, who expressed gratitude to the detectives responsible for eliminating murderers and rapists. Newspapers also reported brutality allegations, especially when African American killers appealed their convictions and charged that John Grosch's detectives had beaten them into signing confessions. "Almost daily," a New Orleans editor noted, "stories and horrible examples of what physical brutality the sworn protectors of the law wreak upon hapless, helpless individuals are brought before the public."[83]

To be sure, white newspapers routinely provided sanitized descriptions of police brutality, highlighting suspects' perceived provocations. Crime-beat reporters emphasized African American resistance and dangerous conduct, particularly attempts to reach for weapons that did not exist, and the heroic efforts of tough cops. Invoking the explanations offered by violent interrogators, white journalists frequently explained that the brutalized suspects were either guilty or hardened criminals, hence justifying their rough treatment. Such "whitewashed" accounts of police violence usually neglected to mention that abuse victims were unarmed, handcuffed, and compliant when detectives slugged them, hammered them with the butts of guns and metal pipes, or shot them. An African American newspaper observed that "one black man after another may be killed or maimed for life by the police, but when the story of the incident reached the [white] newspapers, the black man was always 'resisting arrest' or opening him-self [sic] up in some other way to what he received."[84] In one New Orleans police homicide, white newspaper reports emphasized that the cop killed a predator trying to enter a white woman's bedroom late at night after the prowler ignored his command to "halt."[85] The city's African American newspaper, by contrast, indicated that the policeman shot the suspect with his arms raised from a distance of less than ten feet. The *Louisiana Weekly* added that, according to a witness, "the boy was shot down like a rat."[86] Similarly, white newspapers ordinarily discussed forensic evidence only when it supported the prevailing, racialized narrative, neglecting to mention autopsies that revealed that fleeing felons had been shot in the face from close range and omitting photographic evidence documenting brutal beatings. But even if white newspaper accounts cast violent cops in sympathetic, courageous terms, allegations of police violence were frequent.

For their part, New Orleans law enforcers buttressed the selective reporting and typically insisted that they employed no violent methods, making it easier—or merely more convenient—for white journalists and residents to dismiss abuse allegations as fabricated. Police responses to complaints, however, frequently rejected charges in baldly transparent ways. The ritual for discrediting brutality allegations entailed parading into the courtroom every cop in the precinct or on the patrol shift to testify that no such beatings or shootings had occurred. Another variation relied on desk sergeants gathering statements from dozens of police officers who offered alternate explanations for abuse victims' welts, missing teeth, broken jaws, fractured ribs, and swollen genitals, claiming that clumsy or inebriated suspects had merely tripped and fallen at crime scenes or in station-house cells. One after another, cops often described the causes of the injuries with the exact same language, making little effort to formulate believable accounts. Found dead in a holding cell in the 7th precinct in 1938, Aaron Boyd's body bore unmistakable evidence of a severe beating, his abdomen grotesquely bruised. The coroner attributed the death to "hemorrhage and shock following rupture of liver" and noted the sea of contusions on Boyd's torso.[87] Police officers, however, testified that the thirty-nine-year-old robbery suspect "fell from a back fence in the yard of his home," landing awkwardly on a tree stump.[88] Crime-scene photographs contradicted this explanation, and the officers' formal statements were "identical in grammatical construction."[89]

Police authorities, such as New Orleans's Superintendent Reyer, insisted that their departments did not permit third-degree methods or other violent practices, reinforcing white residents' inclinations to overlook the broken bodies, detailed medical reports, corpses, witness testimony, and photographs that exposed the absurdity of such assertions. Again and again, Reyer and his counterparts throughout the region denied that their detectives extracted confessions with beatings and threats. "The third degree," Reyer bellowed in 1931, "is not permitted in the New Orleans police department," a claim he often repeated.[90] In 1939, after John Grosch boasted to the Rotary Club that he relied on this interrogation technique, Reyer stated, unequivocally, that "no type of third degree methods are used by the New Orleans police department."[91]

Grosch himself offered contradictory explanations, denying, justifying, and "championing" his violent methods.[92] Most often, he contended that vicious criminals fabricated the charges. The "worst offenders" and most "notorious" predators, he argued, filed such complaints. "They will all claim third-degree in their last hope of beating the penitentiary."[93] Grosch even provided explanations for the shattered bones, contusions, and other injuries that blanketed the bodies of suspects shortly after detectives interrogated them. The prisoners, he reported in discounting one affidavit, "inflicted bruises upon themselves in an effort to divert public indignation from themselves to police." In another case, Grosch told a grand jury that "defendants voluntarily exchanged blows with each other for the purpose of presenting 'physical evidence' that they were beaten up by police."[94] In responding to other brutality allegations, however, Grosch boasted that he bludgeoned suspects, knocked out their teeth with the butt of his service revolver, and threatened to kill them to compel them to confess to their vicious predations. During his Rotary Club speech, the chief gloated about his tough methods, emphasizing that he only beat and battered hardened criminals and those guilty of committing violent offenses. These practices, he argued, "curbed" crime, justifying their use.[95]

District attorneys also typically denied that cops mauled suspects, even as they confronted evidence to the contrary in hearings, case files, medical records, depositions, and criminal trials. Eugene Stanley blithely dismissed brutality allegations, including courtroom testimony and affidavits from survivors who claimed they had been beaten in his office, sometimes in his presence. Stanley's successor as the parish prosecutor, Charles Byrne, issued the same blanket denials, as did the assistant district attorneys they supervised. Others in the criminal justice system routinely ignored the abundant, irrefutable evidence of police brutality toward African American suspects as well, reinforcing the pervasive white belief that cops either did not mistreat prisoners or that such actions, if they did occur, were justified and effective. Judges, "in nearly all cases," admitted forced confessions into evidence, and jurors deferred to the testimony of white detectives and signed confessions and discounted conflicting complaints, testimony, and forensic evidence.[96] The "fictitious rubber hose," a Memphis judge grumbled in 1932, "has gotten too many men out of the penitentiary."[97] In describing one especially shocking New Orleans brutality case, Harold Lee revealed to a Justice Department

criminal trials in which judges permitted the introduction of coerced confessions; distorted newspapers accounts of arrests and court proceedings; along with a lattice of protocols that prevented victims' relatives and defense attorneys from seeing abused suspects, precluded private physicians from treating prisoners, discouraged whites from providing testimony at odds with sanitized cops' formal accounts of their violent encounters with African American suspects, forbade African American witnesses from making formal statements, and criminalized public criticism of police methods— enabled white New Orleanians to remain unbothered by allegations of police violence, willfully oblivious to such practices, supportive of aggressive law enforcers, and hence indirectly complicit in the endemic, increasingly normalized, racialized brutality committed on their behalf. Evidence abounded, hidden within plain sight.

Obvious dissembling enraged defense attorneys but proved convincing to New Orleans prosecutors, jurors, and judges, all of them white, and bolstered Manichaean constructions of race and criminality. Brutal cops in other cities employed corresponding, thinly disguised forms of deception and found their supervisors, criminal-court judges, and white residents equally inclined to accept wildly implausible descriptions and justifications. Memphis's police chief Joe Boyle, for example, deferred to detectives' testimony that thirty-five-year-old James Gray, a suspected shoplifter, sustained a "head wound" during his 1941 interrogation when he "ran headlong into a concrete pillar," ruling "I am convinced the officers did not lay a hand on him."[109] In a similar case, Memphis detectives explained that a thirty-year-old robbery suspect sustained a fatal head injury when he "fell into a radiator" during the interrogation session.[110] The routine, casual ways in which criminal justice officials, jurors, and white newspaper readers ignored blatant forensic evidence of extreme brutality reflected white Southerners' willingness to accept racialized, violent law enforcement practices.

White New Orleanians and white Southerners benefitted culturally and legally. Cops' brutality reinforced their inclination to perceive violence as a distinctly African American behavior, and thus the aggressive treatment of African American suspects became necessary, justified, and legitimate. Understanding crime in racial terms buttressed their notions of white supremacy; white society consisted of civilized, law-abiding citizens, while barbaric, savage, criminals filled the African American community. As a result, disregarding the constitutional protections or civil liberties of African American residents was not troubling, inappropriate, or at odds with the rule of law, and coercing confessions from such threats to public safety and empowering cops to employ preemptive deadly force against them merely safeguarded respectable citizens and the constitutional order.

As white officials, particularly those at the helm of legal institutions, exploited this view, white violent crime and white criminals disappeared from public view, making the prophecy of racialized criminality self-fulfilling. Social-scientific research confirmed the connection between crime and race. Racial disparities in criminal justice skyrocketed during the inter-war period. Prosecutors increasingly dismissed charges against white killers, and grand jurors returned "no bill" verdicts against white suspects. Conviction trends seemed to provide definitive evidence that criminals were African American—and that African Americans were criminals. During the 1920s and 1930s, the white homicide conviction rate in New Orleans contracted slightly, while the African American rate ballooned, climbing by 98.4 percent. Racialized interrogation methods to extract confessions and the use of unconstitutional plea-bargaining arrangements with African American suspects contributed to rapidly widening gaps in convictions, incarcerations, and executions.[111] During the 1930s, the death penalty became an exclusively African American punishment in New Orleans, adding weight to the popular view that vicious murderers were African American. Between 1920 and 1930, white residents made up 60 percent of the killers sent to the gallows. But from 1931 until 1945, African Americans comprised 87.5 percent of those executed—and 100 percent after 1933. The proportion of homicides committed by African American residents, however, changed lit-tle during this era, the stark pivot reflecting shifts in criminal justice rather than crime.

These distortions and institutional biases reinforced one another, and white crime and white criminals became increasingly invisible. Between the early 1920s and the early 1940s, the percentage of homicide cases in which white defendants went to trial plunged, dropping by 56.1 percent—from 53.1 percent of court proceedings to 23.3 percent. During the same span, the pro-portion of homicide trials with African American defendants mushroomed. By the World War II years, nearly four-fifths of killers appearing in Orleans Parish courtrooms were African American. As a consequence, newspaper coverage of murder trials seemed to document a white racial frame in which African Americans were criminals, and criminals were African American.[112] The cumulative impact of Jim Crow policing powerfully reinforced racial stereotypes, further magnifying disparities in criminal justice.

When white suspects and defendants disappeared from the courts, from newspaper reports of murders and homicide trials, from the public view, from the Angola State Penal Farm, and from death row, the elision of violence and race hardened. Biases in arrests, indictments, convictions, plea-bargaining practices, and capital punishment produced seemingly irrefutable confirmation for the notion that cops needed and deserved wide discretion in combatting this threat and that racially disparate criminal justice was justified.[113] Perceiving themselves as peaceful and law-abiding, white New Orleanians, and whites throughout the region, celebrated their cultural superiority, extolled their commitment to the rule of law, and embraced police methods of protecting them from natural-born—African American—murderers, rapists, and bandits. White legal privilege and white supremacy worked in unison.[114]

Though hardly new, these views became institutionalized and more pronounced, redounding to the benefit of violent cops. White New Orleanians and, according to ethnographers, white Southerners, ceded the task of racial control to the police and then supported their aggressive crime-fighting methods, confident that law enforcers would continue to employ these practices only to serve the interests of law-abiding citizens—that is, against African Americans. Cops, rather than white civilians and vigilantes, assumed responsibility for preserving white supremacy. In New Orleans, the proportion of white-on-Black killings—the ultimate expression of racial dominance—committed by the police nearly doubled.

In this political and racial environment, challenges to police efforts endangered public safety and could not be tolerated. African American resistance to police methods had to be harnessed or crushed. Cops defended aggressive policing, and city officials, including police administrators, insisted that protest in all forms jeopardized social stability. Both reflecting and reinforcing this view, African American demonstrations against police brutality triggered an explosive response from city officials and cops. Superintendent Reyer's pledge to ban ministers from organizing protest gatherings was typical. Such mass meetings promised to hamstring the police, embolden African American criminals, and undermine law and order. Like defense attorneys, civil rights activists, according to top cops, used complaints against abusive cops and protest meetings to bind the hands of police officers and hence risked unleashing racial turmoil. Policies forbidding protest and the accompanying repression, however, failed to dampen African American demands for police reform and racial justice.

The mayor, police superintendent, and of course John Grosch defined their mandate in capacious terms and instructed detectives to respond forcefully to any effort to foment racial disorder. They not only encouraged the aggressive treatment of African American suspects but also used this law-and-order approach to threaten, arrest, and beat white radicals. Racialized perceptions reshaped white attitudes toward political dissent in the city, and by the late 1930s, cops harassed and brutalized labor organizers, insisting that these "agitators" sought to undermine the racial order. CIO representatives became particular targets (and victims) of Grosch's detectives under the banner of maintaining white dominance. Cops arrested, threatened, and attacked union members, charging that white CIO organizers intended to foment social chaos "by preaching that negroes are the equals of white men" and entitled to "their rights."[115] According to Grosch, the CIO conducted "a campaign of agitation among Negroes and stirring up strife." Nor was he the only police official embracing this belief. Joe Boyle, Memphis's top cop, insisted that "encouraged by foreign Communist agitators, a young element of the negroes has become insolent, reaching a point where their restraint is necessary." This "menace will be stopped," Boyle vowed, and he assigned policemen to all "street cars, buses, and trackless trolleys to 'protect the rights of white passengers.'"[116]

New Orleans's John Grosch unleashed his brother to deploy the methods hitherto reserved for African American crime suspects. In 1938, Willie Grosch beat up a white CIO organizer, ferried him to the detective's favorite execution spot on the Air-Line Highway, held a gun to Bert Nelson's head, and growled "if we ever see you within 50 miles of New Orleans, we'll kill you."[117] To protect white New Orleanians and preserve racial stability, John Grosch pledged to drive radicals from the city.[118]

Louisiana legislators endorsed Grosch's methods and expansive view of racial stability, agreeing that "Communists and reds" imperiled white supremacy and unanimously voting in support of a resolution urging the New Orleans detective chief to maintain his unflinching efforts. "Unless drastic steps are taken at once," their formal resolution asserted, "white supremacy will be endangered."[119] In short, white support, including the explicit approval of Louisiana's state legislature, for preserving the racial order became increasingly open-ended, justifying police brutality in response to any form of resistance, from fleeing suspects and mass protest staged by local ministers to political dissent, for only fierce law enforcement measures could safeguard white supremacy and law and racial order. As resistance and protests intensified, so too did police brutality and repression. Criticism of police brutality and a violent backlash from cops fed one another in the Jim Crow South.[120]

. . .

Police brutality generated determined resistance from African American residents in the region, who refused to submit to beatings, but their protests also ignited a backlash, leading municipal officials and top cops to defend and justify racialized policing in the service of law and order. In turn, most Southern whites expressed gratitude and support for unyielding law enforcers. Brutality begot protest, and protest fueled explicit justifications and greater, more expansive police violence.

But the panoply of racialized policing—beatings, coerced confessions, executions, and omnipresent vulnerability—deployed to produce submission had the opposite effect, provoking dogged, sustained resistance, mobilizing the African American community and energizing the city's nascent civil rights movement. Resistance and opposition to police violence took myriad forms. Some residents nominally cooperated with patrolmen as risk aversion, manipulating beat cops into protecting them from suspicion and therefore shielding them from the Grosch brothers and other barbarous interrogators. Fully aware of the potential to be tortured, taken for "the ride," and murdered, many African American suspects fled from cops, escaping them when possible and actively resisting arrest if apprehended. Such efforts, however, often triggered even greater brutality from police detectives, who frequently responded with preemptive lethal force. Any resistance, by running or more actively preventing arrest, justified killing African American suspects and formed the basis for successful assertions of justified self-defense.

The victims of police brutality, such as Willie Gray, often had committed no unlawful acts or engaged in even vaguely suspicious behavior. Rather, cops hyper-scrutinized their activities because they were African American. This became the foundation of criminal justice in the age of Jim Crow. The majority of victims were also unarmed, and the proportion of unarmed African American victims rose over time as police and white stereotypes of African Americans and crime merged and became institutionalized. Yet policemen murdered in purported self-defense and insisted that they performed their duties in full accordance with the rule of law. As Arthur Raper noted, "the law is white," and maintaining public safety and law and order became euphemisms for preserving racial dominance.

Community leaders, victims' friends, relatives, and witnesses to such brutality, along with a small group of white civil rights activists, shone a bright light on police brutality, waged legal challenges against unlawful, unconstitutional criminal justice practices, and organized protests. But just as police violence sparked a backlash, so did such social justice campaigns. Ironically, any resistance to police authority provided greater justification for police brutality in the name of law and order and generated more vehement white support for such aggressive, racialized law enforcement and greater police legitimacy.

Although local personalities and pressures shaped this process in New Orleans, comparable shifts occurred throughout the South during the interwar period. Early twentieth-century sociologists, ethnographers, legal scholars, and investigative journalists charted parallel trends in other cities and states, documenting the racialization of police brutality, cop homicide, and criminal justice across the region.[121] In 1940, the *Pittsburgh Courier* declared that such practices had become "common in all Southern cities" and concluded that "police brutality—beatings, shootings, arrests on suspicion—constitutes a form of lynching which is more menacing than a mob of citizens which openly lynch."[122]

Police chiefs, elite detectives, and patrolmen throughout the urban South employed and celebrated policies, methods, and brutality that mirrored the practices and violence of the Grosch brothers. Levon Carlock's 1933 execution in Memphis unfolded in ways virtually identical to those that poisoned race relations in New Orleans, for racialized, systemic police brutality in the Louisiana city was typical for the region. On February 24, patrolmen arrested the unemployed nineteen-year-old laborer, who had recently moved to the city from Mississippi. The policemen apprehended him as a "loiterer" and suspected Carlock of committing a series of recent assaults on white women, though the description of the predator was vague. The following day, one of the victims made a tentative identification of her attacker, conceding that she did not recognize him but "his voice" resembled that of the offender. According to the formal police report, Carlock "jerked loose" and ran, compelling two patrolmen to fire one shot apiece at the fleeing criminal, killing him. Police investigators interviewed a dozen witnesses, all of them white, and concluded that the patrolmen had discharged their revolvers in the line of duty. Three days later, a coroner's jury and the local prosecutor concurred, ruling the killing a "justifiable homicide" and exonerating the cops.[123]

But conflicting evidence abounded, as it did in New Orleans cases. African American and labor journalists interviewed African American witnesses, who described the shooting as a "brutal murder." They reported that six patrolmen handcuffed Carlock, forced him "into an alley, beat him and tortured him, then shot him." According to witnesses, the official file "attempted to whitewash their crime with the claim that he had tried to escape."[124] One bystander heard a policeman bellow "we are going to fix you tonight." Then four officers "began beating him over the head with their clubs. They beat him so they broke his neck ... his neck shook like a chickens [*sic*] neck when you break it," and there were four or five shots fired into his body.[125] Forensic evidence corroborated the witnesses' accounts and contradicted the police narrative that they shot twice as he fled. The autopsy revealed that "four or five" bullets struck Carlock in the face, even though four policemen testified that the officers shot the suspect in the back as he tried to escape.[126] African American and labor newspapers also published postmortem photographs showing four bullet holes in Carlock's forehead and cheek.[127]

When African American residents organized a protest campaign, Memphis policemen responded in ways that paralleled the practices of the Grosches and New Orleans police chief George Reyer. One of the shooters, with bluster worthy of Willie Grosch, crowed, "I can't take all the credit, but I was one of them that shot the n-----."[128] Memphis detectives sprung into action as well, arresting, "grilling," and warning Carlock's widow to remain silent.[129] Moreover, Fannie Henderson, a fifty-nine-year-old African American witness, promptly disappeared.[130] Police officials also forbade public demonstrations, vowed to shutter African American newspapers that criticized local cops, and attempted to "stifle the seething resentment of the aroused masses."[131]

White Memphians immediately expressed their fulsome support for the killers, denounced the protesters' "slanderous statements against the police," decried efforts to "prevent the officers from performing their duty," and framed the execution of Levon Carlock as the defense of law and order.[132] Immediately after newspapers published accounts of the murder, one civic organization passed a formal resolution "pledging its support to the police department."[133] Such police violence, repression of protesters, and white endorsement of racialized law enforcement, a sociologist explained in 1943, "is almost standard for the South" and "has occasioned both fear and bitter resentment among all Negroes of all classes."[134]

Police officials throughout the region also exploited their perceived mandate to defend the racial order in expansive ways during the turbulent 1930s. New Orleans cops and their counterparts in other Southern cities harassed and brutalized white labor leaders and political radicals under the same racial mantle, claiming that these "alien agitators" sought to "stir up trouble among the Negro workers of the city" and hence imperil white women and undermine social stability.[135] Containing the threat from African American residents provided the justification for wider political repression.

The cycle of African American resistance and white backlash cemented state-sponsored racial terrorism as the defense of the rule of law. In the Jim Crow South, police crusades to protect "law and order" increasingly operated as a "façade" for white supremacy.[136] Buttressed by voter suppression, the spiral of progress and retrenchment would endure, fraying race relations in New Orleans, the South, and much of the nation for decades.

Conclusion

"KILLERS WHO HIDE BEHIND BADGES"

"AT LEAST ONCE A WEEK," the editor of the *Louisiana Weekly* lamented in 1940, "some poor unfortunate Negro is 'gone over' by our sadistically inclined police department."[1] Beatings, coerced confessions, and summary executions of African American suspects by Willie Grosch and his fellow detectives were not isolated events. Moreover, each of these episodes reverberated through New Orleans's African American community and provided another reminder of the unfettered power of local cops and their systemic use of violence to buttress white supremacy.[2] Municipal cops had become "killers who hide behind badges and uniforms to carry out a scourge of blood and violence. . . . The law," an African American journalist grumbled, granted them boundless "authority and told them to 'keep order' which was another way of saying 'maintain suppression.'"[3] "Negro residents of New Orleans," an African American newspaper groused, "can look to sworn minions of the law for little else than brutality."[4] During the dozen years after the Great War, the rate of police homicides against African American suspects nearly tripled, ballooning to more than quintuple the figure for white New Orleanians. Racial control and crime control became indistinguishable, and local policemen used the defense of law and order to wage state-sponsored racial terrorism.

White New Orleanians, however, viewed surging, racialized police brutality very differently. Violent cops eliminated murderers and ensured the incarceration of African American robbers and rapists, making the city safer for law-abiding residents. And police decisions to dismiss civil rights leaders' demands for due-process protections and to suppress African American demonstrations restrained subversive protest and preserved racial control.

Parallel trends in police brutality and racial repression unfolded across the interwar urban South. Quantitative and qualitative evidence documented virtually identical arrest and interrogation practices and mounting body counts in every city in the region. The Memphis police department used the same procedures for homicide reporting as their New Orleans counterparts, permitting a comparable analysis of police killings. The patterns mirrored one another. In both urban centers, civilian white-on-Black homicide contracted, and cops began to commit the lion's share of interracial killings. The cities experienced similar crime panics, which white residents attributed to a perceived "invasion" by African American predators. Between the mid-1920s and the early 1930s, the number of African American suspects killed by the police rose 3.4-fold in New Orleans and 3.5-fold in Memphis. In the Louisiana city, 46.9 percent of the victims were unarmed, compared with 38.8 percent in the Tennessee metropolis. The suspects were matching as well: 97.2 percent were men, 46.9 percent were unarmed, and their mean age in New Orleans was 29.6. In Memphis, 99.1 percent were men, 40.5 percent were unarmed, and their average age was 29.4. The killer cops were also mirror images, with a mean age of 37.9 in the former city and 36.4 in the latter.[5]

NAACP branch files for New Orleans, Memphis, Washington DC, Mobile, Birmingham, Atlanta, and other Southern cities revealed comparable trends. Just as police brutality spiked in New Orleans during the 1930s, Memphis civil rights leaders described this as the "bloody decade" and decried the "wave of terror" and the "reign of terror."[6] NAACP officials recoiled at the same surging use of third-degree interrogation methods to extract confessions and the preemptive use of lethal force in every city in the region.[7] Even characterizations of police attitudes echoed one another. New Orleans activists complained that local cops treated African American residents "worse than one would a stray mongrel dog," while their counterparts in Mobile reported that policemen "are treating us like dogs."[8]

Early twentieth-century ethnographers documented the same trends and procedures throughout the interwar urban South, revealing systemic racial biases in policing and criminal justice. Across the region, disparities in police shootings, convictions, sentencing, and executions soared. The rate of police homicide against African Americans in the interwar South swelled to seven times the white figure.[9] In New Orleans, white and African American murderers went to the gallows at roughly equivalent rates during the 1920s. By the mid-1930s, however, only African Americans received capital verdicts. Sociologists charting state-level trends found similar shifts throughout the

South.[10] Executions rose sharply during the 1930s, the vast majority of the increase confined to African American convicts.

Discrimination was not new, but it increased dramatically and operated as a state function during the interwar period. Across the region, institutionalized racial repression became intertwined with the preservation of law and order.[11] "The caste order of the South," the sociologist Gunnar Myrdal concluded, developed into an "extension of the law." The Southern policeman "stands not only for civic order as defined in formal laws and regulations, but also for 'white supremacy.'"[12] Cops replaced vigilantes, and prisons and court-sanctioned executions supplanted mob justice. In city after city, African American observers noted the shift but also the continuity, terming police homicides "uniformed lynchings," "police lynchings," "streamlined lynching," and "legal lynchings."[13] The widow of one victim of Memphis police murder in 1933 described Saturday evenings as "lynch night" for local cops.[14] The core activities of Birmingham's NAACP branch pivoted from vigilante violence during the early 1920s to police violence by the early 1930s.[15]

Interwar demographic shifts triggered this racialized sea change in Southern policing. Far more rural African Americans migrated to Southern urban centers during the first stage of the Great Migration than to Northern cities.[16] In 1930, for example, African Americans, most of them newcomers, comprised one-third of New Orleans, Memphis, Birmingham, and Atlanta residents, compared with less than one-eleventh of the Chicago, Detroit, Cleveland, New York City, and Pittsburgh populations. The crime panic of the era fused fears of a massive influx of African Americans and hyperbolic anxieties about murder and rape in Southern cities. Early twentieth-century Northern whites, including cops, embraced horrifying stereotypes of African Americans, but these migrants, according to one scholar, "were not yet a sizable enough population to preoccupy the crafters of police policy" and become institutionalized.[17]

The second stage of the Great Migration, during the middle decades of the century, however, nationalized Jim Crow policing, as African Americans increasingly left the Deep South and relocated to Northern industrial centers. Only in the 1960s did the proportion of African American residents in Chicago, Detroit, Cleveland, New York City, and Pittsburgh reach the share of Southern cities in the pre-Depression era. When the migrants crossed this threshold in the post–World War II period, Northern whites responded with terror and demanded new, urgent, targeted police and criminal justice prescriptions.[18] In cities throughout the United States, fears of an invasion of

African American killers ignited crime panics, and Jim Crow policing infected and redefined law and order in Chicago, New York, and other Northern urban centers. Racialized police brutality, under the guise of the rule of law, fueled exploding disparities in criminal justice across the nation by the 1960s.[19]

Northern mayors and police chiefs, however, did not invent race-targeted policing during the post–World War II era. Instead, interwar officials in cities such as New Orleans and Birmingham had already established a blueprint and had, for decades, crowed about their success at national meetings of police chiefs and other law enforcement conferences. New Orleans's John Grosch had long boasted of his department's commitment to white supremacy; Memphis's police commissioner, Joe Boyle, repeatedly underscored his effort to deploy cops to affirm that "this is white man's country and always will be and any Negro who doesn't agree to this had better move on"; and by the mid-1930s, Birmingham's infamous Bull Connor had assumed the helm of local law enforcement.[20] The interwar policies implemented by the top cops in these cities provided the roadmap for their postwar Northern counterparts, and chiefs such as Los Angeles's William Parker and Daryl Gates invoked the same trope of invasion and threat as had spearheaded the prescriptions forged by an earlier generation of Southern police chiefs.[21]

During the 1960s, Northern police authorities adapted, expanded, renamed, and institutionalized many of the practices developed by Grosch, Boyle, and Connor. They did not explicitly copy earlier procedures, but officials such as Parker and Gates responded to the elision of migration trends and a crime panic in familiar ways and built on well-known, long-established procedures. New versions of late-1920s "disorderly-and-suspicious-character" ordinances became "stop-and-search" (and later "stop-and-frisk") initiatives; New Orleans's Roaring Twenties armored, "death-dealing machines" became military assault vehicles; earlier "Go Get 'Em squads" were reinvented as "S.W.A.T." units; John Grosch's and Joe Boyle's racialized definition of law and order resurfaced as the "War on Crime"; and widening racial disparities in interwar conviction rates eventually ballooned into late twentieth-century mass incarceration.[22]

Remnants of Jim Crow policing remain in early twenty-first-century America. Some racial differentials have narrowed but persist. In the 1930s, Southern cops killed African American suspects at five-to-seven times the rate for white residents. In the last ninety years, the gap has contracted, though the African American rate continues to be considerably higher, hovering at two-to-three times the white figure.[23]

Other racial disparities in law enforcement have remained so deeply entrenched and institutionalized that little change has occurred since the pre–World War II era. Differentials in the preemptive use of deadly force—termed "shooter bias" by modern scholars—have not narrowed, for example. Police officers, then and now, have a far lower threshold for firing their weapons at and killing African American suspects. In early 1930s New Orleans, cops shot unarmed African Americans at four times the rate of white suspects. Early twenty-first-century data reveal 3.5-to-5-fold disparities.[24] Like their predecessors during the early twentieth century, modern police officers react to ambiguous or furtive motions by African American suspects by shooting to kill but are less likely to employ deadly force when white suspects engage in the identical behavior. In the Jim Crow South, the so-called "hip-pocket move" often triggered violent, lethal responses from detectives convinced—or sometimes merely claiming—that the suspect was reaching for a weapon. More recent police officers have shot African American suspects when they have tried to produce their wallets or vehicle registrations to comply with cops' requests, also insisting that they feared that the person was reaching for a handgun. In 1999, for instance, New York City detectives shot Amadou Diallo, a twenty-three-year-old Guinean immigrant, nearly two dozen times after he attempted to remove his wallet from his coat pocket to produce identification.

Shooter bias was and remains bound up with threat perception, which has persisted for a hundred years. Police officers consider African Americans to be dangerous, scrutinize their demeanors more intensely, and misread behavioral cues, imagining threatening conduct when actions are benign.[25] Dogged stereotypes of Black criminality "prime" law enforcers to anticipate violent resistance and to more quickly reach for their firearms and shoot.[26] In some instances, this threat assessment reflects overt, explicit racism, as with Willie Grosch in pre–World War II New Orleans and Derek Chauvin in 2020 Minneapolis. But in other cases, the triggers for "threat-perception failure" are subtler, and "implicit bias" lowers the threshold for the premature use of lethal force. The effect of this process, however, is that police officers shoot unarmed African American suspects at more than quadruple the white rate, a disparity that has not changed since the 1930s.

Though impossible to quantify, other forms of racialized police brutality persist as well. As in Jim Crow New Orleans, Atlanta, and Mobile, modern detectives more frequently employ violent interrogation methods and use force and threats to extract confessions from African Americans.[27] Just as early twentieth-century cops often presumed African American suspects to be deceitful and guilty, their early twenty-first-century counterparts routinely embrace the same stereotypes.[28]

Parallel forms of harassment, frequently inciting racialized police violence, have also contributed to the disturbing and enduring disparities. For example, the race-based cues fueling recent stop-and-frisk interactions are similar to the assumptions that prompted Detective William Drewes to arrest, maul, and shoot sixteen-year-old Willie Gray in New Orleans almost a century ago. In modern America, traffic stops have comparable potential for police violence, based on hyper-scrutiny and threat-perception failure, and cops stop and search African American drivers today at five times the rate of white drivers; every such encounter increases the likelihood that ambiguous movements will be misinterpreted and spark deadly responses from skittish police officers, adding to persistent disparities in violence.[29]

Early twenty-first-century legal and political responses to police brutality have also remained largely static. No New Orleans cops were convicted for killing suspects between 1920 and 1945; prosecutors and jurors determined that all 107 fatal shootings and beatings were "justifiable homicides." Today, less than 1 percent of such killings even lead to felony charges.[30] Political responses to recent police-brutality protests echo those of the 1930s in horrifying ways as well, often igniting repressive backlash initiatives. Many state legislatures have recently criminalized public demonstrations against police violence in the wake of Black Lives Matter protests following the 2020 murder of George Floyd, for example.

In short, the critical inflection point for police violence occurred during the 1930s, when criminal justice institutions expanded, gained authority from anxious white voters, and municipal cops employed racialized violence to enhance their public legitimacy as the protectors of law-abiding citizens. Long before the interwar era, local policemen and sheriffs had often relied on violence, enforced racial dominance, and killed with legal impunity. But the rates of such overlapping forms of brutality soared in the two decades after the Great War, and the trends and practices of that era persist, sometimes in muted fashion, today.

The changing morphology of white-on-Black murder starkly revealed the speed and magnitude of this transformation. During the opening decade of the twentieth century, white civilians committed nearly three-fourths of interracial killings in New Orleans, building on long-established customs of vigilante racial violence. Policemen typically played a secondary role, supporting and supplementing the violence inflicted by white mobs. The proportion of civilian white-on-Black murders remained unchanged through the early 1920s. Within a decade, ignited by the Great Migration and a crime panic, cops committed two-thirds of New Orleans white-on-Black homicides, and by the late 1930s, they committed 100 percent of such murders, a trend mirrored throughout the South and nationalized during the post–World War II era. When professional law enforcers supplanted vigilantes as the foot soldiers for white dominance, racial control became a state function and operated through the criminal justice system. Legal institutions assumed increasing responsibility for preserving white supremacy, enforced under the capacious mantle of maintaining law and order and protecting law-abiding citizens. Racial control and crime blurred, blended, and overlapped. Despite the remarkable achievements of the civil rights movement, "law and order" remains racialized.[31] During the early twenty-first century, police officers continue to commit more than 90 percent of white-on-Black homicides in the United States.[32]

The proportion of total homicides committed by the police offers another measure of the ways in which violence, disproportionately inflicted against African Americans, pivoted during the interwar era and has changed modestly in the last century. Between the 1920s and the 1930s, the percentage of all killing by the New Orleans police doubled and reached 7.8 percent of the total. In early twenty-first-century America, law enforcers commit 8 percent of homicides.[33] Police in the United States kill suspects at forty times the rate of their German counterparts and at one hundred times the rate of British law enforcers.[34]

Most white Americans and most police officers committed (and commit) no violence against African American citizens. But, over the last century, racialized law enforcement has become systemic and produced widening, enduring disparities. Police brutality is not an isolated or rare occurrence, and the social discord it generates frays the fabric of American society and challenges American ideals regarding justice, freedom, and equality. For centuries, white Americans have deployed overt racial violence. The role of law enforcers and legal institutions, however, mushroomed during the early twentieth century, became nationalized during the middle decades of the century, and created the foundation for the horrific police brutality that persists in the early twenty-first century. The recent police murders of Tyre Nichols, George Floyd, Breonna Taylor, Laquan McDonald, Michael Brown, Eric Garner, and Amadou Diallo are grounded in attitudes and practices institutionalized almost a century ago in New Orleans, Memphis, Birmingham, and other Southern cities. The ghost of Jim Crow continues to haunt the nation.

NOTES

INTRODUCTION

1. For "bluecoated terror," see "Charge Two, Though Scores Were Put in Hoosegow for Night," *Louisiana Weekly*, August 3, 1940, 1.

2. Stevenson, "A Presumption of Guilt," 11.

3. Dale, *Criminal Justice in the United States*; Malka, *The Men of Mobtown*.

4. See Johnson, *Street Justice*; Mitrani, *The Rise of the Chicago Police Department*.

5. Wigmore, ed., *The Illinois Crime Survey*; Pound and Frankfurter, eds., *Criminal Justice in Cleveland*; Willrich, "Criminal Justice in the United States."

6. Raper, "Race and Class Pressures"; Davis, Gardner, and Gardner, *Deep South*; Myrdal, *An American Dilemma*; Dollard, *Caste and Class in a Southern Town*.

7. Eckberg, "Crime, Law Enforcement, and Justice," 251.

8. Unless otherwise indicated, the quantitative evidence presented in this book draws from a dataset of 2,118 New Orleans homicides between 1920 and 1945. Combining information from police files, homicide witness transcripts, autopsy reports, court files, prison records, and local newspapers, it includes every homicide in the city during this era.

9. Raper, "Race and Class Pressures," 36–44; Memphis Police Department Homicide Reports; Papers of the National Association for the Advancement of Colored People.

10. Patterson, ed., *We Charge Genocide*, 8.

11. Charles A. J. McPherson to Walter White, April 12, 1940, Memphis Branch Files, Box II:B112, Folder 22, 1940–1955, Papers of the National Association for the Advancement of Colored People.

12. "Brutality and Humiliation Are Charged by Outraged Pair," *Louisiana Weekly*, February 28, 1948, 1.

13. Chafee, Pollak, and Stern, "The Third Degree."

14. Muhammad, *The Condemnation of Blackness*.

15. Kohn, "Report of the Special Citizens Investigating Committee of the Commission Council of New Orleans," 113. Early twenty-first-century social scientists have noted the same transformation. See, for instance, Zimring, *When Police Kill*, 14; Epp, Maynard-Moody, and Haider-Markel, *Pulled Over*, 9.

16. "Police Brutality Common in Southern Cities," *Pittsburgh Courier*, August 3, 1940, 15.

17. Modern social psychologists term this "implicit bias." See Eberhardt, *Biased*.

18. During the opening decades of the twentieth century, more African Americans migrated to Southern than to Northern cities. See Woofter, *Negro Problems in Cities*, 29.

19. Chivers, "Homicides among Negroes in Atlanta, 1934–1938," 1.

20. "344 Murders in N.O. in 5 Years, Record Shows," *New Orleans Item*, September 24, 1924, 4.

21. Maurice B. Gatlin, "Transcript of 'Radio Speech,'" Station WBW, August 9, 1935, Files of the New Orleans Branch of the National Association for the Advancement of Colored People.

22. "Murders, Suicides Increase in 1921," *New Orleans Times-Picayune*, January 1, 1922, 20.

23. "Hanging Only Cure for Homicides, Says Molony," *New Orleans Item*, July 6, 1924, 1.

24. Barnhart, "A Study of Homicide in the United States," 33.

25. "Third Degree Case," *New Orleans States*, May 13, 1932, 6.

26. "Against Third Degree," *New Orleans States*, June 3, 1933, 4; "A Fair Hearing," *New Orleans States*, January 12, 1938, 10; "Police Killings," *New Orleans Item*, August 4, 1927, 12.

27. For recent discussions of this view, see Finkel, *Commonsense Justice*; Carlson, *Policing the Second Amendment*, 177–81.

28. This literature is massive. For example, see McClosky and Brill, *Dimensions of Tolerance*; Sullivan, Piereson, and Marcus, *Political Tolerance and American Democracy*; Marcus, Sullivan, Theiss-Morse, and Wood, *With Malice toward Some*; Mondak and Sanders, "The Complexity of Tolerance and Intolerance Judgments," 325–37.

29. Myrdal, *An American Dilemma*, 498.

30. Raper, "Race and Class Pressures," 8.

31. Legal psychologist Tom R. Tyler has shaped the scholarship exploring the ways in which popular notions of the police serving the needs of the community bolster public attitudes toward law enforcers' legitimacy and authority. But in Jim Crow America, this "public" defined itself as exclusively white. For important examples of this research, see Tyler, "Psychological Perspectives on Legitimacy and Legitimation"; Tyler and Jackson, "Popular Legitimacy and the Exercise of Lethal Authority"; Jackson, Bradford, Huq, and Tyler, "Monopolizing Force?"

32. Dollard, *Caste and Class in a Southern Town*, 361; Johnson, *Patterns of Negro Segregation*, 299.

33. Seigel, *Violence Work*, 9; Wood and Ring, "Introduction," 7.

34. Patterson, ed., *We Charge Genocide*, 9.

35. For example, Balto, *Occupied Territory*, 29, 94.

36. A rich body of recent scholarship charts this backlash and the enhanced racialization of post–World War II policing. For particularly important, insightful analyses, see Balto, *Occupied Territory*; Hinton, *America on Fire*; Balko, *Rise of the Warrior Cop*; Fischer, *The Streets Belong to Us*; Suddler. *Presumed Criminal*; Alexander, *The New Jim Crow*; Simon, *Governing through Crime*.

37. Memphis Police Department Homicide Reports; "Memphis Negroes Aroused to High Pitch of Resentment and Indignation," January 4, 1938, Memphis Branch Files, Box I:G199, Folder 28, 1938, Papers of the National Association for the Advancement of Colored People; Raper, "Race and Class Pressures"; Jett, *Race, Crime, and Policing in the Jim Crow South*; Niedermeier, *The Color of the Third Degree*.

38. See Papers of the National Association for the Advancement of Colored People; Niedermeier, *The Color of the Third Degree*.

39. Myrdal, *An American Dilemma;* Davis, Gardner, and Gardner, *Deep South*; Johnson et al., *To Stem This Tide*; Raper, "Race and Class Pressures."

40. Transcripts of Statements; Papers of the Louisiana League; Criminal District Court Case Files.

41. Scott, Ma, Sadler, and Correll, "A Social Scientific Approach toward Understanding Racial Disparities in Police Shooting," 705; Jones, "Killing Fields," 873.

CHAPTER ONE

1. Homicide Reports, "Report of Homicide of Louis Joseph," December 28, 1927.

2. Homicide Reports, "Report of Homicide of Louis Joseph," December 28, 1927.

3. "Two Charged with Slaying of Newsboy," *New Orleans Item*, December 29, 1927, 1.

4. Homicide Reports, "Report of Homicide of Louis Joseph," December 28, 1927.

5. "Probe of Shooting to Continue Today," *New Orleans Times-Picayune*, December 29, 1928, 25.

6. "Patrolmen Not Guilty of Killing Negro," *New Orleans States*, May 24, 1928, 9; "Two Policemen Questioned on Shooting of Boy," *New Orleans Item*, December 28, 1927, 1.

7. "Probe of Shooting to Continue Today," *New Orleans Times-Picayune*, December 29, 1928, 25.

8. I calculated the city's white-on-Black homicide rate using New Orleanians's African American population as the denominator.

9. Surviving records from interwar New Orleans include police homicide reports, homicide witness transcripts, autopsy reports, court files, prison intake

ledgers, and a variety of local newspapers. I used these sources to create a dataset of 2,118 cases, which included every homicide that occurred in the city between 1920 and 1945. To insure that my evidentiary base was as complete as possible, I compared the case files with tallies in health department reports, federal mortality records, and FBI figures. After I eliminated homicides in which victims died in the city but the violence occurred in New Orleans's hinterland, the number of cases in my dataset came within 1 percent of totals recorded in other sources. For a detailed description of this methodology, see Adler, *Murder in New Orleans*, 183–91. Unless otherwise indicated, the quantitative evidence presented in this book draws from this dataset.

10. "Policemen Freed of Manslaughter," *New Orleans Times-Picayune*, May 24, 1928, 1.

11. Metcalf, "Race Relations and the New Orleans Police Department, 1900–1972," 21.

12. Outrun by Joseph, Hennessey did not fire any shots. McCabe and Dendinger acknowledged discharging their revolvers but insisted that they had "fired three shots in the air and one at his feet": Homicide Reports, "Report of Homicide of Louis Joseph," December 28, 1927. For McCabe and Dendinger's disciplinary transgressions, see "Policeman Drunk," *New Orleans Times-Picayune*, January 10, 1927, 2; "Patrolman Nabbed on Girl's Charge," *New Orleans Times-Picayune*, October 22, 1925, 1. Also see "4 Policemen Are Suspended," *New Orleans Item*, June 20, 1934, 3.

13. "Paint Outside, Inside, 'Fires' 2 Patrolmen," *New Orleans Item*, December 5, 1921, 18; "Fall of Bluecoat Involves Liquor and Green Paint," *New Orleans Times-Picayune*, December 6, 1921, 12.

14. The figure for convictions represents both guilty verdicts from juries and plea agreements. In some cases, the surviving source material does not identify the specific path to incarceration.

15. "Policemen Freed of Manslaughter," *New Orleans Times-Picayune*, May 24, 1928, 1.

16. Brearley, "Ba-ad N-----," 78–79.

17. See Hadden, *Slave Patrols*.

18. Rousey, *Policing the Southern City*, 11–24.

19. Rousey, *Policing the Southern City*, 6, 24–30.

20. Malka, *The Men of Mobtown*.

21. Malka, *The Men of Mobtown*, 19–36.

22. Malka, *The Men of Mobtown*, 37.

23. Prince, *The Ballad of Robert Charles*, 105; Baker, *To Poison a Nation*, 139–40, 247. Prince and Baker focus on the 1900 social crisis revolving around Robert Charles, though their descriptions of white civilians' behavior extend beyond this race riot.

24. Myrdal, *An American Dilemma*, 535.

25. Raper, "Race and Class Pressures," 270.

26. Brearley, "Ba-ad N-----," 79.

27. Johnson, et al., *To Stem This Tide*, 73.

28. Brearley, "Ba-ad N-----," 79.

29. Myrdal, *An American Dilemma*, 535.

30. Brearley, "Ba-ad N-----," 79.

31. Brearley, "Ba-ad N-----," 79; Raper, "Race and Class Pressures," 270.

32. Myrdal, *An American Dilemma*, 541, 535.

33. Brearley, "Ba-ad N-----," 79.

34. Johnson, *Patterns of Negro Segregation*, 127; Dollard, *Caste and Class in a Southern Town*, 320; Moton, *What the Negro Thinks*, 213; Brearley, "Ba-ad N-----," 79.

35. In the overwhelming majority of interracial road-rage incidents, the encounter did not entail a racially subversive element and a challenge to the racial order. But the African American sociologist Charles S. Johnson suspected that some drivers exploited the anonymity of the highway to flout racial boundaries. See Johnson, *Patterns of Negro Segregation*, 127.

36. "Policeman Threatens Editor for Reporting Disorder of a Mob," *Louisiana Weekly*, March 5, 1927, 1.

37. One witness testified that the dispute began when the white conductor ordered the Baptiste brothers "not to smoke on the car" and they "remonstrated with him." See "Killer of Negro Brothers Is on Trial in Algiers," *New Orleans Item*, October 27, 1925, 10.

38. Homicide Reports, "Report of Homicides of Joseph and Ernest Baptiste," November 23, 1923.

39. At his trial, DeRocha denied making the threat, arguing that the Baptistes' aggressive insolence had prompted him to shoot them. A white nurse at Charity Hospital later testified in support of DeRocha and insisted that Ernest Baptiste had succumbed from his injuries without regaining consciousness and hence could not have recounted to his mother the blacksmith's bellicose quip. After deliberating for two hours, the all-white jury convicted DeRocha of "murder without capital punishment," concluding that the blacksmith's racially charged, pre-shooting outburst indicated that he killed without provocation. The *New Orleans Times-Picayune* described the verdict as the "first time in years that a white man has been convicted in New Orleans on a charge of murder in a negro's death." Judge N. E. Humphrey, however, was "not satisfied with the testimony of several negro witnesses," ordered a new trial, and DeRocha was acquitted. See "Man Who Killed Negroes on Car Goes to Trial," *New Orleans Times-Picayune*, November 18, 1925, 20; "Blacksmith Held Guilty in Death of Two Negroes," *New Orleans Times-Picayune*, November 19, 1925, 4; "New Trial Ordered for Blacksmith," *New Orleans Times-Picayune*, December 1, 1925, 10; "Motion for a New Trial," *State of Louisiana v. Frank De Rocha*, Criminal District Court, Section A Case Files, Docket # 26738, November 25, 1925.

40. Louisiana Supreme Court Case Files, "Testimony of Albert Johnson," *State of Louisiana v. Andrew Wiebelt*, Docket # 29325, May 16, 1928, Section A Case Files, 58, 67.

41. Louisiana Supreme Court Case Files, John C. O'Connor, Augustus G. Williams, and William J. O'Hara, "Appeal from the District Court: Original Brief on

Behalf of Defendant and Appellant," *State of Louisiana v. Andrew Wiebelt*, Docket # 29325, May 16, 1928, Section A Case Files, 18–19.

42. Homicide Reports, "Report of Homicide of Lilly Johnson," August 23, 1927.

43. O'Connor, Williams, and O'Hara, "Appeal from the District Court: Original Brief on Behalf of Defendant and Appellant," 18–19.

44. "Our Noble Protectors," *Louisiana Weekly*, March 5, 1927, 6.

45. "Woman Burglar Killer Wants Her Pistol Back," *New Orleans Times-Picayune*, January 9, 1925, 3.

46. W.H. McClendon, "Letter to the Editor," *New Orleans States*, May 25, 1926, 8.

47. "N.O. Policeman Beats, Injures Ex-X.U. Student," *Louisiana Weekly*, February 6, 1937, 1, 2.

48. "Man Beaten in Rear of Store," *Louisiana Weekly*, April 18, 1931, 1.

49. Pfeifer, "At the Hands of Parties Unknown," 835–36; Pfeifer, *Rough Justice*, 139–47; Finnegan, "Politics of Defiance," 851; Campney, *Hostile Heartland*. Some scholars have suggested that formal, legal punishment, particularly the death penalty, substituted for lynching, but a large body of recent scholarship disproves this argument. See Tolnay and Beck, *A Festival of Violence*, 108–11; Massey and Myers, "Patterns of Repressive Social Control," 482; Miller, "Hanging, the Electric Chair, and Death Penalty Reform," 177; Adler, "Justice Is Something That Is Unheard of for the Average Negro."

50. Work, ed., *Negro Year Book*, 295–99.

51. Homicide Reports, "Report of Homicide of John G. Mercier," August 3, 1922.

52. "White Boy, 8, Murdered by a Negro Lad Below Algiers," *New Orleans Item*, March 16, 1925, 1; "Sandwiches, Pop Bring Story of Slaying," *New Orleans States*, March 16, 1925, 2. Also see Dollard, *Caste and Class in a Southern Town*, 336.

53. Johnson, *The Negro in American Civilization*, 351. Also see Raper, "Race and Class Pressures," 274.

54. Nor were these interracial killings undercounted. The police reports provided a remarkably complete records of homicide cases, including white-on-Black murders, during this period. Across time and space, homicide constitutes the least underreported category of crime, for corpses are difficult to ignore. Moreover, few killers faced legal sanction during this era, and therefore assailants had scant reason to flee or deny their actions. Finally, other sources from early twentieth-century New Orleans recorded virtually the same number of cases as police files. Annual tallies from the local health department and from the city coroner revealed almost identical body counts.

55. "The 'Why' of Brutality," *Baton Rouge Advocate*, November 13, 1930, 4.

56. Davis, Gardner, and Gardner, *Deep South*, 501.

57. "Hanging Only Cure for Homicides, Says Molony," *New Orleans Item*, July 6, 1924, 1, 3. Other observers also charged policemen with treating African American assailants "too lightly." See, for example, Chivers, "Homicides Among Negroes in Atlanta, 1934–1938," 1.

58. Daugette, "Homicide in New Orleans," 11–15.

59. "344 Murders in N.O. in 5 Years, Record Shows," *New Orleans Item*, September 24, 1924, 4. Also see "An Unusual Case," *New Orleans Item*, August 22, 1927, 4.

60. Davis, Gardner, and Gardner, *Deep South*, 501.

61. Myrdal, *An American Dilemma, 536.*

62. Raper, "Race and Class Pressures," 269.

63. Davis, Gardner, and Gardner, *Deep South*, 46.

64. Chivers, "Homicides Among Negroes in Atlanta, 1934–1938," 3.

65. Davis, Gardner, and Gardner, *Deep South*, 46.

66. Davis, Gardner, and Gardner, *Deep South*, 46.

67. Davis, Gardner, and Gardner, *Deep South*, 502.

68. Davis, Gardner, and Gardner, *Deep South*, 501, 503.

69. Davis, Gardner, and Gardner, *Deep South*, 510.

70. Johnson et al., *To Stem This Tide*, 72.

71. Johnson, *Patterns of Negro Segregation*, 299; Johnson et al., *To Stem This Tide*, 72.

72. "A Closed Incident," *Louisiana Weekly*, May 20, 1933, 8.

73. Myrdal, *An American Dilemma*, 540.

74. Anonymous, "Memorandum on the Police in a Southern City," 1.

75. The demographic profiles come from New Orleans police files and coroners' reports, while the education data were drawn from census records. Memphis homicide records revealed a similar profile of 1920s killer cops, with 26.7 percent in their twenties and a mean age of 32.6. See Homicide Reports, Memphis Police Department.

76. "Suspension for Officer Gagan," *Louisiana Weekly*, July 22, 1933, 1.

77. Homicide Reports, "Report of Homicide of Albert Colbert," January 25, 1923.

78. "Policemen's Sport," *Louisiana Weekly*, March 20, 1926, 6.

79. Homicide Reports, "Report of Homicide of George Simmons," January 10, 1931.

80. "Negro Mourner at Wake Is Shot by Drunken Cop," *Baton Rouge Advocate*, December 28, 1930, 20; "Policeman Jailed After Terrorizing Negroes at Wake," *New Orleans Times-Picayune*, December 28, 1930, 1.

81. See Brearley, "Ba-ad N-----"; Johnson, *Patterns of Negro Segregation*, 299; Davis, Gardner, and Gardner, *Deep South*, 503.

82. Homicide Reports, "Report of Homicide of George Simmons," January 10, 1931; "Policeman Jailed After Terrorizing Negroes at Wake," *New Orleans Times-Picayune*, December 28, 1930, 1.

83. Homicide Reports, "Report of Homicide of George Simmons," January 10, 1931.

84. "Beyond the Pale," *New Orleans Item*, December 31, 1930, 8.

85. "An Unspeakable Outrage," *New Orleans States*, December 31, 1930, 4.

86. "Cronin Acquitted on Self-Defense Plea in Slaying at Orleans Wake," *New Orleans Times-Picayune*, May 22, 1931, 1.

87. "Evans Shooting Brings Arrests," *New Orleans Times-Picayune*, January 3, 1922, 2.

88. "Policeman Removed for Beating Woman," *New Orleans Times-Picayune*, November 29, 1924, 1; "Policeman Dismissed for Tying, Shooting at Girl," *New Orleans Item*, November 28, 1924, 1; "Elmo Evans Is Suspended, Say He Beat Woman," *New Orleans States*, November 12, 1924, 2.

89. "Officer's Appeal from Dismissal Up," *New Orleans Times-Picayune*, March 13, 1925, 10.

90. "Sleuth Demoted to Patrolman's Rank by Myers," *New Orleans Times-Picayune*, November 2, 1930, 2.

91. "Myers Demotes Detective Who Let Suspect Go," *New Orleans Times-Picayune*, November 1, 1930, 2. "Sleuth Demoted to Patrolman's Rank by Myers," *New Orleans Times-Picayune*, November 2, 1930, 2.

92. Transcripts of Statements, "Statement of Elmo Evans," May 21, 1931.

93. See Homicide Reports, "Report of Homicide of Eugene Brown," May 23, 1931; "Patrolman Evans to Retire Thursday," *New Orleans Times-Picayune*, July 30, 1941, 6.

94. Fichter, "Police Handling of Arrestees," 32.

95. Vyhnanek, *Unorganized Crime*, 29; "How Police Force of New Orleans Ranks with Others of Large Cities of Country," *New Orleans Times-Picayune*, May 30, 1920 (section 2), 1.

96. Vyhnanek, *Unorganized Crime*, 29. Wild fluctuations in the police budget produced numerous expansions and contractions during the decade. See, for example, "Heavy Slash in New Orleans Police Force for 1923 Is Planned," *New Orleans Item*, December 28, 1922, 3.

97. For example, Frank Lannes, who would retire as the chief of the detectives, had been suspended for neglect of duty during his probationary period. See "Police Justice," *New Orleans Times-Picayune*, September 30, 1909, 6. For the virtually automatic promotion of supernumerary patrolmen, see "Supernumerary Policemen to be Raised to Regulars," *New Orleans-Times Picayune* April 26, 1921, 18.

98. "Emergency Police Reserve Recommended for Orleans," *New Orleans Times-Picayune*, December 4, 1921, 12.

99. Smith, *The New Orleans Police Survey*, 34; Woodruff, "The Atlanta Police Officer and Functioning of the Atlanta Police Department," 1.

100. Smith, *The New Orleans Police Survey*, 34.

101. Myrdal, *An American Dilemma*, 539.

102. Fichter, "Police Handling of Arrestees," 50.

103. Davis, Gardner, and Gardner, *Deep South* 503.

104. Raper, "Race and Class Pressures," 50.

105. Brearley, "Ba-ad N-----," 79, 80.

106. "Negro Dead, Man and Woman Cut," *New Orleans Times-Picayune*, February 13, 1922, 5.

107. Homicide Reports, "Report of Homicide of Morris Peterson," February 12, 1922.

108. The figure for Memphis police homicides of African Americans residents during the 1920s was 34.2 percent.

109. Homicide Reports.

110. Memphis Police Department Homicide Reports.

111. Memphis Police Department Homicide Reports; Papers of the National Association for the Advancement of Colored People.

CHAPTER TWO

1. "Bandit Takes $12 from Pocket of Wounded Grocer," *New Orleans Times-Picayune*, March 22, 1932, 1.

2. See Brundage, "Introduction," 4, 10.

3. "Statement of Leaval Hubbard," April 26, 1932, Transcripts of Statements.

4. "Murder Is Solved," *New Orleans States*, April 23, 1932, 2.

5. "Statement of Leaval Hubbard," April 26, 1932, Transcripts of Statements.

6. Coroner's Reports, "Inquest Report on Edward Melancon," March 23, 1932.

7. "Son of Murdered Grocer Picks Out Slaying Suspect," *New Orleans Times-Picayune*, April 27, 1932, 3.

8. "Son of Murdered Man Pleading for Work," *New Orleans States*, April 26, 1932, 1.

9. "Killer at Victim's Funeral," *New Orleans Item*, April 26, 1932, 4; "Family in Want After Robber Kills Father," *New Orleans Times-Picayune*, April 27, 1932, 3.

10. "Son of Murdered Man Pleading for Work," *New Orleans States*, April 26, 1932, 1.

11. "Capture Orleans Crime Gang and Arsenal," *New Orleans States*, April 27, 1932, 2.

12. Campaign advertisement, *New Orleans Times-Picayune*, May 17, 1935, 7.

13. For "marauder," see "Mother and Son, 8, Hacked with Ax in Sleep by Marauder," *New Orleans Times-Picayune*, February 29, 1932, 1.

14. Brearley, "Ba-ad N-----," 79; Raper, "Race and Class Pressures," 54–55.

15. "'Innocent' Says Man Doomed to Hang," *Louisiana Weekly*, November 26, 1932, 1.

16. "Capture Orleans Crime Gang and Arsenal," *New Orleans States*, April 27, 1932, 2; "Killer at Victim's Funeral," *New Orleans Item*, April 26, 1932, 4.

17. Daugette, "Homicide in New Orleans"; Adler, "Justice Is Something That Is Unheard of for the Average Negro," 213–31.

18. Adler, "Justice Is Something That Is Unheard of for the Average Negro."

19. Woofter, *Negro Problems in Cities*, 29.

20. Hall, *Negroes in the United States*, 55.

21. Blalock, *Toward a Theory of Minority-Group Relations*.

22. "How Police Force of New Orleans Ranks with Others of Large Cities of Country," *New Orleans Times-Picayune*, May 30, 1920 (section 2), 1.

23. New Orleans Tax Revision Commission, *A Fiscal and Administrative Survey of the City of New Orleans*, 109.

24. Taeuber and Taeuber, *Negroes in Cities*, 190.

25. Bertrand I. Cahn, "*Amicus Curiae* Brief," Harmon v. Tyler (October 1926), 51–52.

26. Files of the New Orleans Branch of the National Association for the Advancement of Colored People, Maurice B. Gatlin, "Transcript of 'Radio Speech,'" Station WBW, August 9, 1935.

27. "Woman's Cries Bring Capture of Assailant," *New Orleans Times-Picayune*, March 10, 1930, 2; "Woman Holdup Victim Identifies Negro Bandit," *New Orleans Item*, July 25, 1930, 2.

28. "Too Much Interference," *Louisiana Weekly*, August 1, 1936, 6; Johnson, *Patterns of Negro Segregation*, 125, 127, 303; Moton, *What the Negro Thinks*, 213; Dollard, *Caste and Class in a Southern Town*, 320.

29. "Thuggery," *New Orleans Item*, January 9, 1925, 1.

30. Local civil rights activists also attacked institutional mechanisms of racial control, challenging the constitutionality of the city's zoning ordinance and the parish's practices of disfranchising African Americans and excluding them from criminal court juries. These efforts successfully overturned the zoning measure but failed in the other campaigns. Even unsuccessful legal challenges, however, frightened white New Orleanians and put local officials on the defensive. See Devore, *Defying Jim Crow*, 174–90.

31. Homicide Reports, "Report of Homicide of George Stouff," January 21, 1925; "Negro Uses Knife When Reprimanded," *New Orleans Times-Picayune*, January 20, 1925, 13.

32. "Wounded He Crawls to Home; Wife Aids Him," *New Orleans States*, March 9, 1930, 2.

33. "Bandit Pair Shoots Man in Holdup," *New Orleans Item*, March 9, 1930, 1.

34. Edward J. Smith to Theodore A. Ray, "Letter to the Superintendent," March 8, 1930, in Homicide Reports, "Report of Homicide of Wilmer J. Lyons," March 9, 1930; "Murder Charged to Negro Robber Who Blames Pal," *New Orleans Times-Picayune*, July 5, 1930, 13.

35. "Ex-Springhill Football Star Shot by Negro," *Baton Rouge Advocate*, March 9, 1930, 1.

36. "Vengeful Negro Robber Wounds Former Athlete," *New Orleans Times-Picayune*, March 9, 1930, 1.

37. "Negro Assailant of Slain Student Is Found Guilty," *New Orleans Times-Picayune*, May 25, 1930, 1.

38. "Statement of Eddie Herbert," March 5, 1930, Transcripts of Statements.

39. "Two Negroes Jailed, One Resembles Murderer," *New Orleans States*, March 5, 1930, 2.

40. "Negro Assailant of Slain Student Is Found Guilty," *New Orleans Times-Picayune*, May 25, 1930, 1.

41. "Two Negroes Jailed, One Resembles Murderer," *New Orleans States*, March 5, 1930, 2.

42. "Negro Confesses Slaying Student in Carnival Riot," *New Orleans Times-Picayune*, March 6, 1930, 1.

43. "Slayer of Tulane Student Readily Admits Shooting," *Baton Rouge State Times Advocate*, March 6, 1930, 1.

44. "Statement of Louis Tamor," March 5, 1930, Transcripts of Statements; "Statement of Daisy Powell," March 4, 1930, Transcripts of Statements.

45. "Statement of George Johnson," March 5, 1930, Transcripts of Statements.

46. "Straight Talk," *Louisiana Weekly*, March 15, 1930, 6.

47. "Statement of George Johnson," March 5, 1930, Transcripts of Statements.

48. "Slayer of Tulane Student Readily Admits Shooting," *Baton Rouge State Times Advocate*, March 6, 1930, 1.

49. "Statement of Mabel Vincent," March 5, 1930, Transcripts of Statements.

50. "Straight Talk," *Louisiana Weekly*, March 15, 1930, 6.

51. "Two Negroes Jailed, One Resembles Murderer," *New Orleans States*, March 5, 1930, 2.

52. Hoffman, "Homicide Record for 1924," 4.

53. "Action Needed," *New Orleans Item*, October 7, 1929, 10.

54. W. H. McClendon, "Letter to the Editor," *New Orleans States*, May 25, 1926, 8.

55. "Murders, Suicides Increase in 1921," *New Orleans Times-Picayune*, January 1, 1922, 20.

56. "344 Murders in N.O. in 5 Years, Record Shows," *New Orleans Item*, September 24, 1924, 4.

57. "Hanging Only Cure for Homicides, Says Molony," *New Orleans Item*, July 6, 1924, 3.

58. "High Death Rate Due to Influx of Outsiders," *New Orleans Times-Picayune*, January 1, 1924 (section 2), 1.

59. "To the Trial Juries," *New Orleans Item*, February 5, 1926, 12.

60. "Negroes Barred from Building Too Near Whites," *New Orleans Times-Picayune*, September 17, 1924, 14.

61. Harmon v. Tyler, 273 U.S. 668 (1927). For a recent analysis of stereotyping and bias, see O'Flaherty and Sethi, *Shadows of Doubt*, 19.

62. Johnson, *Patterns of Negro Segregation*, 299.

63. Brearley, "Ba-ad N-----," 78.

64. Raper, "Race and Class Pressures," 53–54; Brearley, "Ba-ad N-----," 75.

65. "Healy Plans War on 'Gun Toters,'" *New Orleans Times-Picayune*, July 23, 1925, 12; "Prompt Trials, Death Penalty Urged by Jury," *New Orleans Item*, March 3, 1925, 18.

66. "Managers' Skull Thought to be Fractured," *New Orleans States*, October 15, 1927, 1.

67. "Café Proprietor Is Shot by Bandit," *New Orleans Item*, February 24, 1929, 1.

68. "Merchant Is Shot by Bandit in His Store," *New Orleans States*, July 20, 1930, 1.

69. "Orleans Grocer Seriously Shot by Negro Bandit," *Baton Rouge Advocate*, October 3, 1930, 24.

70. "Capture Orleans Crime Gang and Arsenal," *New Orleans States*, April 27, 1932, 2.

71. "Orgy of Stickups Keeps Police Busy," *Memphis Commercial Appeal*, August 31, 1930, 10; Jett, *Race, Crime, and Policing in the Jim Crow South*, 35.

72. "Women Identify Negro Assailant," *New Orleans Item*, February 20, 1925, 8.

73. "Woman Holdup Victim Identifies Negro Bandit," *New Orleans Item*, July 25, 1930, 2.

74. "Woman's Cries Bring Capture of Assailant," *New Orleans Times-Picayune*, March 10, 1930, 2.

75. "Woman's Cries Rout Fiend," *New Orleans Item*, November 18, 1928, 1.

76. "Woman Is Injured by Negro Robber," *New Orleans Times-Picayune*, September 10, 1929, 4.

77. "State Will Renew Effort to Hang Negro Assailant," *New Orleans Item*, May 21, 1926, 12.

78. "Two Bandits Holdup Women," *New Orleans Item*, January 1, 1929, 1; "Negro Robber Steals Beads Off Woman," *New Orleans States*, January 1, 1929, 4.

79. "Select Jury in Assault Case," *New Orleans Item*, January 20, 1929, 3.

80. "Girl Is Struck by Negro Bandit," *New Orleans Times-Picayune*, January 1, 1931, 29.

81. "Woman, 65, Hurt by Negro Robber," *New Orleans Item*, January 13, 1929, 2; "Woman Beaten in Fight with Burglar," *New Orleans States*, January 13, 1929, 1.

82. "Woman Fires at Negro Burglar," *New Orleans States*, February 22, 1932, 7.

83. "Woman Slugged; Robbed in Home," *New Orleans States*, December 20, 1932, 5.

84. "Photos Solve Robbery of Girl," *New Orleans States*, February 18, 1926, 19.

85. "Suspected Negro Robber Is Shot Down in Flight," *New Orleans Times-Picayune*, February 17, 1926, 25.

86. "Women Identify Negro Assailant," *New Orleans Item*, February 20, 1925, 8.

87. "Negro Gets Life Term for Attacking Young Woman," *New Orleans Item*, June 26, 1929, 1; "Negro Captured Quickly After Robbing Grocery," *New Orleans Times-Picayune*, December 14, 1930, 1.

88. "Negro Bandits Continue Attacks on Women," *New Orleans Item*, June 4, 1929, 4.

89. Local political leaders and criminal justice officials demonstrated no such alarm about white crime or the 51.4 percent spike in New Orleans's white homicide rate during the 1920s.

90. Brearley, "The Negro and Homicide," 247–53. Also see Muhammad, *The Condemnation of Blackness*.

91. See Hoffman, *The Homicide Problem*.

92. For Hoffman's views on race and violence, see "The Increase in Murder," 23.

93. "Hanging Only Cure for Homicides, Says Molony," *New Orleans Item*, July 6, 1924, 1; Frederick L. Hoffman, "The Homicide Record," *New Orleans States*, April 8, 1930, 8.

94. "Hanging Only Cure for Homicides, Says Molony," *New Orleans Item*, July 6, 1924, 1.

95. "Homicide Report of Memphis," 11; "Homicides in Memphis, Tenn.," 7.

96. "Woman Slugged; Robbed in Home," *New Orleans States*, December 20, 1932, 5; "Negro Robber Steals Bead Off Woman," *New Orleans States*, January 1, 1929, 4; "Policemen's Sport," *Louisiana Weekly*, March 20, 1926, 6.

97. "Reyer Warns His Officers to Exercise Extreme Caution in Shooting at Fugitives," *New Orleans Times-Picayune*, March 23, 1936, 1, 3.

98. "Refusing a Whitewash," *Louisiana Weekly*, March 21, 1936, 6.

99. "Robbery Faked by Young Bride, Declare Police," *New Orleans Times-Picayune*, December 21, 1932, 20; "A Call to Arms," *Louisiana Weekly*, May 13, 1933, 1.

100. "The White Man's Burden," *Louisiana Weekly*, May 20, 1933, 8.

101. "Police Discredit Story of Hold-Up," *New Orleans Times-Picayune*, September 17, 1924, 2. When victim accounts seemed fabricated, detectives investigated and interrogated witnesses more aggressively.

102. "Oil Station Manager Is Held by Police in Attendant's Death," *New Orleans Times-Picayune*, August 14, 1936, 1; "Orleans Negro Bandits Shoot Three Whites," *Baton Rouge Star Times Advocate*, August 13, 1936, 1, 8.

103. "Biri Draws Term in Manslaughter," *New Orleans Times-Picayune*, December 12, 1936, 9.

104. Johnson, "The Negro and Crime," 96.

105. "Robbery Faked by Young Bride, Declare Police," *New Orleans Times-Picayune*, December 21, 1932, 20.

106. Potter, *War on Crime*; Walker, *A Critical History of Police Reform*, 139.

107. Files of the New Orleans Branch of the National Association for the Advancement of Colored People, Maurice B. Gatlin, "Transcript of 'Radio Speech,'" Station WBW, August 9, 1935.

108. St. Clair Adams, "Delays Now Strangling Justice in New Orleans' Criminal Courts," *New Orleans Item*, May 8, 1925, 12; "Action Needed," *New Orleans Item*, October 7, 1929, 10.

109. "An Unusual Case," *New Orleans Item*, August 22, 1927, 4.

110. "Wickersham Report Raps Third Degree," *Atlanta Journal*, August 10, 1931, 4.

111. "Negro Criminals Busy in Memphis," *New Orleans Times-Picayune*, November 22, 1920, 11; "Negro Robbers Busy," *Memphis Commercial Appeal*, October 25, 1935, 23; Jett, *Race, Crime, and Policing in the Jim Crow South*, 35.

112. "Girl Names Negroes as Her Assailants," *Memphis Commercial Appeal*, February 28, 1933, 8; "Labor Defense Stirs Up Protest in Killing," *Memphis Commercial Appeal*, February 28, 1933, 8.

113. "Action Needed," *New Orleans Item*, October 7, 1929, 10.

CHAPTER THREE

1. "Prisoners Kills Three Police: Is Slain by Detective," *New Orleans Times-Picayune*, March 10, 1932, 3.

2. "Policemen to be Buried with Full Honors," *New Orleans States*, March 10, 1932, 4; "Prisoners Kills Three Police: Is Slain by Detective," *New Orleans Times-Picayune*, March 10, 1932, 3; "New Orleans' Unsung Police Heroes," *New Orleans Item*, June 30, 1937, 4.

3. "Kills Two, Wounds Two," *New York Times*, March 10, 1932, 12; "New Orleans Fight at Jail Fatal to 3," *Washington Post*, March 10, 1932, 3; "Negro Battles 100 Policemen; Three Are Slain," *Chicago Tribune*, March 10, 1932, 10.

4. "Prisoner Slays 3 Brutal Policemen," *New York Amsterdam News*, March 16, 1932, 3; "Prisoner Fights 200 City Policemen; 3 Are Slain and He Too, Fatally Shot," *Louisiana Weekly*, March 12, 1932, 1.

5. "Prisoner Kills Three Police: Is Slain by Detective," *New Orleans Times-Picayune*, March 10, 1932, 3.

6. Coroner's Reports, "Inquest Report on Percy Thompson," March 9, 1932; Transcripts of Statements, "Statement of Vic Swanson," March 10, 1932.

7. "Prisoner Kills Three Police; Is Slain by Detective," *New Orleans Times-Picayune*, March 10, 1932, 1.

8. Transcripts of Statements, "Statement of James D. Burns," March 9, 1932.

9. Transcripts of Statements, "Statement of Percy Thompson," March 9, 1932.

10. "Louisiana Man Killed After Battle with Cops," *Pittsburgh Courier*, May 19, 1932, 18; "Prisoner Fights 200 City Policemen; 3 Are Slain and He Too, Fatally Shot," *Louisiana Weekly*, March 12, 1932, 1.

11. Transcripts of Statements, "Statement of Percy Thompson," March 9, 1932.

12. "New Orleans' Unsung Police Heroes," *New Orleans Item*, June 30, 1937, 4.

13. Transcripts of Statements, "Statement of Percy Thompson," March 9, 1932.

14. Transcripts of Statements, "Statements of Vic Swanson," March 10, 1932.

15. "Prisoner Slays 3 Brutal Policemen," *New York Amsterdam News*, March 16, 1932, 3; "A Call to Arms," *Louisiana Weekly*, May 13, 1933, 1; "Louisiana Man Killed After Battle with Cops," *Pittsburgh Courier*, May 19, 1932, 18.

16. For Thompson's criminal record, see "In District Court," *Baton Rouge State Times Advocate*, May 6, 1925, 13; "Goes to Throw Wife in River; Is Now in Jail," *Baton Rouge State Times Advocate*, April 28, 1925, 1; "Beats Jury Out of His Case by Pleading Guilty," *Baton Rouge State Times Advocate*, May 25, 1925, 12.

17. Coroner's Reports, "Inquest Report on Percy Thompson," March 9, 1932.

18. "Iron Claw Subdues Unruly Prisoners," *New Orleans Times-Picayune*, March 13, 1932, 58.

19. "It's Happened Again," *Louisiana Weekly*, May 31, 1941, 6.

20. Johnson, "The Negro and Crime," 97.

21. "Police Brutality Common in Southern Cities," *Pittsburgh Courier*, August 3, 1940, 15.

22. Wells-Barnett, *Mob Rule in New Orleans*; Prince, *The Ballad of Robert Charles*; Baker, *To Poison A Nation*.

23. Charles A.J. McPherson to Walter White, April 12, 1940, Papers of the NAACP, Memphis Branch Files, Box II:B112, Folder 22, 1940–1955, Papers of the National Association for the Advancement of Colored People; Kotch, *Lethal State*, 18.

24. Memphis Police Department Homicide Reports.

25. "Labor Defense Stirs Up Protest in Killing, *Memphis Commercial Appeal*, February 28, 1933, 8.

26. "Murder Suspect Tells How Detectives Attempted to Make Him Confess," *Louisiana Weekly*, January 13, 1934, 4.

27. "Ray Warns City Thuggery Looms Under Behrman," *New Orleans Times-Picayune*, January 26, 1925, 25.

28. St. Clair Adams, "Delays Now Strangling Justice in New Orleans' Criminal Courts," *New Orleans Item*, May 8, 1925, 12.

29. "Action Needed," *New Orleans Item*, October 7, 1929, 10.

30. Vyhnanek, *Unorganized Crime*, 29; "How Police Force of New Orleans Ranks with Others of Large Cities of Country," *New Orleans Times-Picayune*, May 30, 1920 (section 2), 1.

31. "Action Needed," *New Orleans Item*, October 7, 1929, 10.

32. Vyhnanek, *Unorganized Crime*, 29–30; *Fourteenth Census of the United States*, 200; *Fifteenth Census of the United States*, 619.

33. "End Crime or Quit, Healy Tells Police," *New Orleans Item*, May 14, 1925, 1; "Our Police and Crime," *New Orleans Item*, October 28, 1925, 12.

34. "Police to Get Machine Guns to Fight Bandits," *New Orleans Item*, March 31, 1926, 1.

35. "Shotguns Called into Play," *New Orleans Times-Picayune*, November 3, 1929, 1.

36. "Bandits, Beware," *New Orleans Item*, July 10, 1929, 1.

37. Journalists typically argue that militarized crime fighting developed in the 1960s. For example, Balko, *Rise of the Warrior Cop*, xvi, 33, 35, 52.

38. "Deadliest Modern Outfit for War on Crime Arrives to Equip Police Gas Squad," *New Orleans Times-Picayune*, June 10, 1928, 33; "Go Get 'Em," *New Orleans Item*, May 16, 1925, 4. Also see Jimenez et al., "Racial Prejudice Predicts Police Militarization."

39. "Here Is the New Police Bandit Squad," *New Orleans States*, August 13, 1926, 7.

40. "County Buys 'Tear Gun,'" *Memphis Commercial Appeal*, December 6, 1930, 4; "Police to Organize Machine Gun Squad," *Memphis Commercial Appeal*, May 22, 1934, 13; "Local Officers Shown New Tear Gas Weapons," *Huntsville Times*, April 20, 1932, 1.

41. "Police Ride Cars Ready to Shoot to Protect Life," *New Orleans Item*, July 5, 1929, 2; "Local Officers Shown New Tear Gas Weapons," *Huntsville Times*, April 20, 1932, 1 "Police to Use Machine Guns to Battle Bandits in Future: 'Shoot to Kill,' Is Order Issued by Superintendent Ray," *New Orleans Item*, July 10, 1929, 1.

42. "Ray to Revive Target Practice So Police Won't Miss Bandits," *New Orleans Item*, June 16, 1929, 10.

43. Smith, *The New Orleans Police Survey*, 34; "How to Kill Bandits to Be Taught Police," *New Orleans Item*, October 28, 1925, 1. Less than one-third of Southern cities mandated formal training during this era. See Raper, "Race and Class Pressures," 17.

44. "Ray to Revive Target Practice So Police Won't Miss Bandits," *New Orleans Item*, June 16, 1929, 10.

45. "Third Degree in Nashville," *Knoxville News-Sentinel*, August 11, 1931, 5.

46. "Police Killings," *New Orleans Item*, August 4, 1927, 12.

47. For example, "Found Shot; May Be Bandit," *New Orleans Item*, April 27, 1929, 1.

48. "Bringing Things to Light," *Louisiana Weekly*, April 2, 1932, 6.

49. "Death of Negro in New Orleans Jail Is Mystery," *Baton Rouge Advocate*, June 18, 1938, 8.

50. Papers of the Louisiana League, Report of Captain Bell relative to registered complaint #6108, May 5, 1945.

51. "Retain 'D & S,'" *New Orleans Times-Picayune*, May 19, 1934, 7.

52. "Constitutionality of D. & S. Law Attacked," *New Orleans Item*, November 2, 1934, 1.

53. "Recorders Talk Over Ordinance," *New Orleans Times-Picayune*, May 19, 1934, 17.

54. City of New Orleans v. Postek, 180 La. 1048 (1934).

55. "Prompt Trials, Death Penalty Urged by Jury," *New Orleans Item*, March 3, 1925, 18; "Molony Scores 'Gun-Toting' Evil in Underworld," *New Orleans Times-Picayune*, May 25, 1923, 3.

56. "Molony Scores 'Gun-Toting' Evil in Underworld," *New Orleans Times-Picayune*, May 25, 1923, 3; "Make It Thorough," *Louisiana Weekly*, January 4, 1930, 6.

57. See Adler, "Guns and Violence," 193.

58. "Stanley Is Pledged to a Relentless War on Crime," *New Orleans Item*, May 4, 1930, 18.

59. "Democrats Work for Big Vote Tuesday," *New Orleans States*, April 6, 1930, 4; "Lays Negro Vote Activity to Long," *New Orleans States*, May 31, 1935, 3; "Warning," *New Orleans States*, May 16, 1935, 7. This also appeared in the *New Orleans Item*, the *New Orleans Times-Picayune*, the *Baton Rouge Advocate*, and the *Baton Rouge State Times Advocate*.

60. W. H. Bentley to Roy Wilkins, July 3, 1933, Birmingham Branch Files, Box I:G199, Folder 13, April-December, 1933, Papers of the National Association for the Advancement of Colored People; Niedermeier, *The Color of the Third Degree*.

61. Article I, Section 11, *Constitution of the State of Louisiana*, 3.

62. Chafee, Pollak, and Stern, "The Third Degree."

63. Niedermeier, *The Color of the Third Degree*; Johnson, *Street Justice*.

64. Coroner's Reports, "Inquest Report on Ross Palumbo," May 10, 1932; "Order Complete Probe of Death of N. O. Prisoners," *Baton Rouge Star Times Advocate*, May 11, 1932, 1.

65. Carnegie-Myrdal Study of the Negro in America Research Memoranda Collection, Anonymous, "Memorandum on the Police in a Southern City," 2.

66. Letter to the Editor, *New Orleans States*, June 14, 1939, 6. Twenty-first-century Americans often share this view of the boundaries of constitutional safeguards. For example, Americans overwhelming oppose the torture of prisoners but were more tolerant after the September 11 violence. Earlier Americans affirmed belief in free speech but not for communists. See McClosky and Brill, *Dimensions of Tolerance*; Sullivan, Piereson, and Marcus, *Political Tolerance and American Democracy*; Marcus, Sullivan, Theiss-Morse, and Wood, *With Malice toward Some*; Boeckmann and Tyler, "Commonsense Justice and Inclusion Within the Moral Community"; Finkel, *Commonsense Justice*.

67. "A Fair Hearing," *New Orleans States*, January 12, 1938, 10.

68. "21st Amendment Study by Special Session Is Urged," *New Orleans Times-Picayune*, May 27, 1933, 2.

69. "Third Degree Case," *New Orleans States*, May 13, 1932, 6.

70. "Against Third Degree," *New Orleans States*, June 3, 1933, 4.

71. "2 Detectives Are Found Guilty," *Louisiana Weekly*, June 3, 1933, 7.

72. "Police Brutality Common in Southern Cities," *Pittsburgh Courier*, August 3, 1940, 15.

73. "Brutality and Humiliation Are Charged by Outraged Pair," *Louisiana Weekly*, February 28, 1948, 1.

74. "Simon Legreeism," *Louisiana Weekly*, May 21, 1932, 6.

75. "Memphis Cop Fined for Slapping Prisoner," *Meridian Weekly Echo*, February 24, 1933, 1.

76. For example, "Police Brutality," *Louisiana Weekly*, February 3, 1940, 8.

77. "Physical Examinations Urged for 'Confessors,'" *New Orleans States*, April 22, 1933, 3. Other Southern cities also ranked poorly; "Survey Finds Americans Enjoy but Half of Guaranteed Rights," *Washington Post*, March 6, 1939, 24; Niedermeier, *The Color of the Third Degree*.

78. "Physical Examinations Urged for 'Confessors,'" *New Orleans States*, April 22, 1933, 3; "Survey Finds Americans Enjoy but Half of Guaranteed Rights," *Washington Post*, March 6, 1939, 24.

79. Kohn, "Report of the Special Citizens Investigating Committee of the Commission Council of New Orleans," 113.

80. "Storm Troopers," *Louisiana Weekly*, April 8, 1933, 8.

81. "Free Policeman in Death of Youth," *Chicago Defender*, June 7, 1941, 8; Letter to the Editor, *New Orleans States*, July 12, 1944, 8.

82. "A Fair Hearing," *New Orleans States*, January 12, 1938, 10.

83. Chisolm and Hart, "Methods of Obtaining Confessions and Information from Persons Accused of Crime," 17.

84. Papers of the Louisiana League, Statement of Mrs. Lottie Williams, April 17, 1944.

85. Papers of the Louisiana League, Statement of Floyd D. T. Washington, September 14, 1939; Leon Lewis, "Says NAACP Asked Membership Free When He

Asked for Aid," *Louisiana Weekly*, August 6, 1938, 2; Papers of the Louisiana League, "Chef Cook Tells of Thirty Days Torture While White Cops Try to Make Him Confess to Crime He Knew Nothing About," Files of the *Pittsburgh Courier*, July 23, 1938.

86. "Held Incommunicado Four Days, Body Black and Blue from Vicious Third Degree," *Louisiana Weekly*, February 4, 1939, 1.

87. "Police Disclaim Use of Force to Get Confession," *New Orleans Times-Picayune*, September 24, 1931, 6.

88. Papers of the Louisiana League, "Bulletin," August 17, 1939.

89. "The 'Hot Tamale' Decision," *Louisiana Weekly*, November 8, 1941, 10.

90. James B. LaFourche, "11-Year-Old Witness Tells Court Cops Beat Him and Promised Bicycle for Lie," *Louisiana Weekly*, May 15, 1937, 1.

91. "Johnson Saved, But Gets Life Imprisonment," *Louisiana Weekly*, August 30, 1930, 1.

92. Davis and Dollard, *Children of Bondage*, 248.

93. Raper, "Race and Class Pressures," 174.

94. W. H. Bentley to Roy Wilkins, July 3, 1933, Birmingham Branch Files, Box I:G199, Folder 13, April–December, 1933, Papers of the National Association for the Advancement of Colored People.

95. Raper, "Race and Class Pressures," 174.

96. "Ice Cream and Cake," *Louisiana Weekly*, June 10, 1939, 8.

97. Brutality victims filed complaints with diverse institutions, ranging from the district attorney to civil rights organizations. Many reports, particularly those made to prosecutors, were ignored or dismissed. Newspapers reported some complaints, and a few private institutions maintained records. Thus, it is impossible to quantify the brutality.

98. "Murder Suspect Tells How Detectives Attempted to Make Him Confess," *Louisiana Weekly*, January 13, 1934, 1, 4.

99. "No Excuse for Police Brutality," *Louisiana Weekly*, February 11, 1939, 8.

100. Raper, "Race and Class Pressures," 174.

101. Papers of the Louisiana League, Harold N. Lee to George Reyer, June 1, 1939.

102. "Giant Lad Declares Sleuth Beat Him All Night Long," *Louisiana Weekly*, March 25, 1933, 4.

103. Papers of the Louisiana League, Statement of Miss Ethel Anderson to John E. Rousseau Jr., April 21, 1945.

104. James B. LaFourche, "11-Year-Old Witness Tells Court Cops Beat Him and Promised Bicycle for Lie," *Louisiana Weekly*, May 15, 1937, 1; Papers of the Louisiana League, Harold N. Lee to John Rousseau Jr., November 1, 1944.

105. Raper, "Race and Class Pressures," 172.

106. Papers of the Louisiana League, Harold N. Lee to Mr. Musgrove, September 24, 1939.

107. "2 Innocent Men Say Police Beat Them in Try at Confession," *Louisiana Weekly*, February 20, 1937, 1.

108. "Astoria Cook Turns Out to be Wrong Man," *Louisiana Weekly*, July 23, 1938, 1.

109. Myrdal, *An American Dilemma*, 541.

110. "No Excuse for Police Brutality," *Louisiana Weekly*, February 11, 1939, 8.

111. Letter to the *Pittsburgh Courier*, March 2, 1943, Administrative File: Police Brutality, Box II: B112, Folder 12, 1940–1955, Papers of the National Association for the Advancement of Colored People.

112. Letter to the Editor, June 10, 1939, *New Orleans States*, June 14, 1939, 6.

113. "Stanley Breaks Record of Court," *New Orleans States*, February 2, 1930, 10; "1101 Convictions Obtained in 1931, Stanley Reports," *New Orleans Times-Picayune*, May 6, 1932, 3.

114. Myrdal, *An American Dilemma*, 535.

115. Among other places, Memphis, Birmingham, and Mobile branch files of the NAACP document the changes. See Papers of the National Association for the Advancement of Colored People; Niedermeier, *The Color of the Third Degree*.

116. Memphis Police Department Homicide Reports; Niedermeier, *The Color of the Third Degree*.

117. Petition to the Birmingham City Commission, January 24, 1933, Birmingham Branch Files, Box I:G1, Folder 1, January–February1933, Papers of the National Association for the Advancement of Colored People.

118. For an important exploration of the concept of "preservation through transformation," see Siegel, "Why Equal Protection No Longer Protects."

119. For Memphis, see Memphis Police Department Homicide Reports.

120. Myrdal, *An American Dilemma*; Raper, "Race and Class Pressures"; Dollard, *Caste and Class in a Southern Town*; Niedermeier, *The Color of the Third Degree*; Pfeifer, *Rough Justice*.

121. J. L. LeFlore to Thurgood Marshall, June 12, 1941, Mobile Branch Files, Box II:B112, Folder 12, 1940–1950, Papers of the National Association for the Advancement of Colored People.

122. For example, "Police Given Praise," *Memphis Commercial Appeal*, March 3, 1933, 5.

123. Papers of the Louisiana League, Harold N. Lee to John Rousseau Jr., November 1, 1944.

124. Fichter, *One-Man Report*, 144.

125. Executive Committee of the Birmingham Branch of the NAACP, "Petition to the Birmingham City Commission," January 31, 1933, Memphis Branch Files, Box I:G2, Folder 1, January–February, 1933, Papers of the National Association for the Advancement of Colored People.

126. For white assertions of being unaware of systemic police brutality, see "Police Brutality Common in Southern Cities," *Pittsburgh Courier*, August 3, 1940, 15. In the evocative phrase "implicated subjects," literary scholar Michael Rothberg describes the process wherein a dominant group secures the tangible benefits of power without dirtying its hands with the repression that sustains that dominance.

See Rothberg, *The Implicated Subject.* Hannah Arendt made a related argument forty years earlier. See Arendt, *On Violence,* 77.

CHAPTER FOUR

1. "Vice Squad Ready for Action," *New Orleans States,* September 19, 1934, 1.
2. "The 'Hot Tamale' Decision," *Louisiana Weekly,* November 8, 1941, 10.
3. "Vicious Young Fiend Is Killed," *New Orleans States,* November 26, 1937, 5; "Assault Suspect Is Shot to Death by Local Police," *New Orleans Times-Picayune,* November 26, 1937, 3.
4. "Orleans Cops Kill Escaping Prisoner," *New Orleans States,* November 25, 1937, 1; "Body of Alleged Rapist Lies in Morgue," *New Orleans Item,* November 26, 1937, 23; "Assault Suspect Is Shot to Death by Local Police," *New Orleans Times-Picayune,* November 26, 1937, 3.
5. "Vicious Young Fiend Is Killed," *New Orleans States,* November 26, 1937, 5.
6. Coroner's Reports, "Inquest Report on Charles Anderson [aka Handy]," November 25, 1937.
7. "Healy Will Set Deadline Limits against Bandits," *New Orleans Times-Picayune,* August 4, 1928, 1.
8. Adler, "Spineless Judges and Shyster Lawyers."
9. "The 'Why' of Brutality," *Baton Rouge Advocate,* November 13, 1930, 4.
10. "Fight on C.I.O. Gets Approval of Lawmakers," *Chattanooga Daily Times,* July 2, 1938, 2.
11. "No Excuse for Police Brutality," *Louisiana Weekly,* February 11, 1939, 8. Cops using violence against white suspects, by contrast, were widely criticized.
12. Papers of the Louisiana League, Harold N. Lee to John Rousseau Jr., November 1, 1944.
13. William Pickens, "Framed," *Louisiana Weekly,* June 6, 1931, 6.
14. "The 'Hot Tamale' Decision," *Louisiana Weekly,* November 8, 1941, 10.
15. Kohn, "Report of the Special Citizens Investigating Committee of the Commission Council of New Orleans," 113; William Pickens, "Police Lawlessness," *Louisiana Weekly,* October 9, 1937, 8.
16. Raper, "Race and Class Pressures," 50–51.
17. "No Excuse for Police Brutality," *Louisiana Weekly,* February 11, 1939, 8.
18. "Rescued," *Louisiana Weekly,* June 3, 1933, 8.
19. "Two Detectives Found Guilty of Beating Boy, 15," *New Orleans Times-Picayune,* May 27, 1933, 1.
20. "Charges Filed against White Sleuths Who Brutally Beat New Orleans Youth," *Pittsburgh Courier,* April 15, 1933, 13; "Reign of Terror in South Grows," *Pittsburgh Courier,* March 25, 1933, 9.
21. For example, Papers of the Louisiana League, Statement of Floyd D. T. Washington, September 14, 1939.

22. Social scientists have described this phenomenon. See Eberhardt, *Biased*, 60; Kahn and McMahon, "Shooting Deaths of Unarmed Racial Minorities," 115; Correll et al., "The Police Officer's Dilemma," 208.

23. Raper, "Race and Class Pressures," 20; Johnson, "The Negro and Crime," 97; Waegel, "How Police Justify the Use of Deadly Force," 147–48.

24. Transcripts of Statements, "Statement of Conrad Neagle," April 6, 1930.

25. "Stanley Will Probe Killing," *New Orleans Item*, May 15, 1933, 4; "Negro Shot in Robbery," *New Orleans Item*, March 28, 1938, 1; "Hip-Pocket Move Brings Death to Attack Suspect," *New Orleans Times-Picayune*, June 18, 1939, 12; Homicide Reports, "Report of Homicide of Willie Battise," May 23, 1942; Transcripts of Statements, "Statement of Joseph Burk," January 25, 1945; Transcripts of Statements, "Statement of Birdie Vesha," July 12, 1937; Homicide Reports, "Report of Homicide of Robert Augusta," August 6, 1945.

26. "Hip-Pocket Move Brings Death to Attack Suspect," *New Orleans Times-Picayune*, June 18, 1939, 12; "Young Boy Is Shot by Detective," *Pittsburgh Courier*, May 20, 1939, 23.

27. Homicide Reports, "Report of Homicide of Milton Battise," June 29, 1930.

28. Transcripts of Statements, "Statement of John Licali," June 17, 1943.

29. Homicide Reports, "Report of Homicide of William P. Forest," November 30, 1923; Homicide Reports, "Report of Homicide of Harold Martin," January 25, 1945.

30. Johnson et al., *To Stem This Tide*, 72.

31. "There Is No Excuse," *Louisiana Weekly*, May 20, 1939, 8.

32. "No Excuse for Police Brutality," *Louisiana Weekly*, February 11, 1939, 8; Johnson et al., *To Stem This Tide*, 72. Perhaps reflecting racial stereotypes of the "bad n-----," men comprised all of the victims in these cases.

33. "It's Happened Again," *Louisiana Weekly*, May 31, 1941, 6.

34. "Shot to Death 'Escaping' Police," *Louisiana Weekly*, January 13, 1945, 2.

35. "Free Policeman in Death of Youth," *Chicago Defender*, June 7, 1941, 8.

36. Executive Committee of the Birmingham Branch of the NAACP, "Petition to the Birmingham City Commission," Memphis Branch Files, Box I:G2, Folder 1, January–February, 1933, Papers of the National Association for the Advancement of Colored People.

37. Recent studies have measured this phenomenon. See Scott et al., "A Social Scientific Approach toward Understanding Racial Disparities in Police Shooting," 705, 717; Kramer and Remster, "Stop, Frisk, and Assault," 967.

38. Scott et al., "A Social Scientific Approach toward Understanding Racial Disparities in Police Shooting," 705; Nix et al., "A Bird's Eye View of Civilians Killed by Police in 2015," 309.

39. Raper, "Race and Class Pressures," 36, 44.

40. Prosecutors secured no convictions against New Orleans policemen who killed African American suspects for allegedly making furtive movements.

41. "Too Thin," *Louisiana Weekly*, March 29, 1930, 6; "Another Joke," *Louisiana Weekly*, August 19, 1933, 8.

42. "No Excuse for Police Brutality," *Louisiana Weekly*, February 11, 1939, 8.

43. John Dickens, Letter to the Editor, *New Orleans Times-Picayune*, June 24, 1938, 10; Patterson, ed., *We Charge Genocide*, 226.

44. "Coppers Shoot to Death Lad They Arrested," *New York Amsterdam News*, December 4, 1937, 2.

45. "Negro Suspect in Death Slain," *Baton Rouge State Times Advocate*, January 16, 1941, 11; "Prisoner Is Shot to Death by Chief in Dash to Escape," *New Orleans Times-Picayune*, December 27, 1936, 16.

46. "Another Killed by Detectives," *Louisiana Weekly*, November 9, 1935, 1.

47. "The 'Hot Tamale' Decision," *Louisiana Weekly*, November 8, 1941, 10.

48. "Say Extradition Victim Beaten to Death," *Chicago Defender*, February 8, 1941, 4; "Demand Probe of L.A. Extradition Murder," *Chicago Defender*, February 1, 1941, 8.

49. Henry W. Hermes, Letter to the Editor, *New Orleans States*, June 9, 1939, 6.

50. "Free Policeman in Death of Youth," *Chicago Defender*, June 7, 1941, 8.

51. They accounted for 41.3 percent of police homicides. This group comprised approximately 20 percent of the detective force.

52. "'Go Get 'Em," *New Orleans Item*, May 16, 1925, 4; "End of Gambling and Vice Ordered Within Five days," *New Orleans Times-Picayune*, September 19, 1934, 1; "New Orleans Squad Instructed to 'Clean Up the Town,'" *New Orleans Times-Picayune*, September 20, 1934, 3.

53. "Counsel Raps Police Brutality; Preacher Held for Perjury," *Louisiana Weekly*, August 7, 1937, 1.

54. "Retired Captain of Police Dead," *New Orleans Times-Picayune*, May 4, 1933, 2.

55. "Healy Promotes 16 on Force, Adds 113 Regular Jobs," *New Orleans Times-Picayune*, September 29, 1928, 3.

56. "Fine Minstrel Show Promised by Police," *New Orleans Times-Picayune*, November 15, 1914, 29; "Capt. James A. 'Buttercup' Burns Dies," *New Orleans States*, May 3, 1933, 1.

57. "Torture Laid to Policemen," *New Orleans Item*, December 1, 1929, 4.

58. "Accuse Police Captain of Brutality," *Louisiana Weekly*, December 7, 1929, 1; "Police Disclaim Use of Force to Get Confession," *New Orleans Times-Picayune*, September 24, 1931, 6.

59. "Board Hears Pleas of 3 Doomed," *Louisiana Weekly*, May 6, 1933, 1.

60. "Detectives Suspected; Death Laid to Brutal Flogging," *Louisiana Weekly*, May 14, 1932, 1.

61. "Accuse Police Captain of Brutality," *Louisiana Weekly*, December 7, 1929, 1.

62. "Court Dismisses Torture Charge against Police," *New Orleans Times-Picayune*, December 7, 1929, 2.

63. "Police Disclaim Use of Force to Get Confession," *New Orleans Times-Picayune*, September 24, 1931, 6.

64. "Reyer, Grosch, Relatives Get $30,000 of Police Payroll," *New Orleans States*, August 26, 1943, 4; "Reyer Denies Laxity in Police Work Here," *New Orleans Times-Picayune*, September 3, 1943, 2.

65. "Grosch Made Chief; Raise for Daniels, Cassard," *New Orleans States*, November 28, 1930, 4; "Grosch, Former Sheriff, Detective Chief Expires," *New Orleans Times-Picayune*, January 20, 1963, 1, 6; "Boyhood Pals Now Shrewd Wreckers of Crime," *New Orleans States*, January 11, 1931 (section 3), 1.

66. "John Grosch Named Aide to Police Superintendent," *New Orleans States*, May 20, 1930, 11.

67. "Death Verdict for Bandits Demanded," *New Orleans States*, July 27, 1937, 2.

68. "Mayor Asks Full Probe of Alleged Violence," *New Orleans States*, May 11, 1932, 7.

69. "On Trials, Lads' Bodies Show Cuts, Bruises; Await Verdict," *Louisiana Weekly*, July 31, 1937, 4.

70. "LA. Investigates Moore's Murder; Body Is Exhumed," *Pittsburgh Courier*, March 15, 1941, 4.

71. "Jury Probes Police Case," *New Orleans Item*, March 12, 1941, 2.

72. "Say Extradition Victim Beaten to Death," *Chicago Defender*, February 8, 1941, 4.

73. "Killing of Negro by Detective Put Under New Probe," *New Orleans Times-Picayune*, March 5, 1941, 5.

74. "LA. Investigates Moore's Murder; Body Is Exhumed," *Pittsburgh Courier*, March 15, 1941, 4.

75. "Body Is Exhumed for Examination After Complaint," *New Orleans Times-Picayune*, March 8, 1941, 5; Papers of the Louisiana League, Harold N. Lee to Fontaine Martin Jr., September 24, 1941. For this lax view, see Papers of the Louisiana League, Case of Charles Sims, October 22, 1942; Papers of the Louisiana League, Harold N. Lee to Henry A. Scheinhaut, October 22, 1942.

76. "Chief John J. Grosch Investigates 'Murder' Here During Brief Visit," *Baton Rouge State Times Advocate*, July 7, 1936, 5; Philip Lord, quoted in "Grosch, Former Sheriff, Detective Chief Expires," *New Orleans Times-Picayune*, January 20, 1963, 6.

77. "Grosch Target of Mrs. Purvis Defense Fire," *New Orleans States*, December 16, 1933, 2.

78. "2 Face Charges in Dupont Attack," *New Orleans States*, July 20, 1937, 23; "Labor Hearing in C.I.O. Row Is Continued," *Baton Rouge State Times Advocate*, July 1, 1938, 6; "Suspect in Hacking Case Is Denied Writ," *New Orleans States*, July 20, 1937, 21; "Bandit in Bank Raid Denies Third Degree Used on Confession," *New Orleans Item*, July 10, 1936, 21.

79. "Third-Degree Champion," *New Orleans Times-Picayune*, June 2, 1939, 12.

80. "Grosch Target of Mrs. Purvis Defense Fire," *New Orleans States*, December 16, 1933, 2; "Accused Woman to Charge 'Third Degree' Tactics," *New Orleans Times-Picayune,* December 15, 1933, 8.

81. "Grosch Upholds 'Third Degree' Use by Police," *Baton Rouge Advocate*, June 1, 1939, 1.

82. "Third-Degree Champion," *New Orleans Times-Picayune*, June 2, 1939, 12.

83. "Press Gets Ice Cream, Cake as Bright Police Plans Go Wrong," *New Orleans Item*, June 3, 1939, 1.

84. "Savagery—Or What?" *New Orleans Item*, June 3, 1939, 4; "Crime Is Curbed by 'Third Degree,' Asserts Grosch," *New Orleans Times-Picayune*, June 1, 1939, 1.

85. "Crime Is Curbed by 'Third Degree,' Asserts Grosch," *New Orleans Times-Picayune*, June 1, 1939, 1.

86. "Testifies Confession Was Forced," *New Orleans Item*, January 13, 1938, 24.

87. "Detectives' Head to Face Queries on 'Brutalities,'" *New Orleans Times-Picayune*, February 26, 1932, 7.

88. "Alleged Confession of Gendusa Is Ruled Out by Judge Oser," *New Orleans States*, November 19, 1937, 4.

89. State v. Silsby 178 LA 663, 671 (1933); State v. Silsby 176 LA 727, 740 (1933).

90. "Beating by N.O. Police Charged," *New Orleans Item*, December 27, 1945, 1.

91. "Crime Is Curbed by 'Third Degree,' Asserts Grosch," *New Orleans Times-Picayune*, June 1, 1939, 1.

92. "Crime Is Curbed by 'Third Degree,' Asserts Grosch," *New Orleans Times-Picayune*, June 1, 1939, 1.

93. "Prisoners Don't Even Get 'Ice Cream and Cake,' Says Reyer," *New Orleans Item*, June 1, 1939, 2.

94. Letter to the Editor, June 10, 1939, *New Orleans States*, June 14, 1939, 6.

95. "Grosch Enter Mayor's Race as Independent," *New Orleans States*, December 2, 1953, 4.

96. "Press Gets Ice Cream, Cake as Bright Police Plans Go Wrong," *New Orleans Item*, June 3, 1939, 1.

97. "Prisoners Don't Even Get 'Ice Cream and Cake,' Says Reyer," *New Orleans Item*, June 1, 1939, 1.

98. Papers of the Louisiana League, Statement of Bernard D. Mintz, August 1, 1938; "Ask State Attorney-General to Make an Investigation," *Louisiana Weekly*, September 23, 1939, 4.

99. Henry W. Hermes, Letter to the Editor, *New Orleans States*, June 9, 1939, 6.

100. "Grosch, Former Sheriff, Detective Chief Expires," *New Orleans Times-Picayune*, January 20, 1963, 6.

101. "Use of Electricity Doubles Local Detective Bureau's Efficiency, Avers Grosch," *New Orleans Times-Picayune*, April 26, 1936, 13.

102. "Legislature Condemns C.I.O.," *Nashville Tennessean*, July 2, 1938, 1.

103. "Huey Starts After N.O. Police," *Tyler Morning Telegraph*, September 15, 1934, 1; Kefauver, *Crime in America*, 175–76; "Grosch Denies He Took Protection Money in N.O.," *Baton Rouge Advocate*, May 19, 1951, 5.

104. Patterson, ed., *We Charge Genocide*, 226. Grosch ran for mayor in 1954.

105. During Grosch's term as the chief of detectives, the city's homicide rate fell by 27 percent, a trend that occurred throughout the nation.

106. "Labor Hearing in C.I.O. Row Is Continued," *Baton Rouge State Times Advocate*, July 1, 1938, 1.

107. William Pickens, "Police Lawlessness," *Louisiana Weekly*, October 9, 1937, 8.

108. Kohn, "Report of the Special Citizens Investigating Committee of the Commission Council of New Orleans," 113.

109. "Patrolman Held on Disorderly Charge," *New Orleans Times-Picayune*, June 4, 1934, 6.

110. See "2 Offer Alibi in Robbery Slaying," *New Orleans States*, July 29, 1937, 2.

111. "Death Verdict For Bandits Demanded," *New Orleans States*, July 27, 1937, 2.

112. "Second Man Shot at Gentilly," *Louisiana Weekly*, August 12, 1933, 4.

113. Homicide Reports, "Report of Homicide of Clarence Thompson," August 17, 1941; "Witnesses Say Man Shot Down in Cold Blood," *Louisiana Weekly*, August 23, 1941, 4.

114. David Marks, quoted in Metcalf, "Race Relations and the New Orleans Police Department," 39.

115. "Policeman Freed by Jury in Death of Roof-Climber," *New Orleans Times-Picayune*, November 26, 1942, 9.

116. "'Justice' Meted Out in Fifteen Minutes by Jury," *Louisiana Weekly*, December 5, 1942, 1.

117. Papers of the Louisiana League, Charles Sims to Fred Weis and Harold N. Lee, August 16, 1941.

118. Kohn, "Report of the Special Citizens Investigating Committee of the Commission Council of New Orleans," 113.

119. "Memphis Police Show Their Teeth as Efforts Are Continued to Expose Their Brutality," *Pittsburgh Courier*, March 18, 1933, A1.

120. Arthur E. Schott, "A Word for the Negro," *New Orleans Times-Picayune*, March 21, 1930, 10.

121. Testimony of Harry J. Daniels, December 21, 1953, in Kohn, "Report of the Special Citizens Investigating Committee of the Commission Council of New Orleans," vol. II, 169.

122. "Establish a Defense Fund," *Louisiana Weekly*, August 18, 1934, 8.

123. Johnson et al., *To Stem This Tide*, 73.

124. Raper, "Race and Class Pressures," 3; "No Excuse for Police Brutality," *Louisiana Weekly*, February 11, 1939, 8; Jett, *Race, Crime, and Policing in the Jim Crow South*.

125. Testimony of Harry J. Daniels, December 21, 1953, in Kohn, "Report of the Special Citizens Investigating Committee of the Commission Council of New Orleans," vol. II, 173.

126. Leon Lewis, "No Action by Civic Bodies on Charge More Police Brutality Here," *Louisiana Weekly*, July 30, 1938, 2.

127. "Counsel for Woman Charges Officers Used 'Third Degree,'" *Shreveport Journal*, December 15, 1933, 17.

128. "Miss. Sheriff Disqualified as Court Officer," *Lafayette Daily Advertiser*, March 13, 1935, 2.

129. "New Orleans Believes 'Voodoo Gods' Getting Revenge on Bad Deputy," *Pittsburgh Courier*, January 27, 1940, 18.

130. Memphis Police Department Homicide Reports; "Memphis Negroes Aroused to High Pitch of Resentment and Indignation," January 4, 1938, Memphis Branch Files, Box I:G199, Folder 28, 1938, Papers of the National Association for the Advancement of Colored People.

131. Raper, "Race and Class Pressures," 51.

132. Davis, Gardner, and Gardner, *Deep South*, 501.

133. Raper, "Race and Class Pressures," 50–51, 41, 44, 52, 53.

134. "Torture Story Unshaken by Questioning," *Atlanta Journal*, February 11, 1941, 28; Niedermeier, *The Color of the Third Degree,* 89.

135. "Third Degree Fails to Halt Sentencing," *Memphis Commercial Appeal*, May 20, 1932, 14; "City Aides Won't Quiz Tri-State Prisoners," *Memphis Commercial Appeal*, August 31, 1937, 3.

136. "City Aides Won't Quiz Tri-State Prisoners," *Memphis Commercial Appeal*, August 31, 1937, 3.

137. See Brown v. Mississippi 297 U.S. 278 (1936); Niedermeier, *The Color of the Third Degree.*

138. See Rothberg, *The Implicated Subject*; Arendt, *On Violence.*

139. Patterson, ed., *We Charge Genocide*, 15.

CHAPTER FIVE

1. Raper, "Race and Class Pressures," 22.

2. "Student Badly Hurt, Bystander Shot by Police," *New Orleans Times-Picayune*, March 15, 1936, 14.

3. "Shot in Battle," *New Orleans Item*, March 15, 1936; "Student Badly Hurt, Bystander Shot by Police," *New Orleans Times-Picayune*, March 15, 1936, 14.

4. "Student Badly Hurt, Bystander Shot by Police," *New Orleans Times-Picayune*, March 15, 1936, 14; "Board Probes Police Shots," *New Orleans Item*, March 16, 1936, 1, 5.

5. "City Rises in Protest at Brutal Shooting of Minister's Innocent Son," *Louisiana Weekly*, March 21, 1936, 1.

6. "Board Probes Police Shots," *New Orleans Item*, March 16, 1936, 5; "Youth Shot, Slugged by Brutal Cops," *Chicago Defender*, March 28, 1936, 2.

7. "Youth Wounded by Sleuth Still in Critical Shape," *New Orleans Times-Picayune*, March 16, 1936, 13.

8. "Protest Shooting," *New Orleans Item*, March 18, 1936, 6; "Youth Shot, Slugged by Brutal Cops," *Chicago Defender*, March 28, 1936, 2.

9. "Police Head Bans Protest Meeting in Shooting Case," *New Orleans Times-Picayune*, March 24, 1936, 3.

10. "Reyer Warns His Officers to Exercise Extreme Care in Shooting at Fugitives," *New Orleans Times-Picayune*, March 23, 1936, 1, 3.

11. "Police Head Bans Protest Meeting in Shooting Case," *New Orleans Times-Picayune*, March 24, 1936, 3.

12. "Reyer Warns His Officers to Exercise Extreme Care in Shooting at Fugitives," *New Orleans Times-Picayune*, March 23, 1936, 1, 3; "Board Probes Police Shots," *New Orleans Item*, March 16, 1936, 5.

13. "Orleans Protest Meeting Banned," *Baton Rouge State Times Advocate*, March 24, 1936, 1.

14. "Ban on Protest Meetings Stands," *New Orleans States*, March 24, 1936, 12.

15. "Protest Shooting," *New Orleans Item*, March 18, 1936, 6.

16. "Shot in Battle," *New Orleans Item*, March 15, 1936, 16.

17. Niedermeier, *The Color of the Third* Degree, 64, Jett, "'We Crave to Become a Vital Force in This Community.'"

18. H.C. Brearley, "Interracial Homicide in the South" (n.d.), 8, in "The Negro and Crime," Guy Benton Johnson Papers; Johnson et al., *To Stem This Tide*, 72.

19. "It's Happened Again," *Louisiana Weekly*, May 31, 1941, 6.

20. "Off-Duty State Trooper Shoots Juvenile in Back," *Louisiana Weekly*, May 31, 1941, 1; Coroner's Reports, "Inquest Report on Jessie [sic] Walton," May 24, 1941; Homicide Reports, "Report of Homicide of Jessie Walton," May 24, 1941.

21. "Freed Policeman in Death of Youth," *Chicago Defender*, June 7, 1941, 8.

22. Executive Committee of the Birmingham Branch of the NAACP, "Petition to the Birmingham City Commission," January 31, 1933, Memphis Branch Files, Box I:G2, Folder 1, January–February, 1933, Papers of the National Association for the Advancement of Colored People.

23. Davis, Gardner, and Gardner, *Deep South*, 503.

24. Johnson, *Patterns of Negro Segregation*, 299.

25. "'Runs Amuck'–Or Desperation?," *Louisiana Weekly*, April 23, 1933, 6.

26. Raper, "Race and Class Pressures," 46.

27. "Physical Examinations Urged for 'Confessors,'" *New Orleans States*, April 22, 1933, 3.

28. Papers of the Louisiana League, Sam Lange, "Report of Criminal Law Division," December 28, 1940, 2.

29. For example, State v. Silsby 178 LA 663, 663 (1933).

30. "Two Confessions Given Death Jury: One Later Denied," *New Orleans Times-Picayune*, July 29, 1937, 2; Papers of the Louisiana League, Case Notes, n.d.

31. "Refusing a Whitewash," *Louisiana Weekly*, March 21, 1936, 6.

32. "No Excuse for Police Brutality," *Louisiana Weekly*, February 11, 1939, 8.

33. "Ruttman Trial Is Resumed; Confession Evidence Is Out," *New Orleans Item*, September 17, 1940, 2.

34. For an important analysis of this strategy, see Jett, *Race, Crime, and Policing in the Jim Crow South*.

35. Raper, "Race and Class Pressures," 21.

36. Louisiana Supreme Court Case Files, Testimony of William Bell, State of Louisiana v. Milton Pierce, Docket # 30045, June 8, 1929.

37. Papers of the Louisiana League, Notes from the interviews of witnesses of the shooting of Felton Robinson, September 10, 1943.

38. "Physical Examinations Urged for 'Confessors,'" *New Orleans States*, April 22, 1933, 3.

39. "Refusing a Whitewash," *Louisiana Weekly*, March 21, 1936, 6.

40. "Not Guilty," *Louisiana Weekly*, May 30, 1931, 6.

41. "Accidental Shootings," *Louisiana Weekly*, September 10, 1932, 6; "A Call to Arms," *Louisiana Weekly*, May 13, 1933, 1.

42. Files of the New Orleans Branch of the NAACP, A. W. Braun to NAACP, August 18, 1938, Papers of the National Association for the Advancement of Colored People.

43. "Both Races Protest Police Brutality in Mass Meeting," *Chicago Defender*, March 28, 1936, 5.

44. DeCuir, "Attacking Jim Crow," 145–47, 153, 173; Maclachlan, "Up from Paternalism," 34; Emanuel and Tureaud Jr., *A More Noble Cause*, 61–88.

45. Leon Lewis, "Says NAACP Asked Membership Fee When He Asked for Aid," *Louisiana Weekly*, August 6, 1938, 1, 2.

46. "Simon Legreeism," *Louisiana Weekly*, May 21, 1932, 6.

47. Leon Lewis, "Says NAACP Asked Membership Fee When He Asked for Aid," *Louisiana Weekly*, August 6, 1938, 1, 2.

48. Files of the New Orleans Branch of the NAACP, A. W. Braun to NAACP, August 18, 1938, Papers of the National Association for the Advancement of Colored People.

49. Moore, *Black Rage in New Orleans*, 3; Niedermeier, *The Color of the Third Degree*, 64.

50. "Claims Evidence of Infringement," *New Orleans States*, August 1, 1939, 5.

51. Papers of the Louisiana League, Important Bulletin, June 30, 1938.

52. Moore, "Civil Liberties in Louisiana," 70–73.

53. Papers of the Louisiana League, Important Bulletin, June 30, 1938.

54. Papers of the Louisiana League, Harold N. Lee to Henry A. Scheinhaut, October 22, 1942.

55. Papers of the Louisiana League, Harold N. Lee to Mr. Musgrove, September 24, 1939.

56. Papers of the Louisiana League, Anonymous to (N----- Loving) Harold Lee, February 1939.

57. "Survey Finds Americans Enjoy But Half of Guaranteed Rights," *Washington Post*, March 6, 1939, 24.

58. "New Orleans Quiz on CIO 'Abuses' Meets Delay," *Pittsburgh Sun Telegraph*, July 1, 1938, 10; "Solons Condemn Communism, Hits C.I.O. Activities," *New Orleans Times-Picayune*, July 2, 1938, 1, 3.

59. For an insightful analysis of these fleeting partnerships, see Bell, "Brown v. Board of Education and the Interest-Convergence Dilemma."

60. "A Red Herring," *Louisiana Weekly*, March 28, 1936, 6.

61. "New Orleans Is Aroused Over Brutality of Policemen," *Chicago Defender*, March 25, 1933, 4.

62. "A Red Herring," *Louisiana Weekly*, March 28, 1936, 6.

63. "Inquiry Slated Into Shooting of High School Boy," *New Orleans Times-Picayune*, March 20, 1936, 3.

64. "A Red Herring," *Louisiana Weekly*, March 28, 1936, 6.

65. "New Orleans Is Aroused Over Brutality of Policemen," *Chicago Defender*, March 25, 1933, 4.

66. "21st Amendment Study by Special Session Is Urged," *New Orleans Times-Picayune*, May 27, 1933, 2.

67. "Groups Are Indignant Over Chief's Stand in Boy's Brutal Shooting," *Louisiana Weekly*, March 28, 1936, 6.

68. "Await Word from District Atty. in La.," *Chicago Defender*, April 4, 1936, 10.

69. "A Fair Hearing," *New Orleans States*, January 12, 1938, 10.

70. "Police Killings," *New Orleans Item*, August 4, 1927, 12.

71. "2 Detectives Are Found Guilty," *Louisiana Weekly*, June 3, 1933, 7.

72. "Theft Victim Boosts Police," *New Orleans Item*, March 19, 1933, 9.

73. Papers of the Louisiana League, Harold N. Lee to Henry A. Scheinhaut, October 22, 1942.

74. "Claims Third Degree Is UnAmerican," *New Orleans States*, June 2, 1939, 11.

75. Anonymous, "Memorandum on the Police in a Southern City," 2.

76. Raper, "Race and Class Pressures," 175.

77. "Lays Negro Vote to Long," *New Orleans States*, May 31, 1935, 5.

78. "Simon Legreeism," *Louisiana Weekly*, May 21, 1932, 6. Also see McClosky and Brill, *Dimensions of* Tolerance, 422; Marcus et al., *With Malice toward Some*, 7.

79. "Legislature Condemns C.I.O.," *Nashville Tennessean*, July 2, 1938, 1.

80. For important perspectives on police legitimacy, see Tyler, "Psychological Perspectives on Legitimacy and Legitimation," 392; Meares, Tyler, and Gardener, "Law of Fair," 297–344; Carlson, *Policing the Second* Amendment, 180–81; Rothberg, *The Implicated Subject*, 34; Baumgartner, Epp, and Shoub, *Suspect Citizens,* 3.

81. For a related analysis, see Epp, Maynard-Moody, and Haider-Markel, *Pulled Over,* 51.

82. "Police Brutality Common in Southern Cities," *Pittsburgh Courier*, August 3, 1940, 15. For a modern version of this argument, see Baumgartner, Epp, and Shoub, *Suspect Citizens*, 3.

83. "No Excuse for Police Brutality," *Louisiana Weekly*, February 11, 1939, 8.

84. "Memphis Police Show Teeth as Efforts Are Continued to Expose Their Brutality," *Pittsburgh Courier*, March 18, 1933, A1.

85. "Prowler Killed When He Invades Policeman's Yard," *New Orleans Times-Picayune*, August 18, 1941, 3.

86. "Witnesses Say Man Shot Down in Cold Blood," *Louisiana Weekly*, August 23, 1941, 4.

87. Coroner's Reports, "Inquest Report on Aaron Boyd," June 17, 1938.

88. "State Attorney Accepts Report in Boyd's Death," *New Orleans Times-Picayune*, June 22, 1938, 15.

89. Papers of the Louisiana League, "Found Lifeless in Jail, Aaron Boyd's Brutal Slaying Is Being Investigated," Associated Negro Press Release of June 30, 1938.

90. "Crime Board Asks Constitution Ban on Third Degree," *New Orleans Times-Picayune*, August 11, 1931, 15.

91. "Reyer Declares Grosch Misquoted on Third Degree," *Baton Rouge State Times Advocate*, June 1, 1939, 6.

92. "'Third-Degree' Champion," *New Orleans Times-Picayune*, June 2, 1939, 12.

93. "Beating Denied by Chief Grosch," *New Orleans Times-Picayune*, December 28, 1945, 28.

94. "'Third Degree' Probe Is Halted," *New Orleans States*, September 29, 1931, 9.

95. "Crime Is Curbed by 'Third Degree,' Asserts Grosch," *New Orleans Times-Picayune*, June 1, 1939, 1.

96. "Police Methods Come Under Fire in Investigation," *New Orleans Times-Picayune*, February 12, 1932, 3.

97. "Third Degree Claims Fail in Plough Case," *Memphis Commercial Appeal*, March 2, 1932, 15.

98. Papers of the Louisiana League, Harold N. Lee to Henry A. Scheinhaut, October 22, 1942.

99. "Demand Probe of LA. Extradition Murder," *Chicago Defender*, February 1, 1941, 8; "Youth Shot as Brother Tries to Catch Him for Officers," *Louisiana Weekly*, August 22, 1936, 1.

100. Fichter, "Police Handling of Arrestees," 57.

101. "On Trials, Lads' Bodies Show Cuts, Bruises; Await Verdict," *Louisiana Weekly*, July 31, 1937, 1; Papers of the Louisiana League, Notes of Harold Lee, August–September, 1941; Papers of the Louisiana League, "Chef Cook Tells of Thirty Days Torture While White Cops Try to Make Him Confess to Crime He Knew Nothing About," Files of the *Pittsburgh Courier*, July 23, 1938.

102. "Student Badly Hurt, Bystander Shot by Police," *New Orleans Times-Picayune*, March 15, 1936, 14.

103. Papers of the Louisiana League, Henry N. Lee, "President's Report," January 30, 1946; Papers of the Louisiana League, Harold N. Lee to George [No Last Name Given], April 23, 1945; Papers of the Louisiana League, Statement of Miss Susie Hauser to Henrietta B. Ross and John Rousseau Jr., April 17, 1944.

104. "Last Pleas Made to Save Slayers from Scaffold," *New Orleans Times-Picayune*, April 29, 1933, 2.

105. Homicide Reports, "Report of Homicide of Clarence Thompson," August 17, 1941.

106. "New Orleans D.A. to Get Police Brutality Case," *Chicago Defender*, March 20, 1943, 9.

107. Homicide Reports, "Report of Homicide of Gladstone Crosier," February 4, 1943.

108. "New Orleans D.A. to Get Police Brutality Case," *Chicago Defender*, March 20, 1943, 9.

109. "Prisoner Rams Pillar," *Memphis Commercial Appeal*, October 16, 1941, 14; "Boyle Will Get Report," *Memphis Commercial Appeal*, October 17, 1941, 15; "Boyle Clears Officers," *Memphis Commercial Appeal*, October 18, 1941, 3.

110. "Memphis Cops Kill Prisoner," *New York Daily Worker*, March 10, 1933, 3.

111. Papers of the Louisiana League, Harold N. Lee to Bernard D. Mintz, March 7, 1940.

112. Feagin, *The White Racial Frame*.

113. See Muhammad, *The Condemnation of Blackness*; Muhammad, "Where Did All the White Criminals Go?"

114. For a related analysis, see Rothberg, *The Implicated Subject*.

115. "Police Nab CIO Leaders," *Jackson Clarion-Ledger*, June 28, 1938, 1.

116. "We'll Have No Race Trouble, Says Boyle," *Memphis Commercial Appeal*, December 12, 1940, 11; "Warn Negroes in Memphis," *Knoxville News-Sentinel*, December 16, 1940, 2.

117. Papers of the Louisiana League, Notarized Statement of Lee Rattner, July 5, 1938.

118. Raper, "Race and Class Pressures," 240.

119. "Legislature Condemns C.I.O.," *Nashville Tennessean*, July 2, 1938, 1.

120. Jett, *Race, Crime and Policing in the Jim Crow South*, 45.

121. Anonymous, "Memorandum on the Police in a Southern City," 2; Raper, "Race and Class Pressures," 38–40; Davis, Gardner, and Gardner, *Deep South*, 501; Brearley, "Interracial Homicide in the South," 6; Niedermeier, *The Color of the Third Degree*; Cole and Ring, eds., *The Folly of Jim Crow*.

122. "Police Brutality Common in Southern Cities," *Pittsburgh Courier*, August 3, 1940, 15.

123. "Report of Homicide of Levon Carlock," February 25, 1933, Memphis Police Department Homicide Reports.

124. "Negro Lad Killed by Tenn. Cops," *New York Daily Worker*, February 28, 1933, 3.

125. Fannie Henderson, sworn deposition, February 1933, Files of the Memphis Branch of the NAACP, Papers of the National Association for the Advancement of Colored People.

126. "Report of Homicide of Levon Carlock," February 25, 1933, Memphis Police Department Homicide Reports.

127. "Murdered Lad," *New York Daily Worker*, March 7, 1933, 1.

128. "Negro Reformists Sabotages the United Front in Carlock Case," *New York Daily Worker*, March 7, 1933, 3; "'We Must Stop Murder of Negro People!' Says Young Widow of Levon Carlock in Memphis," *New York Daily Worker*, March 2, 1933, 1.

129. "Carlock Widow Jailed for Day," *New York Daily Worker*, March 16, 1933, 3.

130. "Carlock Witness Disappears," *New York Daily Worker*, March 17, 1933, 1.

131. "Labor Defense Stirs Up Protest in Killing," *Memphis Commercial Appeal*, February 28, 1933, 8; "No Investigation on Carlock Case," *New York Daily Worker*, March 4, 1933, 1.

132. "Vilifiers of Police Are Condemned by Civic Club," *Memphis Commercial Appeal*, March 7, 1933, 4; "Police Given Praise," *Memphis Commercial Appeal*, March 3, 1933, 5.

133. "Vilifiers of Police Are Condemned by Civic Club," *Memphis Commercial Appeal*, March 7, 1933, 4.

134. Johnson et al., *To Stem This Tide*, 73.

135. "New Orleans Quiz on CIO 'Abuses' Meets Delay," *Pittsburgh Sun Telegraph*, July 1, 1938, 10.

136. Arendt, *On Violence*, 77.

CONCLUSION

1. "Police Brutality," *Louisiana Weekly*, February 3, 1940, 8.

2. For example, see "Jury Probes Police Case," *New Orleans Item*, March 12, 1941, 2.

3. "The Killer behind the Badge," *Louisiana Weekly*, October 3, 1942, 10.

4. "An Uncalled for Killing," *Louisiana Weekly*, August 22, 1936, 6.

5. Homicide Reports; Memphis Police Department Homicide Reports.

6. "Memphis Negroes Aroused to High Pitch of Resentment and Indignation," January 4, 1938, Memphis Branch Files, Box I:G199, Folder 28, 1938, Papers of the National Association for the Advancement of Colored People; "Carlock Witness Disappears," *New York Daily Worker*, March 17, 1933, 1; "Labor Defense Stirs Up Protest in Killing," *Memphis Commercial Appeal*, February 28, 1933, 8.

7. Niedermeier, *The Color of the Third Degree*.

8. "Police Brutality," *Louisiana Weekly*, December 7, 1929, 6; Letter to the *Pittsburgh Courier*, March 2, 1943, Mobile Branch Files, Administrative File: Police Brutality, Box II:B112, Folder 12, 1940–1955, Papers of the National Association for the Advancement of Colored People.

9. Raper, "Race and Class Pressures," 36–38; "Says Law Enforcers Help Increase Murder Rate," *Pittsburgh Courier*, January 16, 1932, 2; Niedermeier, "Forced Confessions," 61.

10. Arthur Franklin Raper Papers, Folder 27; Allen and Clubb, *Race, Class, and the Death Penalty*, 73.

11. Jett, *Race, Crime, and Policing in the Jim Crow South*, 45.

12. Myrdal, *An American Dilemma*, 535.

13. Robert Binkley to Membership of the Memphis Local, March 8, 1933, Memphis Branch Files, Box I:G199, Folder 12, 1933, Papers of the National Association for the Advancement of Colored People; "Georgia Slaying Called Lynching," *Jackson Advocate*, August 16, 1941, 1; "Demand Probe of LA. Extradition Murder," *Chicago Defender*, February 1, 1941, 8; "Carlock Witness Disappears," *New York Daily Worker*, March 17, 1933, 1; Davis and Dollard, *Children of Bondage*, 248.

14. "Memphis Cops Kill Prisoner," *New York Daily Worker*, March 10, 1933, 3.

15. Charles A.J. McPherson to NAACP Publicity Department, June 12, 1922, Birmingham Branch Files, Box I:GI, Folder 12b, 1920–1926, Papers of the National Association for the Advancement of Colored People; Executive Committee of the Birmingham Branch of the NAACP, "Petition to the Birmingham City Commission," January 31, 1933, Memphis Branch Files, Box I:G2, Folder 1, January–February, 1933, Papers of the National Association for the Advancement of Colored People.

16. Woofter, *Negro Problems in Cities*, 29.

17. Balto, *Occupied Territory*, 29; Blalock, *Toward a Theory of Minority-Group Relations*.

18. Balto, *Occupied Territory*, 95.

19. Balto, *Occupied Territory*, 93–94; Fischer, *The Streets Belong to Us*, 29; Dale, *Robert Nixon and Police Torture in Chicago*; Flowe, *Uncontrollable Blackness*, 52; King, "A Murder in Central Park"; Johnson, *Street Justice*.

20. For Boyle, "We'll Have No Race Trouble, Says Boyle," *Memphis Commercial Appeal*, December 12, 1940, 11; "Boyle Rebukes Group for Hurling Charges," *Memphis Commercial Appeal*, December 5, 1940, 10; "Warn Negroes in Memphis," *Knoxville New-Sentinel*, December 16, 1940, 1.

21. Fischer, *The Streets Belong to Us*, 90. Also see Hinton, *America on Fire*, 6, 15, 236.

22. Balto, *Occupied Territory*, 4–5.

23. Zimring, *When Police Kill*, 46; Nix et al., "A Bird's Eye View of Civilians Killed by Police in 2015," 328; "Rate of Fatal Police Shootings in the United States from 2015 to June 2022, by Ethnicity."

24. Scott et al., "A Social Scientific Approach toward Understanding Racial Disparities in Police Shooting," 705; Ross, "A Multi-Level Bayesian Analysis of Racial Bias in Police Shootings at the County-Level in the United States, 2011–14"; Correll et al., "The Police Officer's Dilemma," 202.

25. Brooks, *Tangled Up in Blue*.

26. Johnson, "The Negro and Crime," 97; Correll et al., "The Influence of Stereotypes on Decisions to Shoot," 1103; O'Flaherty and Sethi, *Shadows of Doubt*, 5; Kahn and McMahon, "Shooting Deaths of Unarmed Racial Minorities," 113; Nix et al., "A Bird's Eye View of Civilians Killed by Police in 2015," 324–25; Zimring, *When Police Kill*, 228.

27. See Baer, *Beyond the Usual Beating*; Ralph, *The Torture Letters*.

28. "No Excuse for Police Brutality," *Louisiana Weekly*, February 11, 1939, 8; Ruby and Brigham, "A Criminal Schema," 102.

29. Epp, Maynard-Moody, and Haider-Markel, *Pulled Over*, 105.

30. Zimring, *When Police Kill*, 173.

31. For important, insightful explorations of racial control and crime control, see Simon, *Governing through Crime*; Alexander, *The New Jim Crow*.

32. Data and reporting problems make it difficult to determine with precision the number of homicides committed by law enforcers in the nation. Thus, it is

impossible to provide an exact percentage. But the range is apparent and unmistakable. Lett et al., "Racial Inequality in Fatal U.S. Police Shootings, 2015–2020," 394–97.

33. Edwards, Esposito, and Lee, "Risk of Police-Involved Death by Race/Ethnicity and Place, United States, 2012–2018," 1243; Edwards, Lee, and Esposito, "Risk of Being Killed by Police Use of Force in the United States by Age, Race-Ethnicity, and Sex."

34. Zimring, *When Police Kill*, 87. Racial bias is not the only factor accounting for this transnational disparity. Widespread gun ownership in the United States plays a significant role as well. See Zimring, *When Police Kill*, 248.

BIBLIOGRAPHY

PRIMARY SOURCES

Archival Collections

Arthur Franklin Raper Papers, Southern Historical Collection. Wilson Special Collections Library, University North Carolina, Chapel Hill, NC.

Carnegie-Myrdal Study of the Negro in America Research Memoranda Collection, Schomburg Center for Research in Black Culture, Manuscripts, Archives and Rare Books Division. New York Public Library, New York.

———. Anonymous. "Memorandum on the Police in a Southern City." In "Race and Class Pressures" by Arthur Raper, 1–6.

———. Chivers, Walter Richard. "Homicides among Negroes in Atlanta, 1934–1938." 1–26. In "Race and Class Pressures" by Arthur Raper.

———. Raper, Arthur. "Race and Class Pressures." 1–343. June 1, 1940.

———. Woodruff, William. "The Atlanta Police Officer and Functioning of the Atlanta Police Department," Fall 1939. 1–3. In "Race and Class Pressures" by Arthur Raper.

Criminal District Court Case Files, City Archives/Louisiana Division. New Orleans Public Library, New Orleans, Louisiana.

Files of the New Orleans Branch of the NAACP, Papers of the National Association for the Advancement of Colored People. Part 12, Reel 15, Series A. John H. Bracey, Jr. and August Meier, eds. University Publications. Bethesda, MD, 1991.

Guy Benton Johnson Papers, Southern Historical Collection. Wilson Special Collections Library, University North Carolina, Chapel Hill, NC.

Kohn, Aaron M. "Report of the Special Citizens Investigating Committee of the Commission Council of New Orleans," Vol. III, April, 1954. New Orleans Police Department, Louisiana Research Collection. Tulane University Library, New Orleans, LA.

Louisiana Supreme Court Case Files, Historical Archives of the Supreme Court of Louisiana. Earl K. Long Library, University of New Orleans, New Orleans, LA.

Papers of the Louisiana League for the Preservation of Constitutional Rights. Harold
   Newton Lee Papers, Manuscripts Collection 245, Louisiana Research Collection.
   Howard-Tilton Memorial Library, Tulane University, New Orleans, LA.
Papers of the National Association for the Advancement of Colored People, Manu-
   script Division, Library of Congress, Washington, DC.

Homicide and Coroner Reports

Coroner's Reports. Coroner's Office, City of New Orleans, Parish of Orleans, State
   of Louisiana, City Archives/Louisiana Division. New Orleans Public Library,
   New Orleans, LA.
Homicide Reports, 1893–1947. Department of Police, City of New Orleans, City
   Archives/Louisiana Division. New Orleans Public Library, New Orleans, LA.
Memphis Police Department Homicide Reports, 1920–45. Shelby County Archives,
   Memphis, TN.
Transcripts of Statements of Witnesses to Homicides. New Orleans Police Depart-
   ment, City of New Orleans, City Archives/Louisiana Division. New Orleans
   Public Library, New Orleans, LA.

Published Sources

Barnhart, Kenneth E. "A Study of Homicide in the United States." *Birmingham-
   Southern College Bulletin* 25 (May 1932): 7–38.
Brearley, H. C. "The Negro and Homicide." *Social Forces* 9 (December 1930):
   247–53.
———. "Ba-ad N-----." *South Atlantic Quarterly* 38 (January 1939): 75–81.
Chafee, Zechariah, Jr., Walter H. Pollak, and Carl S. Stern. "The Third Degree." In
   *National Commission on Law Observance and Enforcement, No. 11: Report on
   Lawlessness in Law Enforcement.* Washington, DC: Government Printing Office,
   1931.
Chisolm, B. Ogden, and Hastings H. Hart. "Methods of Obtaining Confessions
   and Information from Persons Accused of Crime." 3–18. Paper Presented at the
   Fifty-First Congress of the American Prison Association. New York: Russell Sage
   Foundation, 1922.
*Constitution of the State of Louisiana, Adopted in Convention at the City of Baton
   Rouge, June 18, 1921.* Baton Rouge: Ramires-Jones, 1921.
Davis, Allison, and John Dollard. *Children of Bondage: The Personality Develop-
   ment of Negro Youth in the Urban South.* Washington, DC: American Council of
   Education, 1940.
Davis, Allison, Burleigh B. Gardner, and Mary Gardner. *Deep South: A Social Anthro-
   pological Study of Caste and Class.* Chicago: University of Chicago Press, 1941.
Dollard, John. *Caste and Class in a Southern Town.* New York: Doubleday Anchor,
   1937.

Fichter, Joseph H. "Police Handling of Arrestees: A Research Study of Police Arrests in New Orleans." Unpublished Report: Department of Sociology, Loyola University of the South, 1964.

Fifteenth Census of the United States: 1930, Occupations, by States, Vol. IV. Washington, DC: Government Printing Office, 1933.

Fourteenth Census of the United States Taken in the Year 1920, Population, Vol. IV. Washington, DC: Government Printing Office, 1923.

Fry, Charles Luther. "The Negro in the United States—A Statistical Statement." *Annals of the American Academy of Political and Social Science* 140 (November 1928): 26–35.

Hall, Charles E. *Negroes in the United States, 1920–32.* Washington, DC: Government Printing Office, 1935.

Harmon v. Tyler (October 1926). Reprinted in *Harmon v. Tyler* (October 1926). *U.S. Supreme Court Transcript of Recording with Supporting Pleadings.* Gale Making of Modern Law Print Editions. Farmington Hill, MI, 2011.

Hoffman, Frederick L. *The Homicide Problem.* Newark, NJ: Prudential Press, 1925.

———. "Homicide Record for 1924." *The Spectator* 114 (May 21, 1925): 1–4, 37.

———. "The Increase in Murder." *Annals of the American Academy of Political and Social Science* 125 (May 1926): 20–29.

"Homicide Report of Memphis." *The Spectator* 112 (May 15, 1924): 11.

"Homicides in Memphis, Tenn." *The Spectator* 114 (June 4, 1925): 7.

Johnson, Charles S. *The Negro in American Civilization: A Study of Negro Life and Race Relations in the Light of Social Research.* New York: Holt, 1930.

———. *Patterns of Negro Segregation.* New York: Harper, 1943.

Johnson, Charles, et al., *To Stem This Tide: A Survey of Racial Tension Areas in the United States.* Boston: Pilgrim Press, 1943.

Johnson, Guy B. "The Negro and Crime." *Annals of the American Academy of Political and Social Science* 217 (September 1941): 93–104.

Kefauver, Estes. *Crime in America.* Garden City, NY: Doubleday, 1951.

Moton, Robert Russa. *What the Negro Thinks.* New York: Doubleday, 1929.

Myrdal, Gunnar. *An American Dilemma: The Negro Problem and Modern Democracy.* New York: Harper and Row, 1944; reprint, with an introduction by Sissela Bok, 1962.

New Orleans Tax Revision Commission. *A Fiscal and Administrative Survey of the City of New Orleans.* New Orleans: Brandao, 1934.

Patterson, William L., ed. *We Charge Genocide: The Crime of Government against the Negro People.* New York: International Publishers, 1951.

Pound, Roscoe, and Felix Frankfurter, eds. *Criminal Justice in Cleveland: Reports of the Cleveland Foundation Survey of the Administration of Justice in Cleveland, Ohio.* Cleveland, OH: Cleveland Foundation, 1922.

Smith, Bruce. *The New Orleans Police Survey.* New Orleans: Bureau of Governmental Research, 1946.

Wells-Barnett, Ida B. *Mob Rule in New Orleans.* 1900; reprinted, Bristol, UK: Read & Co., 2020.

Wigmore, John Henry, ed. *The Illinois Crime Survey*. Chicago: Illinois Association for Criminal Justice in Cooperation with the Chicago Crime Commission & Blakely Printing Company, 1929.

Woofter, T. J., Jr. *Negro Problems in Cities*. New York: Doubleday, Doran, 1928.

Work, Monroe N., ed. *Negro Year Book: An Annual Encyclopedia of the Negro, 1931–1932*. Tuskegee, AL: Tuskegee Institute Press, 1931.

Newspapers

Atlanta Journal
Baton Rouge Advocate
Baton Rouge State Times Advocate
Chattanooga Daily Times
Chicago Defender
Chicago Tribune
Huntsville Times
Jackson Advocate
Jackson Clarion-Ledger
Knoxville News-Sentinel
Lafayette Daily Advertiser
Louisiana Weekly
Memphis Commercial Appeal
Meridian Weekly Echo
Nashville Tennessean
New Orleans Item
New Orleans States
New Orleans Times-Picayune
New York Amsterdam News
New York Daily Worker
New York Times
Pittsburgh Courier
Pittsburgh Sun Telegraph
Shreveport Journal
Tyler Morning Telegraph
Washington Post

SECONDARY SOURCES

Adler, Jeffrey S. "Guns and Violence: Weapon Instrumentality in New Orleans Homicide, 1920–1945." *Journal of Interdisciplinary History* 51 (Autumn 2020): 185–208.

———. "'Justice Is Something That Is Unheard of for the Average Negro': Racial Disparities in New Orleans Criminal Justice, 1920–1945." *Journal of Social History* 54 (Summer 2021): 213–31.

———. *Murder in New Orleans: The Creation of Jim Crow Policing.* Chicago: University of Chicago Press, 2019.

———. "'Spineless Judges and Shyster Lawyers': Criminal Justice in New Orleans, 1920–1945." *Journal of Social History* 49 (Summer 2016): 904–27.

Alexander, Michelle. *The New Jim Crow: Mass Incarceration in the Age of Colorblindness.* New York: New Press, 2010.

Allen, Howard W., and Jerome M. Clubb. *Race, Class, and the Death Penalty: Capital Punishment in American History.* Albany: State University of New York, Press, 2008.

Arendt, Hannah. *On Violence.* Orlando, FL: Harcourt, 1969.

Baer, Andrew S. *Beyond the Usual Beating: The Jon Burge Torture Scandal and Social Movements for Police Accountability in Chicago.* Chicago: University of Chicago Press, 2020.

Baker, Andrew. *To Poison A Nation: The Murder of Robert Charles and the Rise of Jim Crow Policing in America.* New York: New Press, 2021.

Balko, Radley. *Rise of the Warrior Cop: The Militarization of America's Police Forces.* New York: PublicAffairs, 2014.

Balto, Simon. *Occupied Territory: Policing Black Chicago from Red Summer to Black Power.* Chapel Hill: University of North Carolina Press, 2019.

Baumgartner, Frank R., Derek A. Epp, and Kelsey Shoub. *Suspect Citizens: What 20 Million Traffic Stops Tell Us about Policing and Race.* New York: Cambridge University Press, 2018.

Bell, Derrick A. "Brown v. Board of Education and the Interest-Convergence Dilemma." *Harvard Law Review* 93 (January 1980): 518–33.

Blalock, Hubert M. *Toward a Theory of Minority-Group Relations.* New York: John Wiley, 1967.

Boeckmann, Robert J., and Tom R. Tyler. "Commonsense Justice and Inclusion within the Moral Community." *Psychology, Public Policy, and Law* 3 (July–September 1997): 362–80.

Brooks, Rosa. *Tangled Up in Blue: Policing the American City.* New York: Penguin, 2021.

Brundage, W. Fitzhugh. "Introduction." In *The Folly of Jim Crow: Rethinking the Segregated South,* edited by Stephanie Cole and Natalie J. Ring, 1–16. Dallas: Texas A & M Press, 2012.

Campney, Brent M. S. *Hostile Heartland: Racism, Repression, and Resistance in the Midwest.* Urbana: University of Illinois Press, 2019.

Carlson, Jennifer. *Policing the Second Amendment: Guns, Law Enforcement, and the Politics of Race.* Princeton, NJ: Princeton University Press, 2020.

Cole, Stephanie, and Natalie J. Ring, eds. *The Folly of Jim Crow: Rethinking the Segregated South.* Dallas: Texas A & M Press, 2012.

Correll, Joshua, Sean M. Hudson, Stephanie Guillermo, and Debbie S. Ma. "The Police Officer's Dilemma: A Decade of Research on Racial Bias in the Decision to Shoot." *Social and Personality Psychology Compass* 8 (May 2014): 201–13.

Correll, Joshua, Bernadette Park, Charles M. Judd, and Bernd Wittenbrink. "The Influence of Stereotypes on Decisions to Shoot." *European Journal of Social Psychology* 37 (November–December 2007): 1102–17.

Dale, Elizabeth. *Criminal Justice in the United States, 1879–1939.* New York: Cambridge University Press, 2011.

———. *Robert Nixon and Police Torture in Chicago, 1871–1971.* DeKalb: Northern Illinois University Press, 2016.

Daugette, Tennie Erwin. "Homicide in New Orleans." Master's Thesis, Tulane University, 1931.

DeCuir, Sharlene Sinegal. "Attacking Jim Crow: Black Activism in New Orleans." PhD diss., Louisiana State University Press, 2009.

Devore, Donald E. *Defying Jim Crow: African American Community Development and the Struggle for Racial Equality in New Orleans, 1900–1960.* Baton Rouge: Louisiana State University Press, 2015.

Eberhardt, Jennifer L. *Biased: Uncovering the Hidden Prejudice That Shapes What We See, Think, and Do.* New York: Penguin, 2019.

Eckberg, Douglas. "Crime, Law Enforcement, and Justice." Vol. 5 in *Historical Statistics of the United States,* edited by Susan B. Carter, Scott Sigmund Gartner, Michael R. Haines, Alan L. Olmstead, Richard Sutch, and Gavin Wright. New York: Cambridge University Press, 2006.

Edwards, Frank, Michael H. Esposito, and Hedwig Lee. "Risk of Police-Involved Death by Race/Ethnicity and Place, United States, 2012–2018." *American Journal of Public Health* 108 (September 2018): 1241–48.

Edwards, Frank, Hedwig Lee, and Michael Esposito. "Risk of Being Killed by Police Use of Force in the United States by Age, Race-Ethnicity, and Sex." *Proceedings of the National Academy of Sciences* 116 (August 2019): 16793–98.

Emanuel, Rachel L., and Alexander P. Tureaud Jr. *A More Noble Cause: A. P. Tureaud and the Struggle for Civil Rights in Louisiana.* Baton Rouge: Louisiana State University Press, 2011.

Epp, Charles R., Steven Maynard-Moody, and Donald Haider-Markel. *Pulled Over: How Police Stops Define Race and Citizenship.* Chicago: University of Chicago Press, 2014.

Feagin, Joe R. *The White Racial Frame: Centuries of Racial Framing and Counter-Framing.* New York: Routledge, 2020.

Fichter, Joseph H. *One-Man Report: Reminiscences of a Catholic Sociologist.* New York: Wiley, 1973.

Finkel, Norman J. *Commonsense Justice: Jurors' Notions of the Law.* Cambridge, MA: Harvard University Press, 1995.

Finnegan, Terence. "'Politics of Defiance': Uncovering the Causes and Consequences of Lynching and Communal Violence." *Journal of American History* 101 (December 2014): 850–51.

Fischer, Anne Gray. *The Streets Belong to Us: Sex, Race, and Police Power from Segregation to Gentrification*. Chapel Hill: University of North Carolina Press, 2022.

Flowe, Douglas J. *Uncontrollable Blackness: African American Men and Criminality in Jim Crow New York*. Chapel Hill: University of North Carolina Press, 2020.

Hadden, Sally E. *Slave Patrols: Law and Violence in Virginia and the Carolinas*. Cambridge, MA: Harvard University Press, 2001.

Hinton, Elizabeth. *America on Fire: The Untold History of Police Violence and Black Rebellion since the 1960s*. New York: Liveright Press, 2021.

Jackson, Jonathan, Ben Bradford, Aziz Z. Huq, and Tom R. Tyler. "Monopolizing Force? Police Legitimacy and Public Attitudes toward the Acceptability of Violence." *Psychology, Public Policy, and Law* 19 (November 2013): 479–97.

Jett, Brandon T. *Race, Crime, and Policing in the Jim Crow South: African Americans and Law Enforcement in Birmingham, Memphis, and New Orleans, 1920–1945*. Baton Rouge: Louisiana State University Press, 2021.

———. "'We Crave to Become a Vital Force in This Community': Police Brutality and African American Activism in Birmingham, Alabama, 1920–1945." *Alabama Review* 75 (January 2022): 50–72.

Jimenez, Tyler, Peter J. Helm, and Jamie Arndt, "Racial Prejudice Predicts Police Militarization." *Psychological Science* 33 (December 2022): 2009–26.

Johnson, Marilynn S. *Street Justice: A History of Police Violence in New York City*. Boston: Beacon Press, 2003.

Jones, James M. "Killing Fields: Explaining Police Violence against Persons of Color." *Journal of Social Issues* 73 (December 2017): 872–83.

Kahn, Kimberly Barsamian, and Jean M. McMahon, "Shooting Deaths of Unarmed Racial Minorities: Understanding the Role of Racial Stereotypes on Decisions to Shoot." *Translational Issues in Psychological Science* 1 (December 2015): 310–20.

King, Shannon. "A Murder in Central Park: Racial Violence and the Crime Wave in New York during the 1930s and 1940s." In *The Strange Careers of the Jim Crow North: Segregation and Struggle Outside of the South*, edited by Brian Purnell, Jeanne Theoharis, and Komozi Woodward, 43–66. New York: New York University Press, 2019.

Kolsky, Elizabeth. *Colonial Justice in British India: White Violence and the Rule of Law*. Cambridge, UK: Cambridge University Press, 2010.

Kotch, Seth. *Lethal State: A History of the Death Penalty in North Carolina*. Chapel Hill: University of North Carolina Press, 2019.

Kramer, Rory, and Brianna Remster, "Stop, Frisk, and Assault: Racial Disparities in Police Use of Force During Investigatory Stops." *Law and Society Review* 52 (December 2018): 960–93.

Lett, Elle, Emmanuella Ngozi, Theodore Corbin, and Dowin Boatright. "Racial Inequality in Fatal U.S. Police Shootings, 2015–2020." *Journal of Epidemiology and Community Health* 75 (April 2021): 394–97.

Maclachlan, Alan. "Up from Paternalism: The New Deal and Race Relations in New Orleans." PhD diss., University of New Orleans, 1998.

Malka, Adam. *The Men of Mobtown: Policing Baltimore in the Age of Slavery and Emancipation*. Chapel Hill: University of North Carolina Press, 2018.

Marcus, George E., John L. Sullivan, Elizabeth Theiss-Morse, and Sandra L. Wood. *With Malice toward Some: How People Make Civil Judgments*. Cambridge, UK: Cambridge University Press, 1995.

Massey, James L., and Martha A. Myers. "Patterns of Repressive Social Control in Post-Reconstruction Georgia, 1882–1935." *Social Forces* 68 (December 1989): 458–88.

McClosky, Herbert, and Alida Brill. *Dimensions of Tolerance: What Americans Believe about Civil Liberties*. New York: Russell Sage Foundation, 1983.

Meares, Tracey L., Tom R. Tyler, and Jacob Gardener. "Law of Fair: How Cops and Laypeople Perceive Good Policing." *Journal of Criminal Law and Criminology* 105 (Spring 2015): 297–343.

Metcalf, Christina. "Race Relations and the New Orleans Police Department, 1900–1972." Undergraduate Honors Thesis, Tulane University, 1985.

Miller, Vivien. "Hanging, the Electric Chair, and Death Penalty Reform in the Early Twentieth-Century South." In *Crime and Punishment in the Jim Crow South*, edited by Amy Louise Wood and Natalie J. Ring, 170–91. Urbana: University of Illinois Press, 2019.

Mitrani, Sam. *The Rise of the Chicago Police Department: Class and Conflict, 1850–1894*. Urbana: University of Illinois Press, 2013.

Mondak, Jeffery J., and Mitchell S. Sanders. "The Complexity of Tolerance and Intolerance Judgments: A Response to Gibson." *Political Behavior* 27 (December 2005): 325–37.

Moore, Leonard N. *Black Rage in New Orleans: Police Brutality and African American Activism from World War II to Hurricane Katrina*. Baton Rouge: Louisiana State University Press, 2010.

Moore, William V. "Civil Liberties in Louisiana: The Louisiana League for the Preservation of Constitutional Rights." *Louisiana History* 31 (Winter 1990): 59–81.

Muhammad, Khalil Gibran. *The Condemnation of Blackness: Race, Crime, and the Making of Urban America*. Cambridge, MA: Harvard University Press, 2010.

———. "Where Did All the White Criminals Go? Reconfiguring Race and Crime on the Road to Mass Incarceration." *Souls* 13 (March 2011): 72–90.

Niedermeier, Silvan. *The Color of the Third Degree: Racism, Police Torture, and Civil Rights in the American South, 1930–1955*. Chapel Hill: University of North Carolina Press, 2019.

———. "Forced Confessions: Police Torture and the African American Struggle for Civil Rights in the 1930 and 1940s South." In *Crime and Punishment in the Jim Crow South*, edited by Amy Louise Wood and Natalie J. Ring, 58–78. Urbana: University of Illinois Press, 2019.

Nix, Justin, Bradley A. Campbell, Edward H. Byers, and Geoffrey P. Alpert. "A Bird's Eye View of Civilians Killed by Police in 2015: Further Evidence of Implicit Bias." *Criminology and Public Policy* 16 (February 2017): 309–40.

O'Flaherty, Brendan, and Rajiv Sethi. *Shadows of Doubt: Stereotypes, Crime, and the Pursuit of Justice.* Cambridge, MA: Harvard University Press, 2019.

Pfeifer, Michael J. "At the Hands of Parties Unknown? The State of the Field of Lynching Scholarship." *Journal of American History* 101 (December 2014): 832–46.

———. *Rough Justice: Lynching and American Society, 1874–1947.* Urbana: University of Illinois Press, 2004.

Potter, Claire Bond. *War on Crime: Bandits, G-Men, and the Politics of Mass Culture.* New Brunswick, NJ: Rutgers University Press, 1998.

Prince, K. Stephen. *The Ballad of Robert Charles: Searching for the New Orleans Riot of 1900.* Chapel Hill: University of North Carolina Press, 2021.

Ralph, Laurence. *The Torture Letters: Reckoning with Police Violence.* Chicago: University of Chicago Press, 2020.

"Rate of Fatal Police Shootings in the United States from 2015 to June 2022, by Ethnicity." Statista. https://www.statista.com/statistics/1123070/police-shootings-rate-ethnicity-us/.

Ross, Cody T. "A Multi-Level Bayesian Analysis of Racial Bias in Police Shootings at the County-Level in the United States, 2011–14." *PLoS One* 10 (November 2015): e0141854. https://doi.org/10.1371/journal.pone.0141854.

Rothberg, Michael. *The Implicated Subject: Beyond Victims and Perpetrators.* Stanford, CA: Stanford University Press, 2019.

Rousey, Dennis C. *Policing the Southern City: New Orleans, 1805–1889.* Baton Rouge: Louisiana State University Press, 1996.

Ruby, C. L., and John C. Brigham. "A Criminal Schema: The Role of Chronicity, Race, and Socioeconomic Status in Law Enforcement Officials' Perceptions of Others." *Journal of Applied Social Psychology* 26 (January 1996): 95–112.

Scott, Kendra, Debbie S. Ma, Melody S. Sadler, and Joshua Correll. "A Social Scientific Approach toward Understanding Racial Disparities in Police Shooting: Data from the Department of Justice (1980–2000)." *Journal of Social Issues* 73 (December 2017): 701–22.

Seigel, Micol. *Violence Work: State Power and the Limits of Police.* Durham, NC: Duke University Press, 2018.

Seo, Sarah A. *Policing the Open Road: How Cars Transformed American Freedom.* Cambridge, MA: Harvard University Press, 2019.

Siegel, Reva. "Why Equal Protection No Longer Protects: The Evolving Forms of Status-Enforcing State Action." *Stanford Law Review* 49 (May 1997): 1111–48.

Simon, Jonathan. *Governing through Crime: How the War on Crime Transformed American Democracy and Created a Culture of Fear.* New York: Oxford University Press, 2007.

Stevenson, Bryan. "A Presumption of Guilt: The Legacy of America's History of Racial Injustice." In *Policing the Black Man: Arrest, Prosecution, and Imprisonment*, edited by Angela J. Davis, 3–30. New York: Vintage Press, 2017.

Suddler, Carl. *Presumed Criminal: Black Youth and the Justice System in Postwar New York.* New York: New York University Press, 2019.

Sullivan, John L., James Piereson, and George E. Marcus, *Political Tolerance and American Democracy*. Chicago: University of Chicago Press, 1982.

Taeuber, Karl E., and Alma F. Taeuber. *Negroes in Cities: Residential Segregation and Neighborhood Change*. Chicago: Aldine, 1965.

Tolnay, Stewart E., and E. M. Beck. *A Festival of Violence: An Analysis of Southern Lynchings, 1882–1930*. Urbana: University of Illinois Press, 1995.

Tyler, Tom R. "Psychological Perspectives on Legitimacy and Legitimation." *Annual Review of Psychology* 57 (2006): 375–400.

Tyler, Tom R., and Jonathan Jackson. "Popular Legitimacy and the Exercise of Lethal Authority: Motivating Compliance, Cooperation, and Engagement." *Psychology, Public Policy, and the Law* 20 (February 2014): 78–95.

Vyhnanek, Louis. *Unorganized Crime: New Orleans in the 1920s*. Lafayette, LA: Center for Louisiana Studies, 1998.

Waegel, William B. "How Police Justify the Use of Deadly Force." *Social Problems* 32 (December 1984): 144–55.

Walker, Samuel. *A Critical History of Police Reform: The Emergence of Professionalism*. Lexington, MA: Lexington Books, 1977.

Willrich, Michael. "Criminal Justice in the United States." In *The Cambridge History of Law in America*, Vol. 3, edited by Michael Grossberg and Christopher Tomlins, 195–231. New York: Cambridge University Press, 2008.

Wood, Amy Louise, and Natalie J. Ring. "Introduction." In *Crime and Punishment in the Jim Crow South*, edited by Amy Louise Wood and Natalie J. Ring, 1–16. Urbana: University of Illinois Press, 2019.

Zimring, Franklin E. *When Police Kill*. Cambridge, MA: Harvard University Press, 2017.

INDEX

African Americans: civilian homicide of, 1,
14–16, 34–35; crime, 39–57; interracial
violence against, 3, 4, 34–35; police
violence against, 4, 31, 59–83, 91–110,
139–45
Atlanta: homicide, 57; police violence, 3, 9,
69, 93, 108, 140
automobiles and racial custom, 17–19, 42,
151n35

Birmingham: criminal justice, 69; homicide, 57; police department, 57; police
homicide, 3, 79, 140; police violence
during interrogations, 9, 69; police
violence in defense of racial dominance,
4, 8, 25, 34, 63, 65, 81, 142, 146; population, 41, 141; protests against police
violence, 92, 116, 141
Boyle, Joe, 131, 134, 142
Burns, James, 95–97, 107, 108

Charles, Robert, 62–63
Chicago, 40, 45, 46, 101, 141, 142
commonsense justice, 6, 71
Congress of Industrial Organizations, 121,
134
Connor, Eugene "Bull," 63, 142
constitutional rights and civil liberties, 73,
163n66; race-based exceptions, 6, 67,
71–73, 102, 123–25, 131–32, 139
crime: African American crime, 48–49;
panic about murders, 47, 52–57, 62, 67,
141; panic about robberies, 48–49,

52–53, 56–57; panic about sexual
assaults, 51, 141; panic about threats to
racial custom, 47, 49, 53–55, 57, 65, 80,
86–87, 142, 145
criminal justice, 64; capital punishment,
69, 81, 82, 132, 140–41, 152n49; conviction rates, 2, 13, 23, 28, 39, 68–69, 78, 81,
82, 87, 132; juries, 23, 118; racial disparities, 1–3, 8, 10, 67–69, 132, 140–46

Detroit, 40, 46, 141
disfranchisement and voter suppression, 6,
7, 56, 82, 109, 124–25, 138, 156n30

Floyd, George, 1, 11, 143, 144, 146

Gray, Willie, 112–16, 119–23, 129, 135, 144
Great Migration, 8; into Northern cities, 8,
141; into Southern cities, 5, 40–41, 57,
141
Grosch, John, 97–107, 111, 123–29, 134–37,
142
Grosch, William: background and police
career, 84, 87, 95, 97–98, 105, 137; brutal
interrogation methods, 70, 74, 84–85,
89, 95, 98–99, 104–6, 111, 117, 121, 135;
murder of suspects, 70–71, 84–89,
94–98, 105, 108, 116, 126, 129, 138–39,
143; public image, 85–86, 99, 108–9,
125

Handy, Charles, 1, 85, 88, 94, 98, 109
Hoover, J. Edgar, 54

Founded in 1893,
UNIVERSITY OF CALIFORNIA PRESS
publishes bold, progressive books and journals
on topics in the arts, humanities, social sciences,
and natural sciences—with a focus on social
justice issues—that inspire thought and action
among readers worldwide.

The UC PRESS FOUNDATION
raises funds to uphold the press's vital role
as an independent, nonprofit publisher, and
receives philanthropic support from a wide
range of individuals and institutions—and from
committed readers like you. To learn more, visit
ucpress.edu/supportus.